Creative Kids Zone

2

Brighter Child®
An imprint of Carson-Dellosa Publishing LLC
Greensboro, North Carolina

Brighter Child®
An imprint of Carson-Dellosa Publishing, LLC
P.O. Box 35665
Greensboro, NC 27425-5665

© 2012, Carson-Dellosa Publishing, LLC. Except as permitted under the United States Copyright Act, no part of this publication may be reproduced, stored, or distributed in any form or by any means (mechanically, electronically, recording, etc.) without the prior written consent of Carson-Dellosa Publishing LLC. Brighter Child® is an imprint of Carson-Dellosa Publishing LLC.

carsondellosa.com

Printed in the USA. All rights reserved.   ISBN 978-1-60996-826-7

02-366121151

Table of Contents

Welcome to *Creative Kids Zone* 4

Craft Zone 5–50

Math Zone 51–100

Story Zone: "The Great Butterfly Search" 101–106

Story Zone: "Tyler's Invention" 107–112

Story Zone: "Kayla and the Class Pet" 113–118

Science Zone 119–158

Game Zone 159–226

Answer Zone 227–256

Introduction

Welcome to *Creative Kids Zone*!

Five different exciting zones await your child. Each zone features fun activities designed to stimulate your child's mind and entertain him or her for hours. The standards-based content in *Creative Kids Zone* expands on math, science, and reading content being taught in the 21st century, second grade classroom. Through interactive stories, crafts, games, math puzzles, and science experiments your child will make connections to learning in exciting ways. Each zone is unique so your child can:

Be creative in the Craft Zone!

- The Craft Zone features beautiful nature crafts, fun tie-dye projects, musical instruments, origami, and puppets! Each craft is a useful and creative expression of your child's individuality.

Get logical in the Math Zone!

- The Math Zone features fun activities that reinforce place value, addition, subtraction, simple multiplication, fractions, and shapes. Your child will help Tyler and Kayla make graphs, count change, and crack codes while becoming a stronger math student.

Use imagination in the Story Zone!

- The Story Zone features three removable story books about Tyler and Kayla, two fun creative kids in the second grade! Each story includes open-ended activities that involve your child in the story telling process and interactive comprehension questions.

Experiment in the Science Zone!

- The Science Zone features interesting learning pages about the different states of matter, the solar system, weather, the water cycle, plants, birds, and insects. Not to mention an engaging science experiment for each topic takes the learning off the page!

Have fun in the Game Zone!

- The Game Zone features mazes, hidden pictures, how to draw, secret codes, crossword puzzles, and more! Everything your child needs to stay entertained, and what seems like a diversion to your child actually reinforces the learning concepts taught in the other zones.

Check it out in the Answer Zone!

- A complete answer key is included to check your child's answers.

Craft Zone

Dip 'n' Dye Designs

Have you ever seen colors move and blend on their own? In this project, the colors flow and change! Experiment to create colorful patterns and pictures.

What you'll need:
- Flattened coffee filters or paper towels
- Food coloring
- Empty margarine tubs or muffin tins
- Water
- Toothpicks
- Scissors (optional)

What to do:

1. Fill the tubs with water. Add a few drops of food coloring to each one. Mix each with a toothpick.

2. Fold the coffee filter in half several times.

3. If you want, cut out patterns on the folded edges. Be careful not to cut off the entire fold.

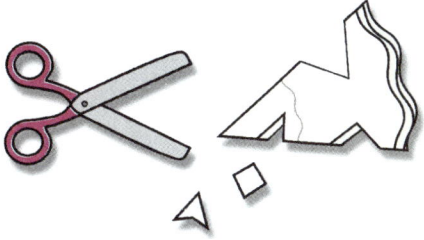

4. Dip each corner into a different color. The color will spread and run into other colors. You may see two colors mixing together to make a new color.

5. Unfold the filter to dry.

Add the flowers to the vase on pages 28 and 29 in Craft Zone!

Suggestion

- Cut the dried designs into flower shapes. Add green construction paper stems and leaves.

Starry Night Scene

Draw the stars and planets in the night sky. This project sparkles even more with florescent or glitter crayons.

What you'll need:
- Watercolor paint
- Paintbrush (a flat 1 inch brush works best)
- Crayons
- White construction paper
- Poster board or heavy paper
- Scissors

CRAFT ZONE

8

What to do:

1. Draw and cut out several star shapes from the poster board to use as stencils or patterns to trace.

2. Use crayons to trace your stars and draw a night sky design on the paper. Make sure to draw enough stars to fill the entire page. Color heavily.

3. Use dark **blue** or **black** watercolors to paint over the entire paper. Paint over your design only one time.

Suggestion

- Add planets, moons, shooting stars, or anything else you can think of to your starry night.

CRAFT ZONE

Tie Dyeing

Imagine you are sleeping in a swirling space galaxy! Decorate a pillowcase using this special project. Be sure to get your parent's permission first!

What you'll need:
- A cotton pillowcase, a *white* one works best*
- Fabric dye**
- Buckets or other containers for dye, one for each color
- Large plastic bag or piece of plastic
- Rubber gloves
- Rubber bands (optional)
- Eyedropper, squeeze bottle, or paintbrush (optional)
- An adult

* Have an adult wash the pillowcase before doing this project. Do not use fabric softeners or dryer sheets.

** Any kind will do, but make sure to read the label before buying it; some dyes call for extra ingredients.

What to do:

1. Have an adult make the dye, following the directions on the package. Anyone working with the dye throughout the project should wear rubber gloves. Doing the project outside is ideal.

2. Tie off the pillowcase. You can knot or bundle up sections and put rubber bands on them. See page 12 for different ways to tie it off. Whichever way you choose, make sure to do it tightly, so that dye stays out of those areas.

3. Have an adult dye your pillowcase. See page 13 for different ways to dye it. Whichever way you choose, remember that the longer you leave the fabric in the dye, the darker the color will be. Also, the dye will be lighter when dry. To mix colors on your pillowcase, dye it with a new color. If you want the colors separated, let them dry first.

4. Dry the fabric completely in plastic for one to three days.

5. Rinse your project in warm water, one section at a time, then in cool water. Take off the rubber bands (or untie the knots) and rinse the pillowcase again.

6. Have an adult wash the pillowcase alone before adding it to the regular laundry.

Suggestions

- Some dyes will set better if you have an adult place the pillowcase between two sheets of paper and steam it with an iron.

- Tie-dye scarves, socks, hats, shirts, and fabric napkins—anything made with cotton fabric.

Ways to Wrap the Pillowcase

Each pillowcase is its own original project and will be different even if you wrap it the same way.

Regular Tie Dye:

Tie knots in sections of the fabric all over the pillowcase. Dip different sections into the dye, switching colors as you choose.

Sunburst:

Pinch the fabric near the center of the pillowcase. Lift up and twist it into a tight spiral. Then, roll it into the shape of a donut. Keep it in place with rubber bands. Drip dye on top, then turn it over and drip dye on top again or dip it into one color.

Star:

Choose five places on the pillowcase to be the points of your star. Bring the edges of them to the center of the pillowcase. Put rubber bands around the rest of the star's arms. Dye the center using a squeeze bottle or eyedropper. Use a different color on the next sections out from the center. Change colors when you get to the second set of sections from the center, and so on.

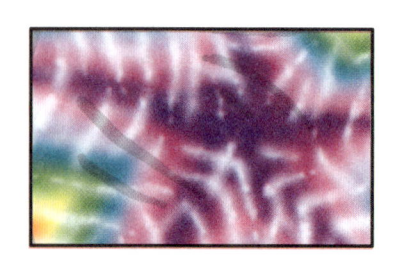

Ways to Dye the Pillowcase

- Dunk the entire pillowcase in one color. If you want to change the color, dunk it in another color afterward.

- Dip sections into a color. Dip sections into different colors, if desired. The colors will probably run together depending on how close they are.

- Use an eyedropper or a squeeze bottle to make designs and keep the colors separate.

Stained Glass Butterfly

Create your own rare and beautiful butterfly! Hang it in the window to see a colorful stained glass design.

What you'll need:
- 12 x 18 inch **black** construction paper
- Tissue paper in assorted colors
- Pencil
- Scissors
- Glue
- String or yarn
- Paper hole punch

Read about Tyler and Kayla's "Great Butterfly Search" in the Story Zone, starting on page 101!

CRAFT ZONE

14

What to do:

1. Fold the **black** paper in half lengthwise.

2. Draw half an outline of a butterfly.

3. Repeat the outline 1 inch inside the first outline, as shown. Leave space between the outlines.

4. With the design still folded in half, cut out the outline and inside of the shapes. Leave the borders uncut.

5. Unfold the butterfly and cut tissue paper to cover each opening. Make the tissue paper slightly larger than the opening.

6. Glue the tissue paper to the back of the butterfly covering each opening.

7. Punch a hole near the top and tie on a string.

8. Hang the butterfly from the ceiling or in a window.

Suggestion

- If you hang your butterfly, you may want to glue another **black** construction paper frame onto the back so it looks nice from both sides.

Leaf Designs

Collect your favorite kinds of leaves to make this colorful nature picture. Use all sorts of shapes, sizes, and colors of leaves.

What you'll need:
- Fresh leaves, various shapes and sizes
- Watercolor paints in fall leaf colors
- Paintbrushes
- Pencil
- **Black** crayon
- **White** construction paper

CRAFT ZONE

16

What to do:

1. With your pencil, trace the outlines of leaves onto **white** construction paper. Make sure to fill the entire page.

2. Trace over each leaf shape with a thick line of **black** crayon.

3. Paint the inside of each leaf shape with different fall colors. The **black** crayon will keep the colors from running together.

Suggestions

- Use different color crayons for the leaf outlines.
- Paint the **white** background area.

CRAFT ZONE

Self-Hardening Clay

Create your very own statue! This clay hardens over time, so you will have a strong sculpture without even using an oven.

What you'll need:
- 4 cups flour
- 1 teaspoon alum
- 1½ cups salt
- 1½ cups water
- Mixing bowl
- Resealable plastic bag
- Spoon

What to do:

1. Mix the salt, flour, and alum in a bowl.

2. Add the water gradually to form a ball.

3. Knead (pound, roll, and pull) the clay, adding water until it no longer falls apart.

4. Store in a sealed plastic bag in the refrigerator. Wait for the clay to become room temperature for easy use.

5. Let your finished project dry at room temperature for two days. It will be very hard and can be painted.

Suggestion

- Try sculpting your favorite animal or toy. See how close you can make the sculpture to the real thing!

Clay Creations

Now that you have your own clay recipe, there are a million things you can make with it. Here are a few ideas!

Octopus

- Divide your clay in half and make a ball with one half.
- Use the other half to make eight long legs. Roll the clay between your hands or on a flat surface.
- Attach each leg by pinching it to the body.

Snail

- First, roll a long piece of clay.
- Turn up one end to make the snail's head.
- Then, roll up the other end to make the shell.
- Two small pieces of uncooked spaghetti or pipe cleaners can be stuck into the head to make feelers.

Prickly Porcupine

- Shape your clay like an egg.
- Stretch out one end to make the head.
- Break up uncooked spaghetti and stick it on the porcupine's back.
- Next, add four pretzel pieces for the legs.
- Add eyes by pressing beads into the clay.

Flower Pot

Grow your own flowers in this pot! This pot takes several days to make, but once it is finished you can fill it with soil and seeds to grow flowers.

What you'll need:
- Self-hardening clay (see page 18)
- Tempera paint
- Paintbrushes and paint dishes
- Glue
- Water
- Soil
- Flower seeds

What to do:

1. Roll the clay into a ball.
2. Poke your thumb into the center of the ball to make an opening for the pot.
3. Turn the clay in your hand and pinch the opening wider with your thumbs.
4. Allow the pot to dry for two days.
5. When your pot is hardened and completely dry, paint it.
6. When your pot dries again, mix equal amounts of glue and water together.
7. Brush the mixture on the pot to protect the finish.
8. Pour soil into the pot.
9. Plant a few seeds in the soil and water. Place the pot in a window where there is sunlight.
10. Water your plant every few days and watch it grow!

Can you name the parts of a plant? Learn all about plants on pages 148 and 149 in the Science Zone!

CRAFT ZONE

Leaf Prints

Turn outdoor treasures into indoor art! Make natural wall hangings using leaves, twigs, and even sturdy flowers.

What you'll need:
- 2 cups cornstarch
- 1½ cups flour
- A leaf
- Wax paper
- 1 cup warm water
- Spoon
- Rolling pin
- Plastic drinking straw
- Yarn
- Mixing bowl
- Food coloring (optional)

Pick your favorite leaf from your leaf collection in the Science Zone! Check out pages 150–151 for more information.

CRAFT ZONE

What to do:

1. Mix the cornstarch and flour in a bowl.

2. If desired, add the food coloring to the water.

3. Make a hollow dent in the center, and stir in the warm water a little at a time.

4. Mix the dough all together.

5. Knead (press, pull, and fold) the mixture on wax paper. Sprinkle it with more flour if the dough is too sticky.

6. Flatten the dough and smooth it out with a rolling pin. Be careful not to roll it too thin.

7. Place a leaf, veined side down, onto the dough. Press it into the dough with a rolling pin, and then remove it carefully.

8. Poke a hole in the top of the dough with a straw.

9. When the print is dry, tie a loop of yarn through the hole to hang it.

Origami Sailboat

Origami is the ancient art of folding paper. Amazing creations can be made without even cutting or gluing.

What you'll need:
- Construction paper or any unlined paper
- Crayons or markers
- Scissors

Boy Oh Buoy!

CRAFT ZONE

24

What to do:

1. Cut the construction paper into a square with four-inch sides.

2. Fold your paper in half diagonally, and then fold it in half diagonally again.

3. Unfold the paper once to make a triangle.

4. Fold one edge up to meet the halfway line (see diagram on the right).

5. Fold the bottom corners on the boat back behind, as shown. Tuck them in together to keep them in place.

6. Decorate your sail with crayons or markers.

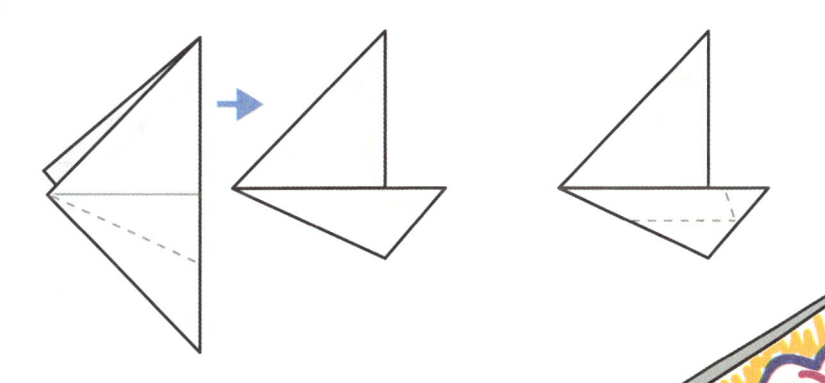

Suggestion

- Give your boat a name! Write it on the side.

Spring Flowers

Use these colorful flowers to create a beautiful bouquet. Give them to a friend or put them in the vase on page 28.

What you'll need:
- Construction paper, **green** and other colors
- Crayons or markers
- Scissors
- Glue
- Paper hole punch (optional)

What to do:

1. Cut a circle about 1½ inches across out of construction paper.

2. Glue dots from a hole punch or color a design in the center of the flower.

3. Cut out ½ inch by 1½ inch strips of construction paper to make petals.

4. Glue the ends of the petal together, as shown.

5. Glue each petal onto the back of the circle. You may need to hold it for a minute while it dries.

6. Cut a stem and some leaves from the **green** construction paper and glue them to the flower.

Suggestions

- Glue another ring of petals behind the first set.

- Use longer strips to make longer petals.

CRAFT ZONE

27

Flower Vase

Use this vase for dried or paper flowers. Decorate it with brightly colored paper to make it look like stained glass.

What you'll need:
- Round cardboard box (such as oatmeal or bread crumb boxes)
- Colored paper, wallpaper, or wrapping paper
- Old paintbrush
- Glue
- Scissors

What to do:

1. Cut or tear the paper into small pieces about the same size.

2. Decorate the box by gluing pieces of the colored paper over the entire box.

3. Brush glue over the whole vase to smooth it out.

Suggestion

- Use masking tape to cover the box, and then rub it with shoe polish to give it the look of leather.

Make a flower arrangement with the flowers from pages 7 and 26 in the Craft Zone!

Homemade Kazoo

If you can hum, you can already play this easy-to-make instrument! Make a kazoo for a friend, and you can play music together!

What you'll need:
- Cardboard roll
- Wax paper
- Rubber bands
- Crayons, markers, stickers, or paint
- Paper hole punch or scissors
- An adult

What to do:

1. Decorate the cardboard roll using crayons.

2. Have an adult punch out or poke several holes in one end of the roll.

3. Cover the end and the holes with wax paper held on tightly with a rubber band.

4. Hum into the open end of the roll with fingers placed lightly over the wax paper. Put your fingers over one or several holes.

5. Experiment with covering and uncovering the holes as you hum.

Suggestion

- Use a comb instead of the cardboard roll. Loosely wrap the wax paper around the comb. Fasten it on with a rubber band. Hold the comb to your lips and hum!

CRAFT ZONE

31

Box Guitar

You can make a guitar with things you have around the house. You'll be strumming tunes in no time!

What you'll need:
- A shoebox (no lid needed)
- Rubber bands of varying widths
- Tempera paint
- Paintbrushes with stiff bristles
- Paper towel roll
- Glue

What to do:

1. Paint the paper towel roll and entire shoebox, a few sides at a time, with a dark **brown** color. Let it dry.

2. Paint over the dark **brown** with lighter **brown** paint. This makes it look like wood. Let it dry.

3. Glue the paper towel roll to a short end of the shoebox.

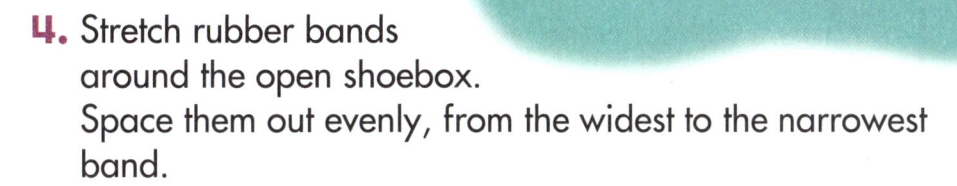

4. Stretch rubber bands around the open shoebox. Space them out evenly, from the widest to the narrowest band.

5. Experiment by plucking the strings one at a time as well as by strumming the strings all at once.

Foil Fun

This project will really make your creativity shine! Use the yarn to spell your name or make unique designs.

What you'll need:
- Aluminum foil
- Cardboard
- Permanent felt-tipped markers (water based markers will not work)
- Yarn
- Glue
- Tape
- Scissors
- Ruler

CRAFT ZONE

34

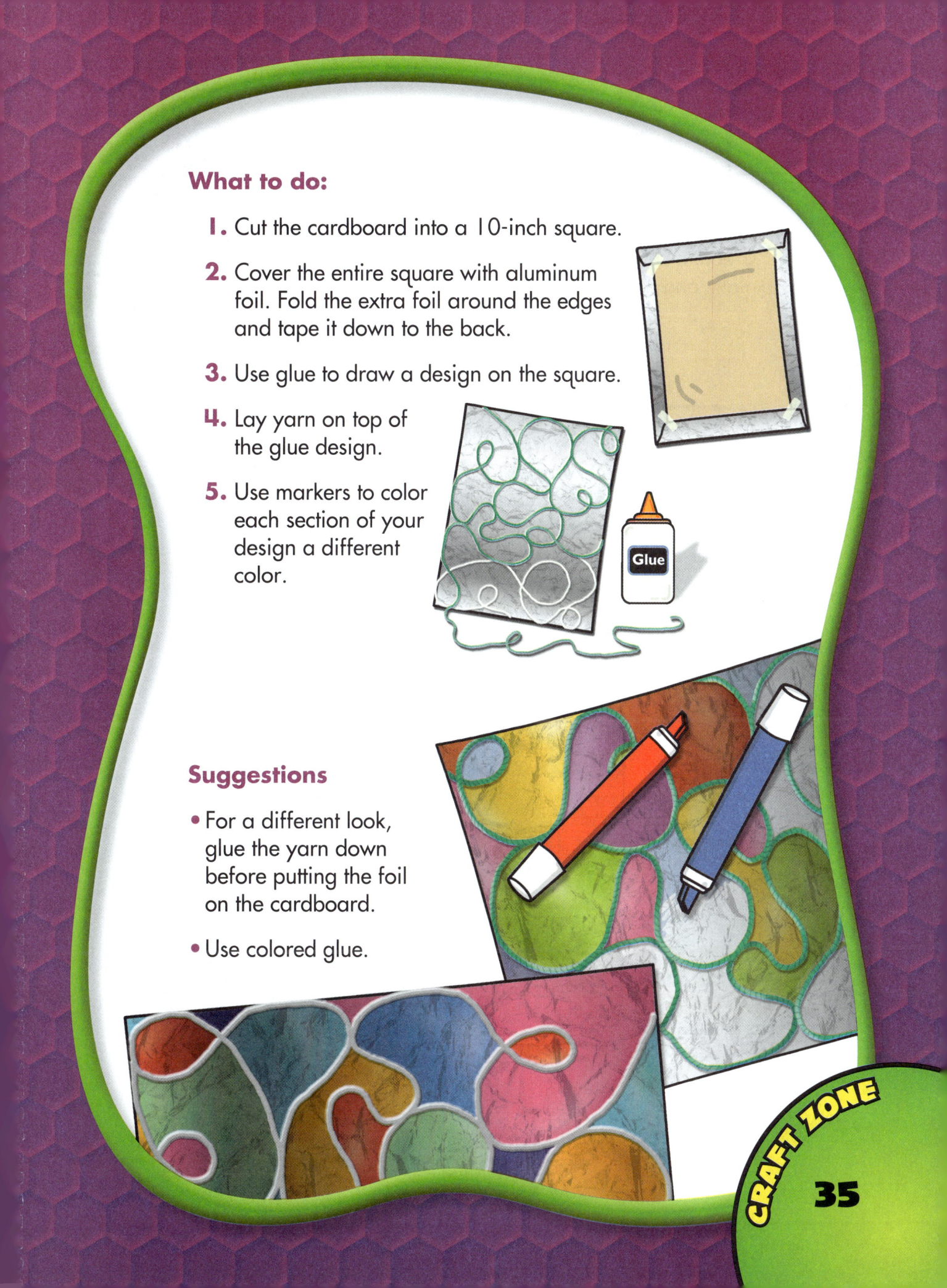

What to do:

1. Cut the cardboard into a 10-inch square.
2. Cover the entire square with aluminum foil. Fold the extra foil around the edges and tape it down to the back.
3. Use glue to draw a design on the square.
4. Lay yarn on top of the glue design.
5. Use markers to color each section of your design a different color.

Suggestions

- For a different look, glue the yarn down before putting the foil on the cardboard.
- Use colored glue.

CRAFT ZONE

Sand Painting

Create a colorful beach in a jar! Sand paintings are fun to make and easy to clean up.

What you'll need:
- Sand (white sand from garden shops works best)
- Baby food jar or another glass jar with a lid
- Food coloring
- Paper cups
- Spoon

What to do:

1. Fill paper cups about three-quarters full of sand.

2. Add a few drops of food coloring to each cup and mix well. Prepare at least three different colors of sand.

3. Carefully, spoon the sand into the jar, forming one layer of color at a time.

4. When the jar is full, screw on the lid tightly.

Suggestion

- After you fill your jar, take a toothpick and slowly poke into the sand along the sides. This will create wavy lines of different colors without completely mixing them.

CRAFT ZONE

37

Pinecone Bird Feeder

Fun to make and fun to watch! This bird feeder may become a favorite spot for the birds right outside your window.

What you'll need:
- Pinecone
- Peanut butter
- Birdseed or bread crumbs
- Butter knife or spoon
- String

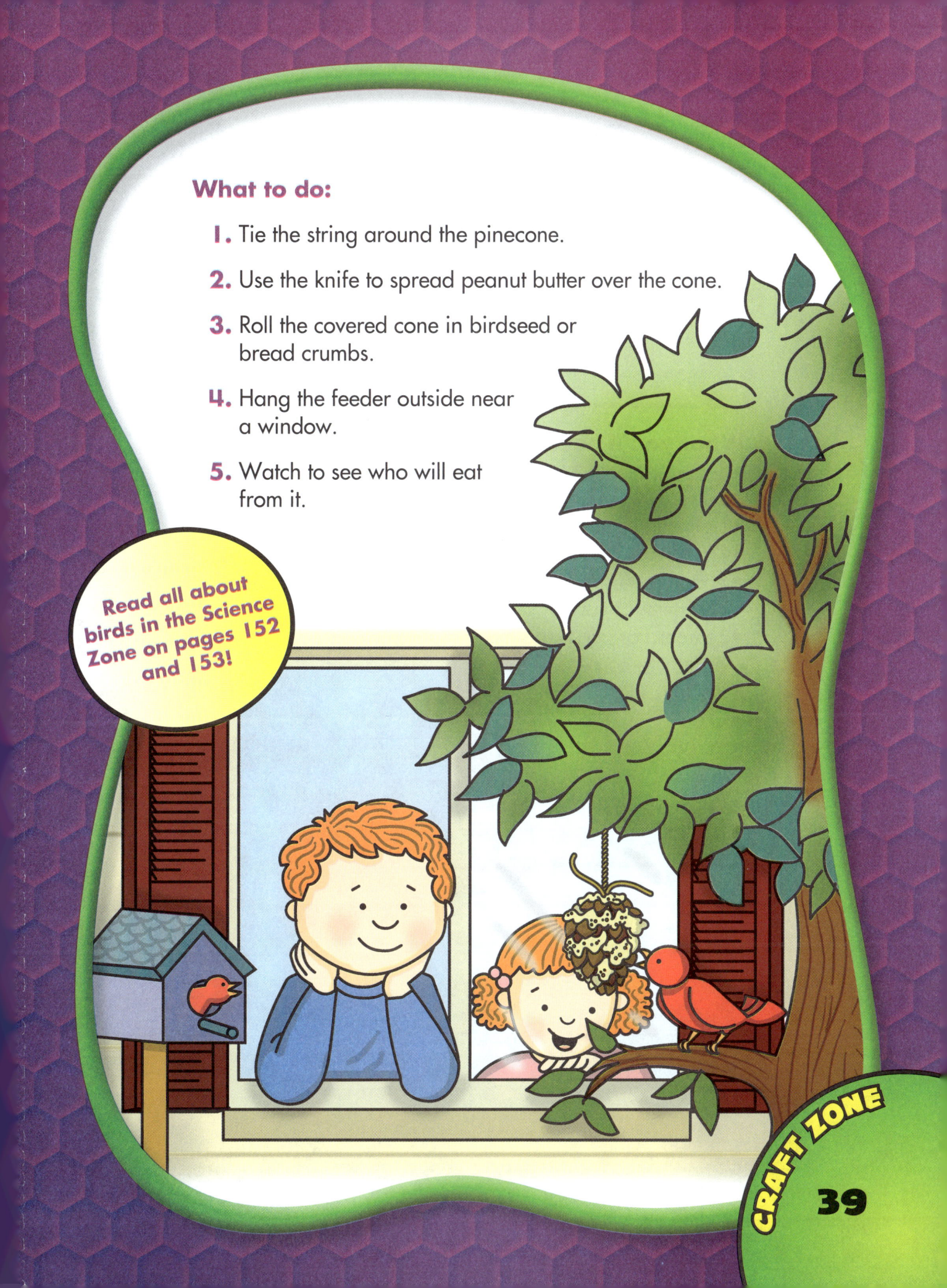

What to do:

1. Tie the string around the pinecone.
2. Use the knife to spread peanut butter over the cone.
3. Roll the covered cone in birdseed or bread crumbs.
4. Hang the feeder outside near a window.
5. Watch to see who will eat from it.

Read all about birds in the Science Zone on pages 152 and 153!

CRAFT ZONE

39

Piggy Bank

This pig is hungry! Saving money is much more fun when you are feeding a porky pig.

What you'll need:
- Two disposable soup bowls
- Lightweight cardboard
- Pipe cleaner
- Four thread spools, film canisters, or corks
- Tempera or acrylic paints, or felt-tipped pens
- Paintbrushes
- Glue
- Pencil
- Scissors
- Paper hole punch
- An adult

CRAFT ZONE

40

What to do:

1. Make a drawing of the pig's head on cardboard, including the tabs, as shown. Then, cut it.

2. Cut a $1\frac{1}{4}$ inch slit at the side of one bowl.

3. Slide the head into the slit and bend out the tabs and glue them to the inside of the bowl, as shown.

4. Punch a small hole in the bowl on the side opposite the head and insert a curled pipe cleaner as a tail. Glue or tape the pipe cleaner to the inside of the bowl to secure it.

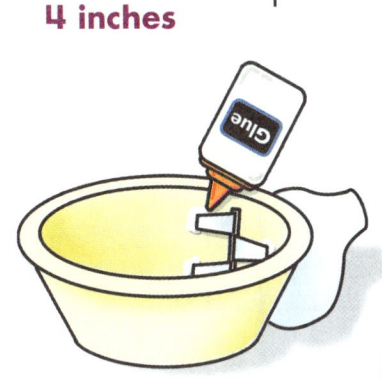

5. Have an adult cut a slit in the center of the pig's back, large enough for a quarter to fall through.

6. To make the body, apply glue to the rim of the other bowl and put the bowl with the pig's head directly on it, as shown. Let them dry.

7. To make legs, glue four thread spools to the bottom of the pig. Let them dry.

8. Paint your pig!

3 inches
4 inches

Help Kayla count the change from her piggy bank on page 92 in the Math Zone!

CRAFT ZONE
41

Bug Out

Is it an insect from the dinosaur era? A rare and deadly bug? Or just something silly from your imagination? You decide!

What you'll need:
- Crayons
- Various natural objects such as leaves, twigs, small pinecones, or tree bark
- Construction paper
- Glue

What to do:

1. Go outside and collect objects from nature, such as: twigs, leaves, bark, and pinecones.

2. Sort through your collection and arrange them in different ways. Make different kinds of bugs.

3. Draw a background on the construction paper. Include details to show where the bugs live and what they eat. Ideas may be scientifically correct or artistically creative.

4. Glue the bugs to the background paper.

Make an insect collection in the Science Zone! Check out pages 156–158.

Suggestion

- Arrange and glue the leftover natural objects to the background.

CRAFT ZONE

43

Quick and Easy Puppets

These are some of the fastest puppets you can make!

Greeting Card Puppet

- Cut out a person or animal from a greeting card.
- Glue it onto a craft stick or a plastic drinking straw for an instant puppet.

Cardboard Roll People Puppet

- Draw a face on a cardboard roll.
- Add a paper baking cup skirt by cutting out the bottom of a cup and then gluing it to the roll.
- Glue on yarn or cotton balls for hair and baking cups or paper scraps for hats and other simple features.

Envelope Shark Puppet

- Seal a long, business-sized envelope.
- Cut a triangle from one of the short edges to make a mouth.
- Tape the triangle to the top for the fin.
- Trim off the edge of the envelope opposite the mouth, making an opening for your hand.
- Decorate your shark with eyes, stripes, and sharp teeth!

Paper Plate Puppet

- Glue or draw a face onto a paper plate. You may want to use yarn hair, button eyes, ribbon eyebrows, and so on.
- When all is dry, tape a wooden paint stirring stick to the back of the plate.

Paper Plate Hand Puppet

Did you know you can make a paper plate talk? Use your imagination to make this silly puppet. Adding buttons, beads, or macaroni will make this puppet even more special.

What you'll need:
- Two 9 inch paper plates
- Watercolor, tempera, or acrylic paints or felt-tipped pens
- Paintbrush
- Glue
- Scissors

Suggested trims:

Buttons, beads, sections of egg cartons, bottle caps, foam balls, plastic wiggly eyes, paper nut cups, cardboard roll, cork, pieces of sponge, thread spool, paper cup, plastic cup, pom-poms, beans, popcorn packing foam, macaroni, yarn, curled gift ribbon, fur, raffia, cotton, fiberfill, construction paper, crepe paper strips, pipe cleaners, broom straws, drinking straws, fabric trims, sequins, foil, paper doilies, veiling, feathers, or old costume jewelry

CRAFT ZONE
46

What to do:

1. Fold a 9-inch paper plate in half to form a large mouth.

2. Cut the other paper plate in half.

3. Glue the rim of the halved plate to the rim of the folded plate. Leave the cut edge of the plate unglued, this forms a place for your hand, as shown. (Note: Do not try to stick your hand in until the glue is completely dry.)

4. Use your imagination as you glue some of the suggested trims to the paper plates to make the face. Be careful not to add yarn, feathers, or such items that may accidentally get paint on them. These can be glued in place after the paint is dry.

5. Paint your puppet. Let it dry.

6. Add the trims that do not need painting.

7. Cut a 1-inch by 3-inch strip from the paper plate scrap and glue it to the folded plate, as shown. This will give you a thumb hold, so that you will be better able to open and close the mouth of the puppet.

CRAFT ZONE

47

Treasure Box

Do you have any treasures you want to keep safe? Create your very own treasure box that opens and closes. Use it to hide your favorite treasures!

What you'll need:
- Two disposable soup bowls
- Hairpin or twisty tie
- Crayons, felt-tipped pens, watercolors, tempera or acrylic paints
- Glue
- Small round button or bead
- Paper hole punch
- Decorative stickers, glitter, ribbon, etc. (optional)

What to do:

1. To make a hinged box, punch two holes about 1 inch apart through the rims of the two bowls.

2. Thread a hair pin through each pair of holes and twist the ends to make it secure, as shown.

3. Decorate the box. Use an idea shown here or create your own design.

4. Add stickers or other decorations, if desired.

5. Glue the button to the front of the lid to make opening and closing easier.

Have a treasure hunt! Hide your treasure box and make a map for a friend to find it.

CRAFT ZONE

49

Thumbprint Animals

These animals are original since you use your own fingerprints to make them! See how many different animals you can create.

What you'll need:
- Several stamp pads (**black** or **purple** work well)
- Paper
- Crayons, colored pencils, or markers

What to do:

1. Roll your fingertip or thumb over the stamp pad.
2. Press it onto paper.
3. Add animal details (eyes, nose, whiskers, teeth, etc.) with the crayons.

Suggestions

- Staple several sheets together at the top to form a notepad.
- Use your stamped paper to make greeting cards, book covers, or wrapping paper.
- Write a story and illustrate it with these simple characters.

Math Zone

= 41¢

Number Recognition: Dot-to-Dot Fun

Directions: Connect the dots from **1** to **50**. Color the picture.

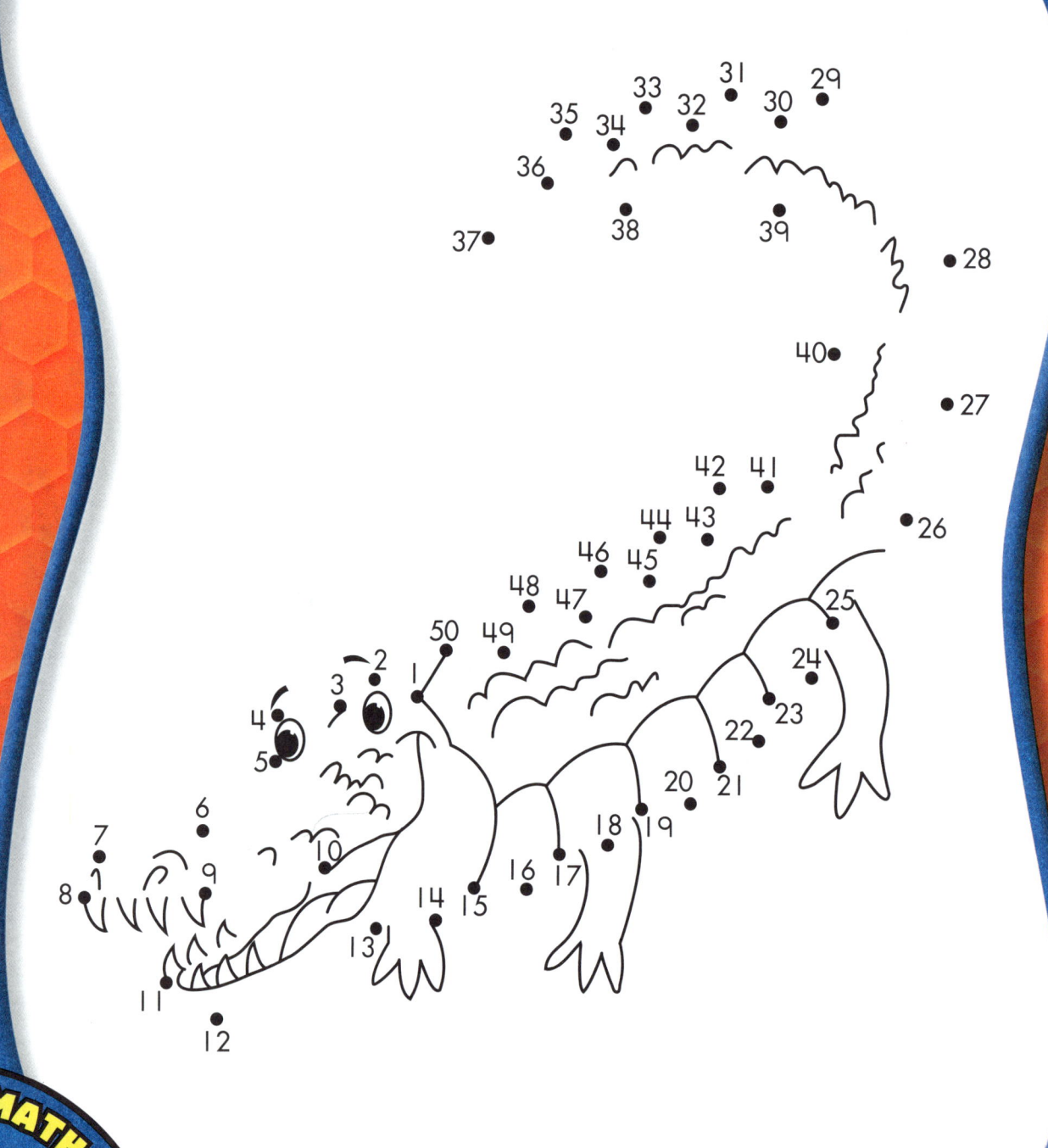

52

Number Recognition: Matching Game

Directions: Cut out the pictures and number words below. Mix them up and match them.

one	six		
two	seven		
three	eight		
four	nine		
five	ten		

MATH ZONE

53

Ordinal Numbers: Tyler's Toy Chest

Directions: Count Tyler's toys. Write your answers.

Where are the teddy bears?

eighth

seventeenth

Where are the dinosaurs?

_____

_____

Underline the **seventh** toy.

Circle the **thirteenth** toy.

Which toy do you think is Tyler's favorite? Draw it below.

Place Value: Ones, Tens

Place value refers to the position of each digit in a number. For example, if a monkey has **23** bananas, it has two sets of 10 bananas plus 3 bananas. The number **2** has the place value of **tens** and the number **3** is **ones**.

2 tens + 3 ones = 23

Directions: Add the tens and ones and write your answers on the lines.

7 tens + 5 ones = _____

5 tens + 2 ones = _____

9 tens + 5 ones = _____

8 tens + 1 one = _____

6 tens + 3 ones = _____

Directions: Draw a line to the correct number. The first one is done for you.

6 tens + 7 ones	73
4 tens + 2 ones	67
8 tens + 0 ones	51
7 tens + 3 ones	80
5 tens + 1 ones	42

Place Value: Ones and Tens

Kayla opened her piggy bank. She wants to use her change to count tens and ones. Help Kayla count.

10 ones = 1 ten

Directions: Write how many tens and ones.

____ tens ____ ones = ____

____ tens ____ ones = ____

____ tens ____ ones = ____

____ tens ____ ones = ____

____ tens ____ ones = ____

____ tens ____ ones = ____

Place Value: Shooting Stars

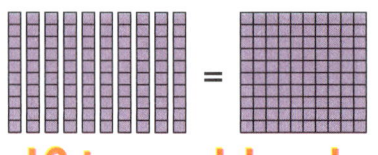

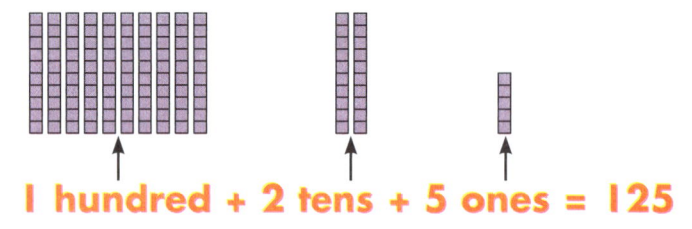

10 tens = 1 hundred

1 hundred + 2 tens + 5 ones = 125

Directions: Write how many hundreds, tens, and ones.

137 = ____ hundred ____ tens ____ ones

109 = ____ hundred ____ tens ____ ones

122 = ____ hundred ____ tens ____ ones

146 = ____ hundred ____ tens ____ ones

114 = ____ hundred ____ tens ____ ones

130 = ____ hundred ____ tens ____ ones

Place Value: Up, Up, and Away

Directions: Use the code to color the balloons.

Color Code:

7 hundreds = red

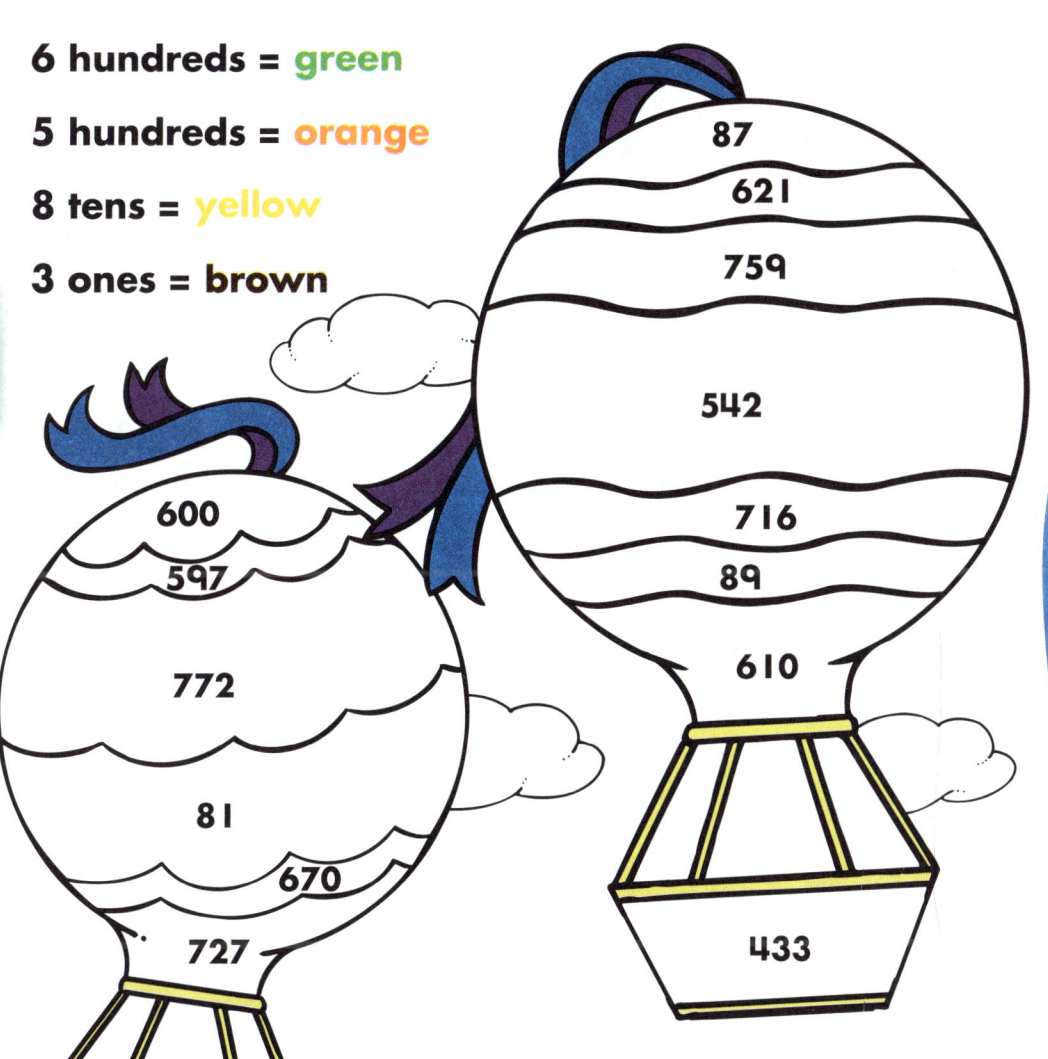

6 hundreds = green

5 hundreds = orange

8 tens = yellow

3 ones = brown

87
621
759
542
716
89
610
433

600
597
772
81
670
727
13

MATH ZONE

59

Addition: Apple Picking

Directions: Add the numbers. Write the answer on the apples.

- 7 + 9 = 16
- 5 + 2 = 7
- 9 + 3 = 12
- 4 + 6 = 10
- 3 + 1 = 4
- 4 + 4 = 8
- 8 + 9 = 17
- 6 + 0 = 6

MATH ZONE

60

Addition: Solve the Riddle

Directions: Add to find the sums. Use the code to answer the riddle. One is done for you. *Excellent*

11	18	3	9	13	10	4	12	6	14	7	20
E	U	H	A	S	F	D	T	R	Y	L	W

Why are teddy bears never hungry?

8 + 4 = 12 → T
1 + 2 = 3 → H
5 + 6 = 11 → E
7 + 7 = 14 → Y

5 + 4 = 9 → A
1 + 5 = 6 → R
9 + 2 = 11 → E

7 + 2 = 9 → A
4 + 3 = 7 → L
10 + 10 = 20 → W
6 + 3 = 9 → A
11 + 3 = 14 → Y
7 + 6 = 13 → S

10 + 3 = 13 → S
9 + 3 = 12 → T
9 + 9 = 18 → U
5 + 5 = 10 → F
6 + 4 = 10 → F
11 + 0 = 11 → E
2 + 2 = 4 → D!

Ha, Ha, Ha

Addition: 2-Digit

Kayla wrote some 2-digit addition problems for Tyler! Help Tyler solve them. Look at the example. Then, follow the directions.

Example:

Step 1: Add the ones.

```
  25
+ 43
———
   8
```

Step 2: Add the tens.

```
  25
+ 43
———
sum = 68
```

Directions: Add to find the sum.

```
  53      36      74      82      25
+ 11    + 43    + 15    + 12    + 14
```

```
  66      28      31      27      84
+ 22    + 41    + 60    + 50    + 11
```

Directions: Create your own 2-digit addition problem. Give it to a friend to solve.

_____ + _____ = _____

Addition: Problem Solving

Directions: Solve each problem using 2-digit addition. Show your work next to the problem. The first one is done for you.

Marti catches 10 in one pond.

She catches 11 in another pond.

How many does she catch in all? __21__

```
  10
+ 11
```

There are 42 in one tree.

There are 33 in another tree.

How many are in both trees? _____

Craig finds 13 .

Zach finds 20 .

How many do they find in all? _____

There were 14 in the park this morning.

There were 22 in the park last night.

How many were in the park in all? _____

Addition

Addition is putting together or adding two or more numbers to find the sum. **Regrouping** is using 10 ones to form one ten, 10 tens to form one 100, 15 ones to form one ten and five ones, for example.

Example:

Step 1: Add the ones.

```
  37
+ 45
----
  12
```
12 = 1 ten 2 ones

Step 2: Regroup the tens.

```
   1
  37
+ 45
----
   2
```

Step 3: Add the tens.

```
   1
  37
+ 45
----
  82
```

Directions: Follow the steps to add.

```
  15      48      29      19      43
+ 66    + 44    + 35    + 18    + 39
```

```
  75      88      47      26      27
+ 17    +  8    + 37    + 55    +  9
```

Addition: Follow the Path

Directions: Write each sum. Connect the sums of **83** to make a road for the truck.

$$\begin{array}{r}17\\+66\\\hline\end{array} \quad \begin{array}{r}48\\+26\\\hline\end{array} \quad \begin{array}{r}42\\+19\\\hline\end{array}$$

$$\begin{array}{r}28\\+38\\\hline\end{array} \quad \begin{array}{r}64\\+19\\\hline\end{array} \quad \begin{array}{r}26\\+57\\\hline\end{array} \quad \begin{array}{r}58\\+25\\\hline\end{array} \quad \begin{array}{r}17\\+75\\\hline\end{array} \quad \begin{array}{r}65\\+29\\\hline\end{array}$$

$$\begin{array}{r}37\\+39\\\hline\end{array} \quad \begin{array}{r}48\\+35\\\hline\end{array} \quad \begin{array}{r}58\\+37\\\hline\end{array} \quad \begin{array}{r}65\\+16\\\hline\end{array} \quad \begin{array}{r}38\\+25\\\hline\end{array} \quad \begin{array}{r}39\\+59\\\hline\end{array}$$

$$\begin{array}{r}59\\+27\\\hline\end{array} \quad \begin{array}{r}55\\+28\\\hline\end{array} \quad \begin{array}{r}39\\+44\\\hline\end{array}$$

Subtraction: Hidden Differences

Directions: Circle the pairs that have a difference of **3**. One is done for you.

7 10 (5 2) 0 11 14 17
15 12 16 1 4 8 10 13
18 10 4 11 2 1 12 9
7 6 6 9 0 18 15 18
16 13 3 1 3 16 5 15
14 8 17 6 6 8 13 0
11 3 5 4 1 17 12 3
7 4 2 5 2 14 0 9

Subtraction

Tyler wrote some subtraction problems for Kayla. Help Kayla solve the problems!

Directions: Subtract to find the difference.

```
 13     7     4    14    10     5
- 4   - 1   - 2   - 8   - 9   - 0
```

```
 11    15     6    17     8    12
- 4   - 6   - 6   - 8   - 2   - 5
```

Directions: Create your own subtraction problem. Give it to a friend to solve.

_____ − _____ = _____

Subtraction: 2-Digit Numbers

Looks like a storm is coming! Look at the example and follow the directions to create some math storm clouds.

Example:

Step 1: Subtract the ones.

$$\begin{array}{r} 77 \\ -26 \\ \hline 1 \end{array}$$

Step 2: Subtract the tens.

$$\begin{array}{r} 77 \\ -26 \\ \hline \end{array}$$
difference = 51

Directions: Subtract to find the difference. Write the answers on the clouds. Use the color code to color the clouds.

Color Code:

12 = gray
21 = black
24 = purple
33 = blue

$$\begin{array}{r} 36 \\ -24 \\ \hline \end{array}$$

$$\begin{array}{r} 74 \\ -50 \\ \hline \end{array}$$

$$\begin{array}{r} 95 \\ -62 \\ \hline \end{array}$$

$$\begin{array}{r} 59 \\ -38 \\ \hline \end{array}$$

$$\begin{array}{r} 69 \\ -36 \\ \hline \end{array}$$

$$\begin{array}{r} 78 \\ -66 \\ \hline \end{array}$$

$$\begin{array}{r} 82 \\ -61 \\ \hline \end{array}$$

$$\begin{array}{r} 35 \\ -11 \\ \hline \end{array}$$

Subtraction: Color Code

Directions: Solve the subtraction problems. Use the code to color the picture.

Color Code:

25 = blue   57 = green
31 = yellow   14 = orange
21 = brown   11 = red

47 − 22 = 25

52 − 21 = 31

25 − 11 = 14

62 − 31 = 31

77 − 20 = 57

51 − 40 = 11

55 − 34 = 21

69 − 12 = 57

98 − 41 = 57

Subtraction: Regrouping

Subtraction is taking away or subtracting one number from another to find the difference. **Regrouping** is using one ten to form 10 ones, one 100 to form 10 tens, for example.

Example:

Step 1: Regroup.

$$\begin{array}{r}{\scriptstyle 2\ 13}\\ \cancel{33}\\ -19\\ \hline \end{array}$$

Step 2: Subtract the ones.

$$\begin{array}{r}{\scriptstyle 2\ 13}\\ \cancel{33}\\ -19\\ \hline 4\end{array}$$

Step 3: Subtract the tens.

$$\begin{array}{r}{\scriptstyle 2\ 13}\\ \cancel{33}\\ -19\\ \hline \end{array}$$
difference = 14

3 tens 3 ones =
2 tens 13 ones

Directions: Follow the steps to subtract.

```
  36      51      44      84      72
- 17    - 39    - 15    - 47    - 65
```

```
  76      90      53      94      75
- 19    - 78    - 26    - 85    - 18
```

70

Subtraction: Fruit Picking Fun

Tyler and Kayla are on a class field trip to a fruit farm! Follow the directions to solve the problems below.

Directions: Solve the problems. Show your work. The first one is done for you.

Tyler picks 50 .

Kayla picks 38 .

How many more does Tyler pick? __12__

$$\begin{array}{r} 50 \\ -38 \\ \hline \end{array}$$

The farm sold 37 yesterday.

It sells 29 so far today.

How many more were sold yesterday? _____

Kayla buys 60 for her mom.

51 are ripe.

How many of the are not ripe? _____

Tyler picks 42 .

He gives 18 away.

How many does he have left? _____

3-Digit Addition

Example:

Step 1:
Add the ones.

```
  623
+ 156
-----
    9
```

Step 2:
Add the tens.

```
  623
+ 156
-----
   79
```

Step 3:
Add the hundreds.

```
  623
+ 156
-----
  779
```

Directions: Add to find the sum. Circle answers that are even in **red**. Circle answers that are odd in **blue**.

```
  415        566        373        160
+ 342      + 333      + 221      + 334


  835        642        287        723
+ 142      + 251      + 412      + 245


  133        454        314        654
+ 522      + 324      + 602      + 235
```

72

3-Digit Subtraction

Example:

Step 1: Subtract the ones.

```
  586
- 142
----
    4
```

Step 2: Subtract the tens.

```
  586
- 142
----
   44
```

Step 3: Subtract the hundreds.

```
  586
- 142
----
  444
```

Directions: Subtract to find the difference. Use the code to answer the riddle. One is done for you.

212	237	311	152	521	255	511	236	200	512
L	I	S	E	N	A	M	O	G	T

What did the beach say when the tide came in?

```
  635       569       846       818
- 423     - 333     - 325     - 618
  212
   L
```

```
  936       478       653       297              611       579
- 424     - 241     - 142     - 145            -  90     - 343
```

```
  338       292       769
-  27     - 140     - 514
```

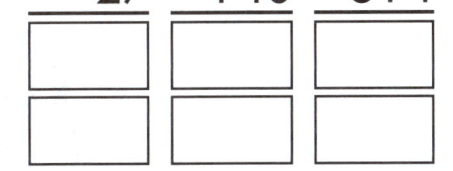

73

Review Addition and Subtraction

An elephant is given 91 peanuts.
It eats 76 peanuts.
How many are left? _____

Directions: Now, draw the elephant with the correct number of peanuts.

Kayla and Tyler are picking flowers.
Kayla picks 6 flowers.
Tyler picks 12 flowers.
How many flowers in all? _____

Directions: Now, draw Kayla and Tyler with the correct number of flowers.

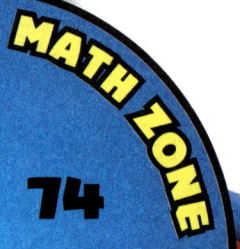

Review: Monster Math

Monsters are only afraid of one thing, math! Help the monsters solve the problems.

Directions: Add or subtract using regrouping.

```
  84         41         64         65
- 56       - 17       + 17       - 28
```

```
  33         25         57         72
+ 18       + 35       - 39       - 19
```

Directions: Draw your own monster!

Multiplication

Multiplication is a short way to find the sum of adding the same number a certain amount of times. For example, 7 x 4 = 28 instead of 7+7+7+7 = 28.

Example:
3 + 3 + 3 = 9
3 threes = 9
3 x 3 = 9

Directions: Study the example. Solve the problems.

7 + 7 = _____

2 sevens = _____

2 x 7 = _____

---

4 + 4 + 4 + 4 = _____

4 fours = _____

4 x _____ = _____

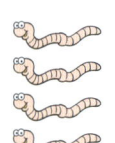

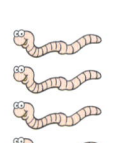

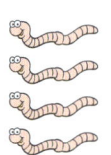

---

2 + 2 + 2 + 2 = _____

4 twos = _____

4 x _____ = _____

---

6 + 6 = _____

2 sixes = _____

2 x _____ = _____

Multiplication

Tyler draws pictures to help him understand multiplication. You can try it, too!

Directions: Draw a picture for each problem. Write the missing numbers.

Draw 3 groups of four balloons.

4 + 4 + 4 = _____

or 3 x 4 = _____

Draw 6 groups of two hats.

2 + _____ + _____ + _____ + _____ + _____

or 6 x _____ = _____

Draw 6 groups of three cupcakes.

3 + _____ + _____ + _____ + _____ + _____

or _____ x _____ = _____

Multiplication

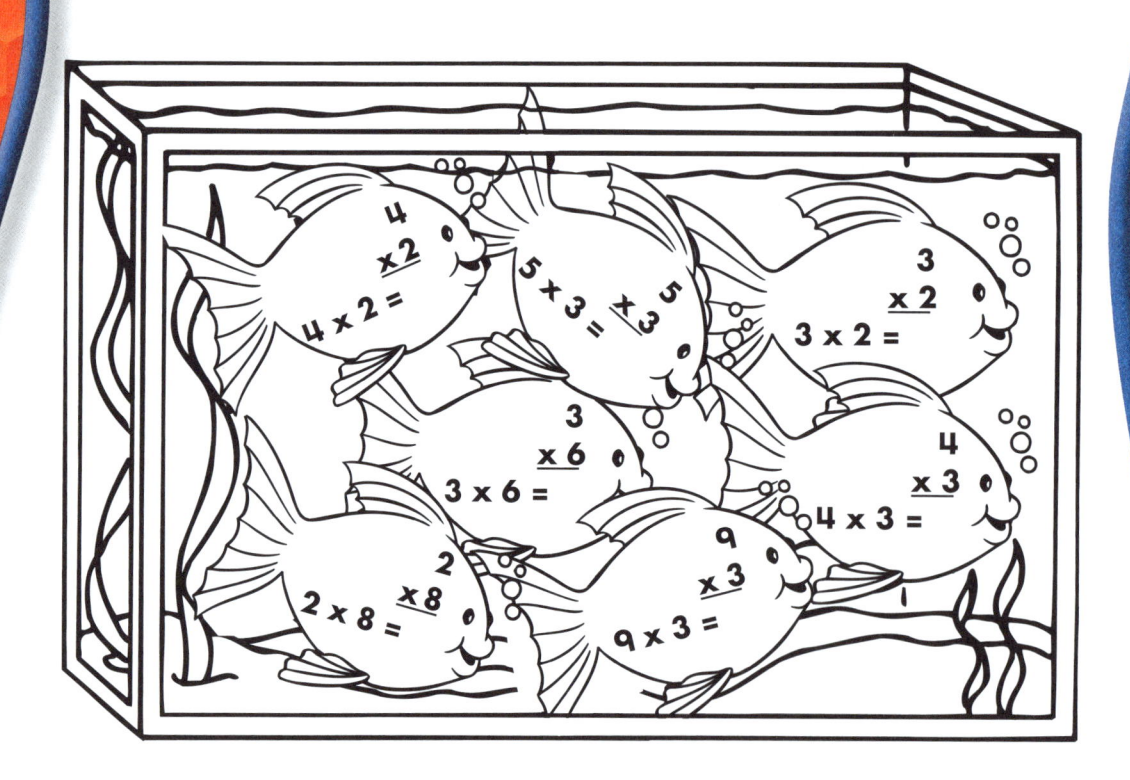

Directions: Solve the multiplication problems. Use the code to color the picture.

Color Code:
6 = red   27 = brown   18 = purple
12 = orange   8 = yellow
16 = blue   15 = green

4 × 2 =   4
            ×2

5 × 3 =   5
            ×3

3 × 2 =   3
            ×2

3 × 6 =   3
            ×6

4 × 3 =   4
            ×3

2 × 8 =   2
            ×8

9 × 3 =   9
            ×3

Multiplication

Directions: Solve the multiplication problems. Use the code to color the picture.

Color Code:
6 = green
8 = purple
9 = red

16 = pink
18 = white
21 = brown

25 = orange
27 = blue

3 x 3 =
4 x 2 =
8 x 2 =
5 x 5 =
2 x 3 =
9 x 3 =

3 x 6 =

2 x 9 =

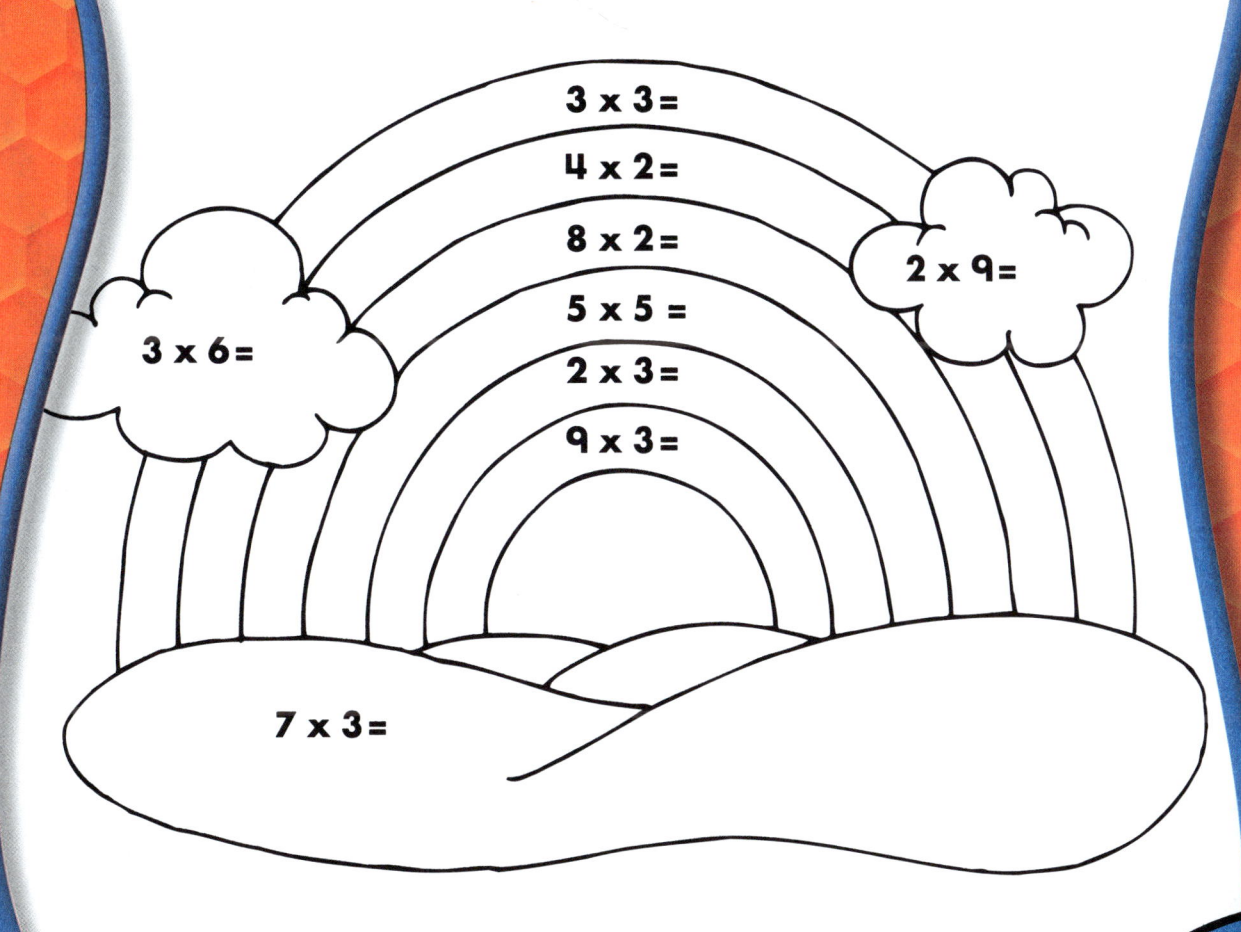

7 x 3 =

Problem Solving: Addition, Subtraction, and Multiplication

Directions: Tell if you add, subtract, or multiply. Write the answer on the lines. "In all" means to add. "Left" means to subtract. Groups with the same number in each means to multiply.

Example:

There are 6 brown dogs and 6 gray dogs.
How many dogs in all?

_____**add**_____ ___**12**___ dogs

Tyler counted 15 basketballs on the playground.
He picked up 3 of them.
How many are left on the playground?

_____ _____ basketballs

There are 5 cages of snakes.
There are 2 snakes in each cage.
How many snakes are there in the store?

_____ _____ snakes

Kayla saw 18 school buses waiting for children.
When she checked again, 7 buses had driven away.
How many buses are left?

_____ _____ buses

Problem Solving: Addition and Subtraction

Directions: Add or subtract to solve each problem. Show your work. The first one is done for you.

Marcus has 12 📕.

He gives 3 📕 to Tyler.

How many 📕 does Marcus have left? __9__

$$\begin{array}{r} 12 \\ -3 \\ \hline \end{array}$$

There are 15 students with ⚽.

There are 9 students with 🏈.

How many students have ⚽ or 🏈? _____

The earth club plants 14 🌳 on Saturday

and 18 🌳 on Sunday.

How many 🌳 do they plant in all? _____

Then, the earth club plants 45 🌼.

24 of the 🌼 are tulips.

How many of the 🌼 are not tulips? _____

MATH ZONE

81

Shapes: Circles and Squares

A **circle** is a shape that is round.

This is a circle ●.

Directions: Look around you. Find something that is a circle. Draw it below.

A **square** is a shape with four right angles and four sides of the same length.

This is a square ■.

Directions: Look around you. Find something that is a square. Draw it below.

Shape Spill: Rectangles and Triangles

Tyler and Kayla mixed up all the rectangles and triangles! Sort the shapes below.

A **rectangle** is a shape with four corners and four sides.

This is a rectangle.

A **triangle** is a shape with three corners and three sides.

This is a triangle.

Directions: Help Tyler color the rectangles **blue**. Help Kayla color the triangles **purple**.

Shape Chef

The Shape Chef is cooking a meal using his favorite shapes. Help create a yummy shape meal.

Directions: Practice tracing and drawing triangles and squares. Then, draw one triangle and one square on the plate. Turn the shapes into foods!

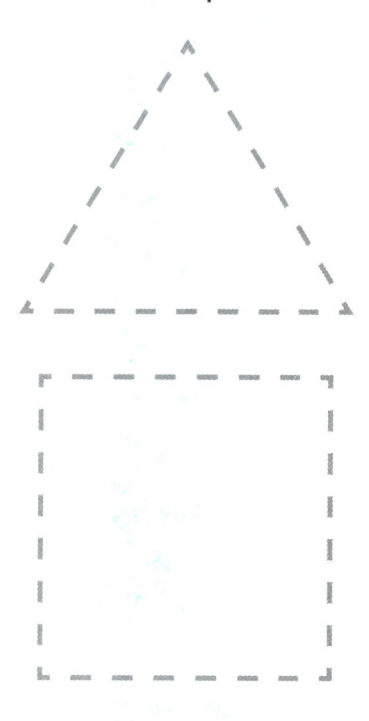

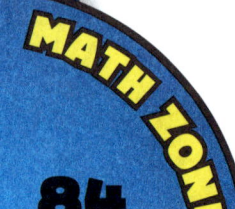

MATH ZONE

84

Robot Shapes

Two shape robots want to help you learn about ovals. An **oval** is egg-shaped. This is an oval.

Directions: Use a **green** crayon to color all the **circles** on the robots. Use an **orange** crayon to color all the **ovals**. Color the other shapes any way you like!

MATH ZONE

85

Fractions: Half, Third, Fourth

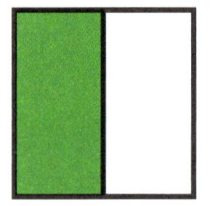

shaded part 1
equal part   2

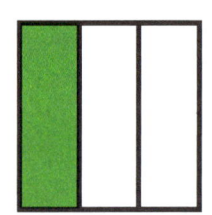

$\dfrac{1}{2}$ (one-half)

shaded part 1
equal part   3

$\dfrac{1}{3}$ (one-third)

shaded part 1
equal part   4

$\dfrac{1}{4}$ (one-fourth)

Directions: Color the correct fraction.

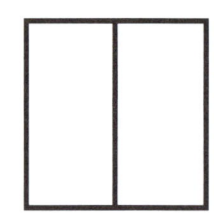

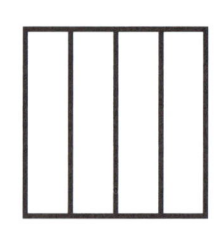

Color $\dfrac{1}{3}$ **red**

Color $\dfrac{1}{4}$ **blue**

Color $\dfrac{1}{2}$ **orange**

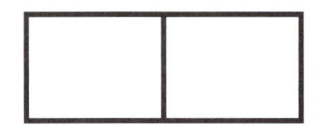

Fractions: Shaded Shapes

Directions: Draw a line to match each fraction with its correct shape.

$\frac{1}{3}$

$\frac{2}{4}$

$\frac{1}{4}$

$\frac{1}{2}$

$\frac{3}{4}$

$\frac{2}{3}$

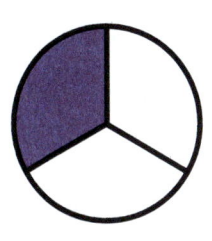

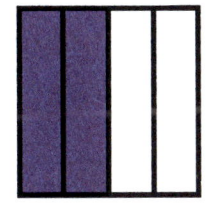

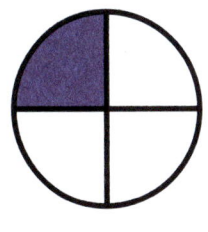

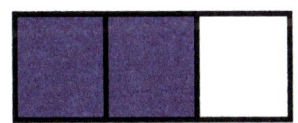

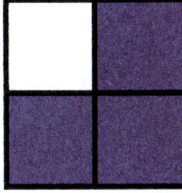

Time: Time to the Hour and Half Hour

Hour:
4 o'clock
4:00

Half Hour:
Half past 4
4:30

Directions: Write the time two ways.

_____ o'clock

_____ : _____

_____ o'clock

_____ : _____

Half past _____

_____ : _____

Half past _____

_____ : _____

Half past _____

_____ : _____

_____ o'clock

_____ : _____

MATH ZONE

88

Time: Your Schedule

Directions: Look at the time on the clocks. Write the number that tells the time. Then, draw a picture of something you do at that time.

_____ : _____

_____ : _____

_____ : _____

Money: Pennies and Nickels

penny
1¢

nickel
5¢

Directions: Look at each amount of money. Draw the correct number of pennies and nickels.

3¢

7¢

5¢

9¢

2¢

Money: Dimes

dime

10¢

Directions: Count by 10s. Write the number. Circle the group with more.

_____ ¢   or   _____ ¢

_____ ¢   or   _____ ¢

_____ ¢   or   _____ ¢

_____ ¢   or   _____ ¢

Money: Quarters

Kayla is counting the quarters she has in her piggy bank! Help Kayla count the quarters.

quarter

25¢

Directions: Count the quarters. Write the answer on the line.

_____ ¢

_____ ¢

_____ ¢

What should Kayla buy with her quarters? Draw it below.

Make your own piggy bank in the Craft Zone! Check it out on pages 40 and 41!

Money: Counting Change

Directions: Elephants never forget how much change they have! Draw a line from the change to the elephant with the correct number.

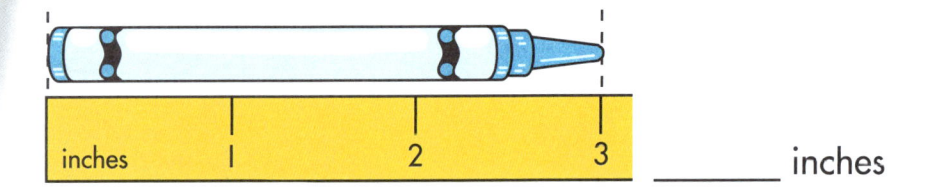

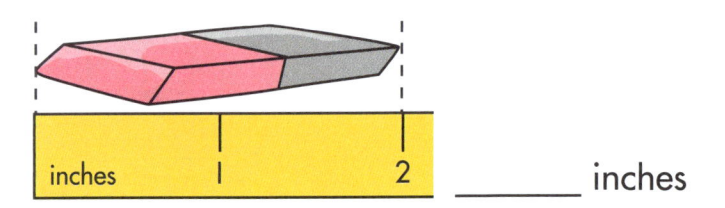

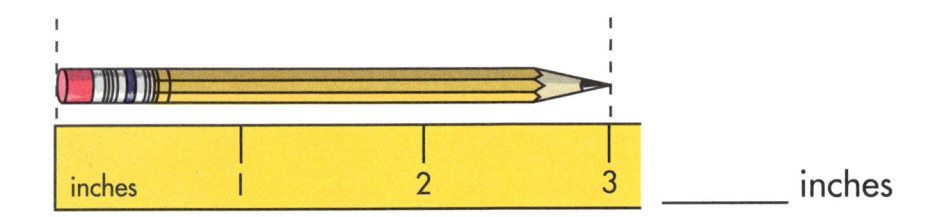

Measurement: Inches

Kayla is measuring things in her desk at school. See if you can find the correct length in inches of each object.

Directions: Write the length of each object in inches. The first one is done for you.

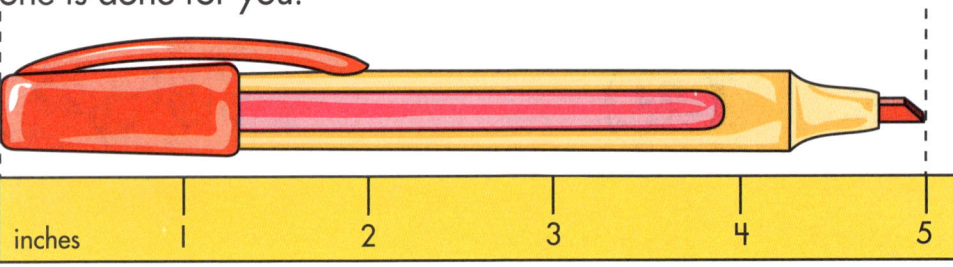

__5__ inches

_____ inches

_____ inches

_____ inches

Measurement: Centimeters

Look around your house for objects you can measure in centimeters. Measure the objects below for practice.

Directions: Write the length of each object in centimeters. The first one is done for you.

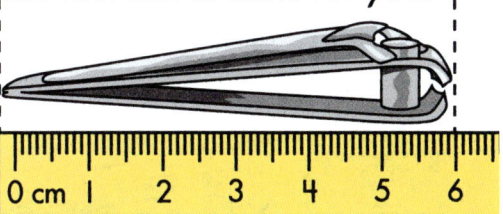

___6___ centimeters

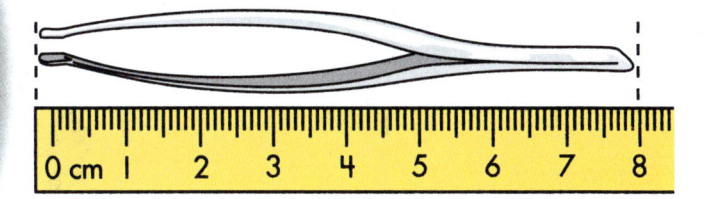

_____ centimeters

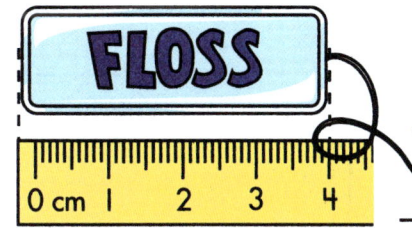

_____ centimeters

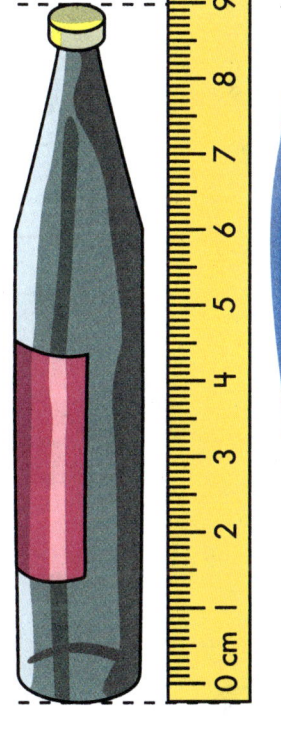

_____ centimeters

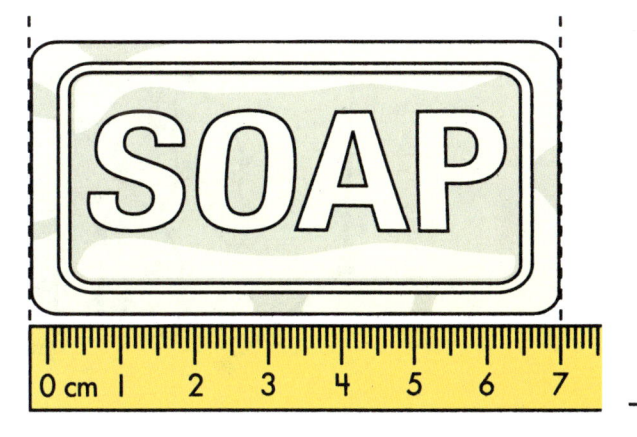

_____ centimeters

MATH ZONE

95

Measurement

Directions: Use a centimeter ruler to measure the distance each animal has to travel to reach the watering hole. Write the answer on each line.

_____ cm

_____ cm

_____ cm

_____ cm

_____ cm

_____ cm

Measurement

Directions: Search your house and find an object to measure. Measure it in inches first. Write the inches. Then, measure it in centimeters. Write the centimeters. Draw the object.

_____ inches

_____ centimeters

Graph: Picture Graph

Tyler is making a picture graph about his friends' favorite sports. Can you make one, too?

Directions: Use the picture graph to answer the questions. Each picture means one person likes the sport.

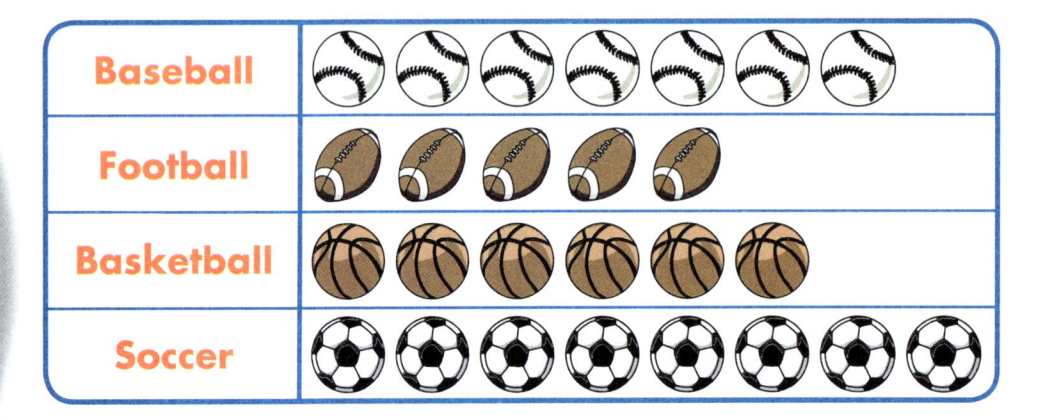

Baseball	⚾⚾⚾⚾⚾⚾⚾
Football	🏈🏈🏈🏈🏈
Basketball	🏀🏀🏀🏀🏀🏀
Soccer	⚽⚽⚽⚽⚽⚽⚽⚽

Which sport did most people choose? _____

Which sport did 7 people choose? _____

How many people chose football or basketball? _____

Circle the sport that had more people choose it.   ⚾ ⚽

What is your favorite sport? _____

Graph: Bar Graph

Kayla is taking care of her class pet rabbit, Flash! She made a bar graph to show how many carrots he ate in one school week.

Directions: Count the carrots in each column. Color the boxes **green** to show how many carrots the rabbit ate.

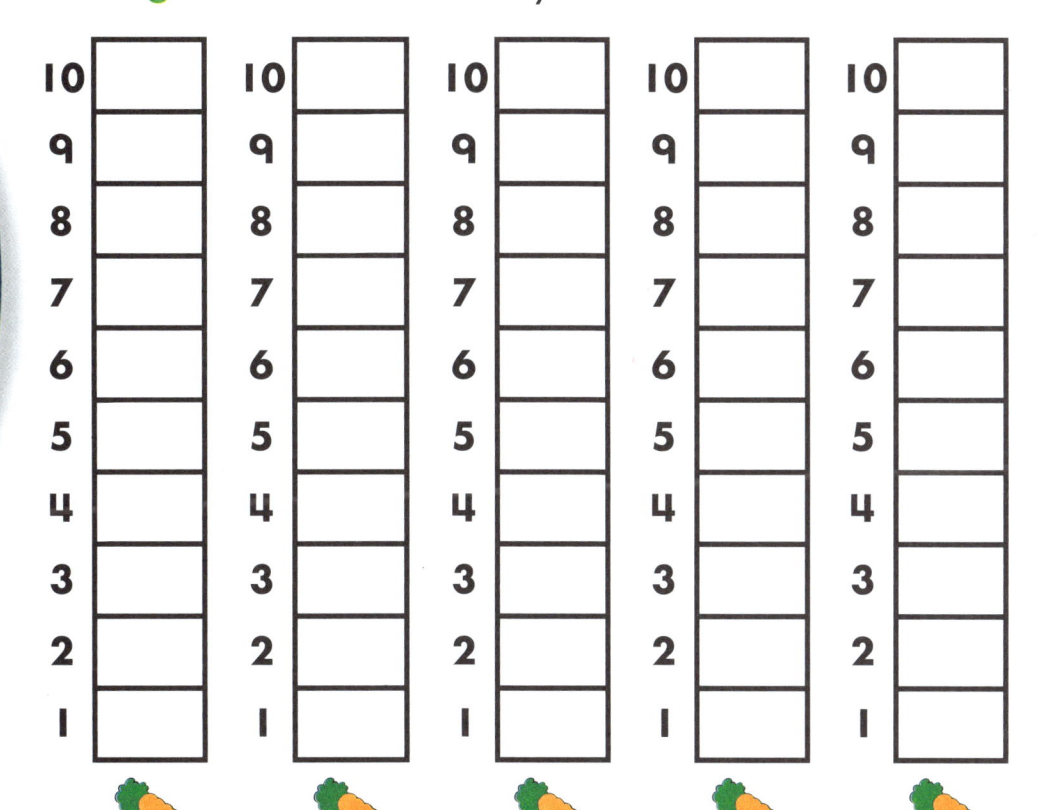

Read "Kayla and the Class Pet" in the Story Zone, starting on page 113!

Graph: Breakfast Graph

What kind of cereal is your favorite? What is your friend's favorite? Make your own bar graph to find out!

Directions: List five kinds of cereal on the graph below. Ask five people to vote for one cereal. Color one space for each vote. Use the information to answer the questions.

cereals

　　　　　1　2　3　4　5
　　　　　number of people

Which cereal was the favorite? _____

Which cereal had the fewest votes? _____

How many more voted for _____ than
　　　　　　　　　　　　　　name of cereal

for _____ ? _____
　　name of cereal

How many people chose _____ and
　　　　　　　　　　　　　　name of cereal

_____ altogether? _____
name of cereal

MATH ZONE

100

The Great Butterfly Search

STORY ZONE
101

"Hi Kayla," Tyler said. "Can I sit with you?"

"Sure!" Kayla said.

Miss Garcia's second grade class was going to the conservatory for a field trip.

"I hope we see lots of bugs!" Tyler said excitedly. He loved to collect insects.

"We should go in the tropical room," Kayla said. "There are so many butterflies in there." Then, Kayla whispered, "including a very rare one."

"Let's be the first ones to find it!" Tyler said with a smile.

Directions: What do you think the rare butterfly looks like? Draw it below.

Soon, Miss Garcia's class was in the tropical room.

"Listen closely everyone," Miss Garcia said. "Explore the tropical room and fill out your worksheets. We will meet again in a half hour."

"If you are lucky," Miss Garcia said with a smile. "You might see a rare orange and blue butterfly called the Pipevine Swallowtail."

"Let's go Ty!" Kayla said. Kayla and Tyler began their search.

"Don't worry Kayla. I'm the best at hide and seek," Tyler said. "I'll find it."

Directions: Help Kayla and Tyler fill out their worksheets. Fill in the blanks below. Use the words from the word box to help.

Butterfly Conservatory Worksheet
Miss Garcia's Class

| blue | insect | colors | egg |

A butterfly is an *insect*.

A butterfly's life cycle is *egg*, larva, pupa, and adult.

Butterflies come in many different *colors*.

The Pipevine Swallowtail is orange and *blue*.

STORY ZONE

103

"There are so many cool butterflies in here!" Kayla said. She and Tyler were drawing and coloring every butterfly they saw. But they did not see the Pipevine Swallowtail.

"There are more butterflies in here than I thought," Tyler said. "We only have five minutes left. I need to draw one on my worksheet."

"Me too," said Kayla. "How about this one?" She pointed to a pretty butterfly.

Directions: Color the butterfly.

"Looks good to me," Tyler said. He was disappointed he could not find the Pipevine Swallowtail.

"Ty, don't move," Kayla whispered.

"Why?" he asked, frozen.

"The Pipevine Swallowtail is on your head!" Kayla began drawing it. After a minute, it flew away.

"Well, I found it after all," Tyler laughed as he watched it flutter into the bushes.

"Nope, I think it found you!" said Kayla with a smile. "Let's go tell Miss Garcia!"

Directions: Help Kayla and Tyler think of some adjectives to describe the butterfly. **Adjectives** are describing words. Write some on the lines. Then, plug them into the sentences below. You can be silly or serious!

Adjectives

1. _pretty_
2. _colorful_
3. _weird_

The _____ butterfly was on Tyler's head.
   adjective 1

It had _____ wings.
   adjective 2

The _____ conservatory was very fun!
   adjective 3

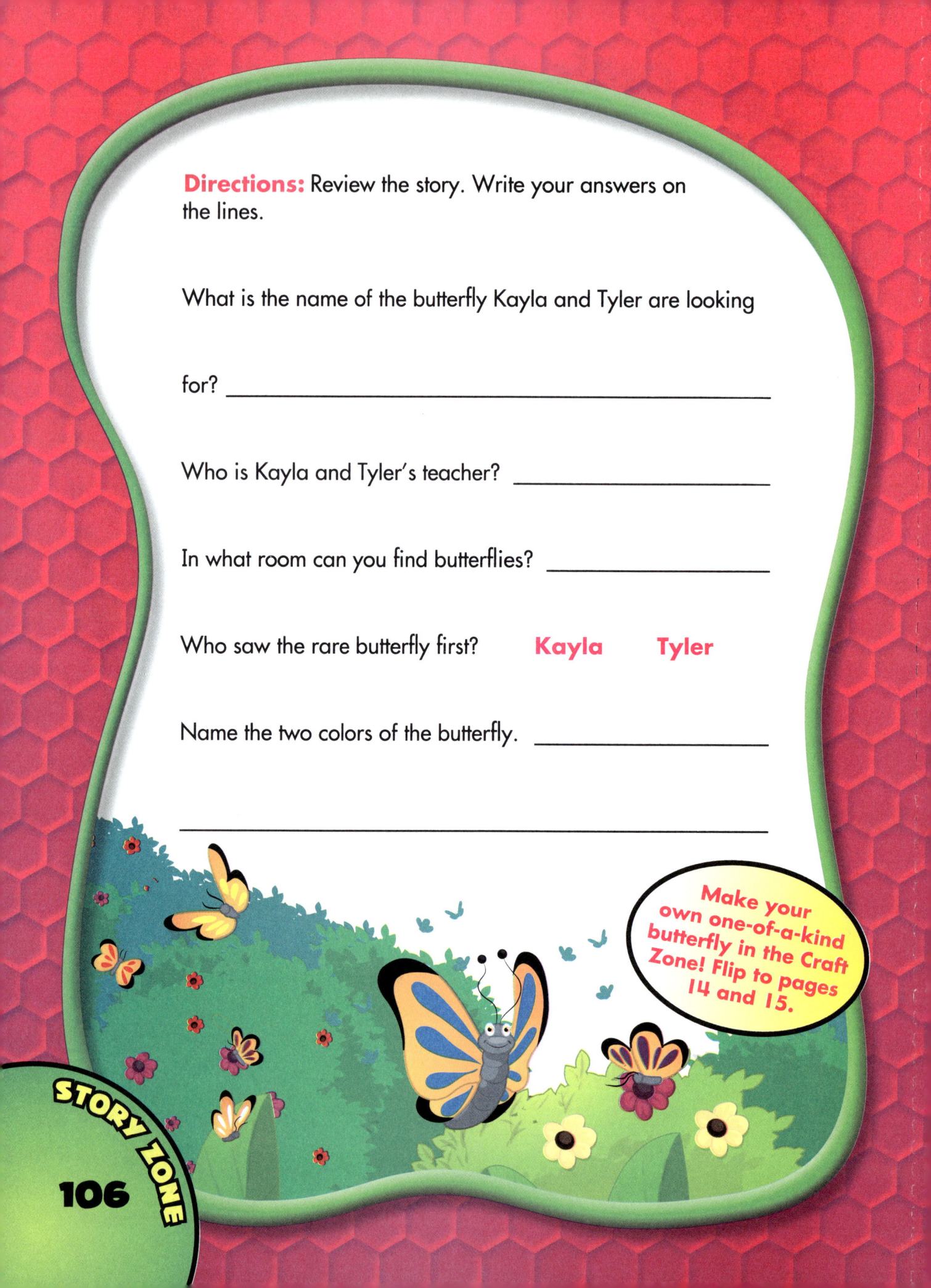

Directions: Review the story. Write your answers on the lines.

What is the name of the butterfly Kayla and Tyler are looking for? _____

Who is Kayla and Tyler's teacher? _____

In what room can you find butterflies? _____

Who saw the rare butterfly first?   **Kayla**   **Tyler**

Name the two colors of the butterfly. _____

_____

Make your own one-of-a-kind butterfly in the Craft Zone! Flip to pages 14 and 15.

STORY ZONE
106

Tyler's Invention

STORY ZONE
107

Ding-dong. The doorbell rang and Tyler opened the door.

"Hi Ty," Kayla said. "Thanks for letting me come over."

"No problem," said Tyler. "I have a fun game for us to try." Tyler handed Kayla a compass.

"What's this?" Kayla asked.

"A compass, you use it to find north," Tyler said. "Okay, I hid five things in the living room. Use the compass to help you find them!" Tyler said.

Directions: Help Kayla find the hidden objects. Follow the directions below. Circle the objects when you find them.

Find the apple. Look north of the couch, then look east.
Find the hat. Look south of the table.
Find the orange. Look north of the **blue** book, then look west.
Find the fork. Look north of the couch.

"Good job!" Tyler said. "Do you know what makes a compass work?"

"What?" asked Kayla.

"Magnets," Tyler said. "My dad just gave me some to make my inventions with." Tyler loved to make his own wacky inventions.

"Let's see what we can find that is magnetic," Kayla suggested.

They tested magnetic objects like coins and paperclips and non-magnetic ones like wood and plastic.

"Let's try this," Kayla said as she took off her necklace.

Directions: What do you know about magnets? Draw things you think are magnetic below. Test them out!

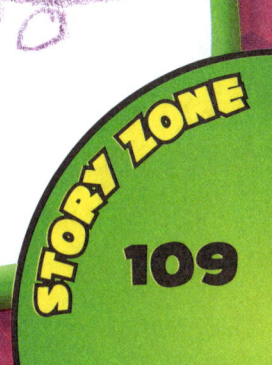

"It works," Tyler said holding up Kayla's necklace with the magnet.

"Cool," said Kyla with a smile. She set the necklace on top of the couch.

"Let's get a snack," Tyler said. They went into the kitchen. They came back twenty minutes later.

"I almost forgot!" Kayla said reaching for her necklace. But it was gone. "Oh no! I lost it," Kayla said. Tyler looked behind the couch.

"I see it, but I can't reach it," he said. "Don't worry, I have an idea!"

Directions: How did Kayla's necklace fall? Use the context clues to fill in the blank below. **Context clues** can help you figure out a missing word just by looking at the other words in the sentence.

Tyler's _____ jumped on the couch. It loves to take a nap on top of the couch. Its tail pushed the necklace behind the couch.

mom   **cat**   **goat**   **magnets**

Directions: Draw a picture of how Kayla's necklace fell behind the couch.

"Ta-dah!" Tyler said as he held out a fishing pole.

"Good idea Ty," Kayla said. "We can tie a magnet to the end." Kayla and Tyler tied the strongest magnet to the end of the fishing pole.

"Looks like you have a new invention," said Kayla.

"Here goes," Tyler said. He lowered the line behind the couch. "I have something!" Tyler pulled the fishing pole up, and right on the bottom was…

Directions: Finish the story. Does Tyler get Kayla's necklace? What else might they find? Draw what happens next below.

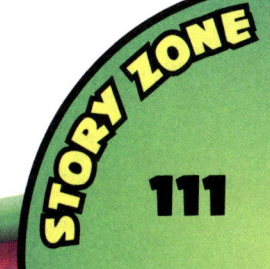

Directions: Review the story. Write your answers on the lines.

Where are Kayla and Tyler playing? _____

What makes a compass work? _____

What does Kayla lose? _____

Who knocks it behind the couch? _____

What is Tyler's new invention?

_____

_____

What does Tyler pull out from behind the couch?

_____

_____

Want to learn about magnets and make your own compass? Turn to pages 128 through 131 in the Science Zone!

Kayla and the Class Pet

STORY ZONE

113

"Okay, Kayla," Miss Garcia said, handing Kayla a bag of rabbit food. "Here is his food." It was Kayla's turn to take home Flash, the class pet.

"I am so excited," Kayla said. "I will take good care of him, Miss Garcia."

"Remember, he is very fast," Miss Garcia smiled. "That's why his name is Flash!"

Miss Garcia gave Kayla an instruction sheet. Kayla was ready to take Flash home. "See you on Monday!" Kayla said as she waved goodbye.

Directions: Help Kayla read the instructions to take care of Flash. Some words are scrambled. Unscramble the words and write them on the lines.

Step 1: Clean Flash's _cage_ **geca** every day.

Step 2: Feed Flash one cup of food in the _morning_ **rmnoign**.

Step 3: Flash loves _carrots_ **crotras**. You can give him one a day.

Step 4: Check Flash's _water_ **trewa** bottle twice a day.

Step 5: Let Flash get some _exrsisze_ **xerisece**.

Step 6: Do not let Flash out of his cage, unless you are in a very small space!

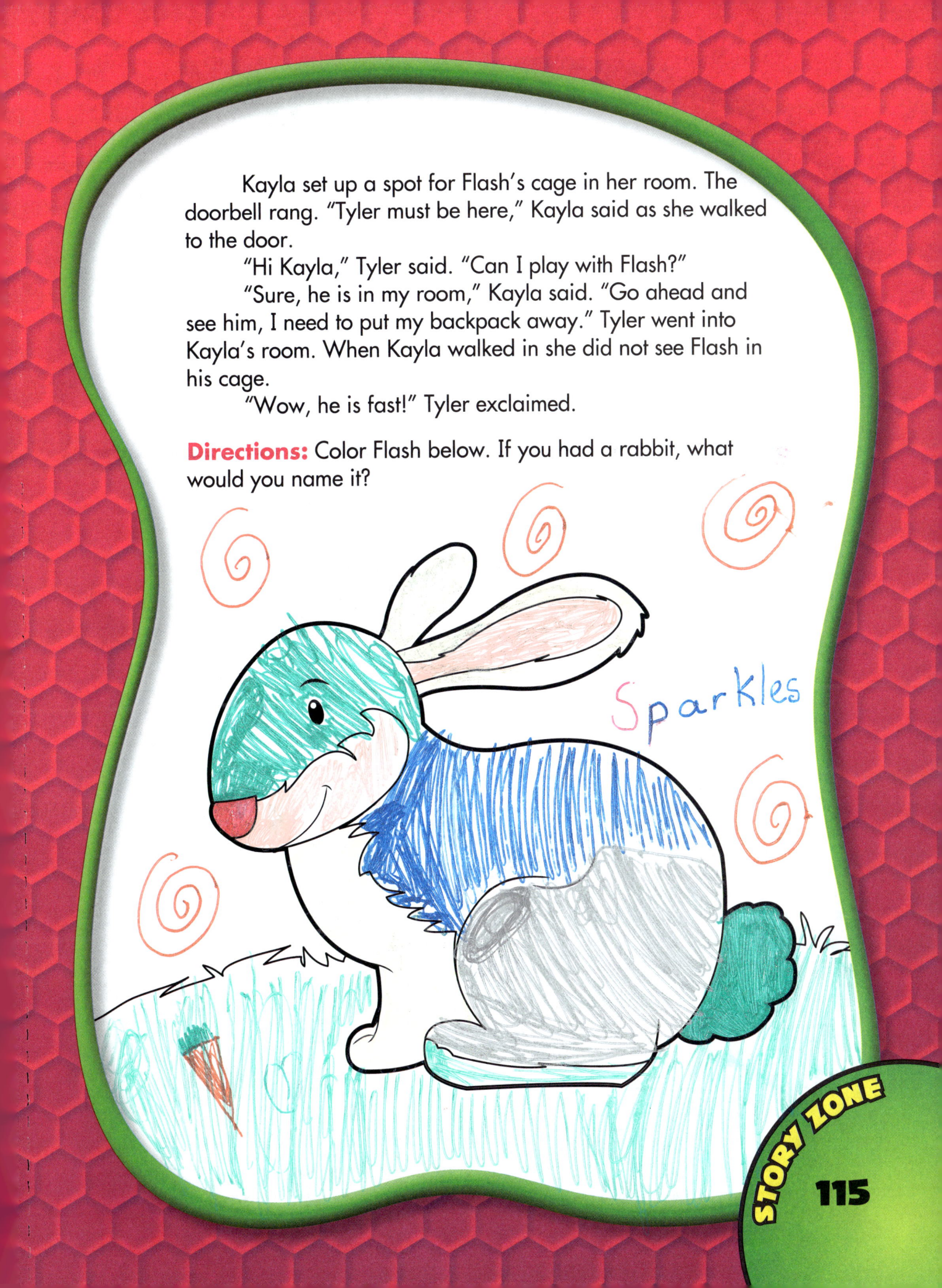

Kayla set up a spot for Flash's cage in her room. The doorbell rang. "Tyler must be here," Kayla said as she walked to the door.

"Hi Kayla," Tyler said. "Can I play with Flash?"

"Sure, he is in my room," Kayla said. "Go ahead and see him, I need to put my backpack away." Tyler went into Kayla's room. When Kayla walked in she did not see Flash in his cage.

"Wow, he is fast!" Tyler exclaimed.

Directions: Color Flash below. If you had a rabbit, what would you name it?

"Uh oh," Kayla said. "Did he get out of my room?"

"No," Tyler said, "but he is hiding!"

"Ty!" Kayla said. "We are not supposed to let him out of the cage unless we are in a smaller room."

"Sorry," Tyler said. "I will help you catch him though." Suddenly, Flash ran past them.

"It's okay," Kayla said. "At least he is getting his exercise, but where is he now?"

Directions: Find and circle Flash.

"I think he likes your room, Kayla," Tyler laughed. Flash was bouncing over all of Kayla's toys.

"Yeah, but we need to eat dinner," said Kayla. "I'm starving!"

"That's it!" Kayla said. "I know what to do." She carefully left the room then came back with a carrot. Kayla held it out and Flash came to her. She put him away.

"I think when it's my turn to watch Flash, I will keep him in the cage!" Tyler said. They both laughed as Flash happily munched on his carrot.

Directions: Imagine another adventure with Flash. Tell a story about it. Draw a picture from your story below.

One day, Nisa was playing with Flash. She had lost balance and let Flash go! He had went in the woods to find food. But Nisa caut him and went back home.

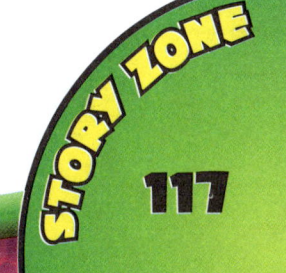

Directions: Review the story. Write your answers on the lines.

Why is the rabbit named Flash? _____

Name two things from the instruction sheet Kayla needs to do.

_____

_____

Chase Flash through mazes in the Game Zone! Try the maze on page 160.

What is Flash's favorite food? _____

Where is Flash hiding? _____

Who let Flash out of his cage? _____

What will Tyler do when he watches Flash?

_____

_____

Science Zone

water drops become heavy

rain falls

clouds form

water vapor rises

water flows back into ocean

States of Matter: Liquids

Matter is everywhere. Everything on Earth is made of matter. All matter takes up space. There are three types of matter: liquids, solids, and gases. Each type of matter is made of tiny **molecules**.

A **liquid** does not have a shape. Molecules move around easily in liquid. Liquids take the shape of the container they are in. Water is a liquid. If you pour water in a glass, it takes the shape of the glass.

Directions: Circle the liquids below. Can you think of another liquid? Draw it.

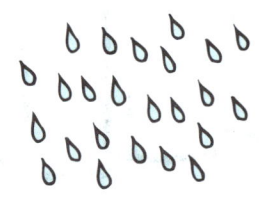

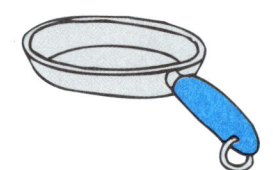

Liquid Motion

Directions: Some liquids have more molecules than others. **Speed** is the term used to describe how fast an object moves. Try this experiment to see if the same object moves through different liquids at the same speed.

What you'll need:
- two identical jars
- vegetable oil
- stopwatch
- water
- two identical marbles
- ruler

What to do:

1. Fill one jar with water and one jar with vegetable oil. Make sure the same amount of liquid is in each jar.

2. Hold the marble so the bottom of it touches the top of the vegetable oil.

3. Drop the marble.

4. Use the stopwatch to record the time in seconds that it takes the marble to reach the bottom of the jar.

5. Use the ruler to measure the distance the marble travels.

6. Follow the same procedure for the second marble and the jar of water.

Which marble traveled faster? _____

What is the difference between the speed of the first marble and the speed of the second marble?

_____

States of Matter: Solids

A **solid** has its own shape. The molecules are very close together. Solids can be hard, soft, stretchy, or bouncy. Many things are solids, such as rocks, apples, and you!

Directions: Draw a solid.

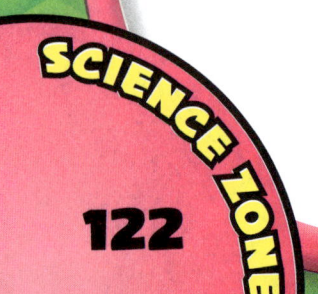

Tyler's Goopy Goo

Directions: Solids have their own shape. However, you can change the shape of a solid by pounding, twisting, or stretching it. Make this fun goo and practice changing its shape.

What you'll need:
- 1 cup liquid starch
- 2 cups glue
- Resealable plastic bag
- Food coloring (optional)

What to do:

1. Pour the glue and liquid starch into a plastic bag and seal it. Gently, knead (press and squeeze) the bag to mix the ingredients.

2. Add food coloring, if desired, and continue kneading the bag for about 20 minutes. If the mixture seems too thin (like a liquid), add more starch. Add glue if it gets too thick (it should stretch easily).

3. Roll the goo on the table into a long shape. Is it a solid or a liquid? _____

4. Now, use your hands or a rolling pin to flatten the goo. Is it still a solid? Describe the shape now. _____

5. Continue shaping and stretching the goo to make different shapes. What kinds of things can change a solid's shape?
_____

6. Store the goo in an airtight plastic bag when finished.

SCIENCE ZONE
123

Matter and Temperature

Matter can change forms. It can go from a solid to a liquid, then back to a solid. One thing that changes matter is temperature. Try this simple experiment for a solid example of changing matter.

What you'll need:
- Ice cube tray
- Water
- Resealable sandwich bag
- Powdered drink mix
- Tape

What to do:

1. Make a colorful batch of powdered drink mix. Fill an ice cube tray with the mix and put it in the freezer until frozen.

2. Place the frozen ice cubes into a resealable plastic bag. Touch the ice cubes, what state of matter are they in?

   _____

3. Tape the bag to a window that faces direct sunlight.

4. Observe the bag every hour, what is happening to the solid?

   _____

5. After the ice melts the solid becomes a liquid again. Open the bag and let it sit open for a while. The liquid will evaporate slowly.

What happened?
The cold temperature changed the matter from a liquid to a solid. The warm temperature created a gas that turned the solid back to a liquid. Turn to page 146 to learn more about evaporation!

Gas Blast

Kayla is learning about gases. She poured cold water on something very hot. What happened? Steam rose off the object. The steam is a **gas**. Gas has no shape. The molecules are very far apart in gases. Gases will fill the shape of the container they are in.

Try this experiment that mixes liquids and solids to create a gas. It is a real blast!

What you'll need:
- A sandwich bag (make sure there are no holes and it can seal completely)
- Paper towel
- $\frac{1}{2}$ cup white vinegar
- $1\frac{1}{2}$ tablespoons baking soda
- $\frac{1}{2}$ cup warm water
- Scissors
- A clear outdoor area
- An adult

What to do:

1. On a paper towel, draw a square that is about 5 inches on each side. Then, cut it out.

2. With an adult, measure the baking soda and spoon it onto the paper towel. Fold the corners inward so the powder is contained in a little pouch, as shown.

3. Mix the vinegar and warm water together.

4. Pour the vinegar mixture into the sandwich bag.

5. Go outside.

6. Quickly and carefully, drop the paper towel packet into the bag. Seal it shut right away.

7. Shake the bag a bit. Then, put it on the ground and stand back for a surprise!

What happened? _____

The **liquid** vinegar and the **solid** baking soda created a **gas**. There was too much gas in the bag, so the bag burst to let it out!

SCIENCE ZONE

127

Magnets

Have you ever used a magnet to pick something up? A **magnet** has one north pole and one south pole.

Sometimes, two magnets **attract** each other. When a magnet's north pole is close to another magnet's south pole, they connect.

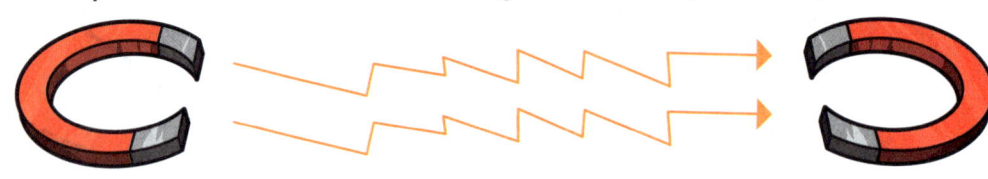

When a north pole tries to touch another north pole, the magnets will not connect. This is called **repulsion**.

Directions: Use the words from the word box to fill in the blanks.

| north | south | repulsion | attract | two |

You need _____ magnets to attract or repulse each other.

Magnets _____ each other if the north and south poles connect.

Every magnet has a north and _____ pole.

If magnets do not connect it is called _____.

When a north pole and a _____ pole meet, the magnets will not touch.

Magnets

What objects do you think are magnetic? You will need a magnet for this activity. Collect several objects from around your house like paper clips, silverware, coins, marbles, wood blocks, and a pencil. Test them to see if they are magnetic.

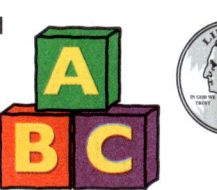

Directions: Draw the items that are magnetic in one column. Draw the items that are not magnetic in the other column.

Magnetic	Not Magnetic
A B C	

Read about magnets in the Story Zone! "Tyler's Invention" begins on page 107.

Make a Compass

Earth also has a North Pole and a South Pole. Did you know they were magnetic, too? If you hold a compass you will see the needle point north. The magnetic North Pole of Earth attracts the needle, so it pulls toward north.

Tyler has a compass in his story. Make your own compass. Follow the simple experiment below to test Earth's magnetic poles.

What you'll need:
- Needle
- Clay or play dough
- Water
- Paper bowl
- Small piece of cork
- A compass (to test your compass)
- An adult

What to do:

1. Roll the clay into a small ball.
2. Attach the ball of clay to the cork.
3. With an adult, carefully take the needle and press it into the top of the clay. Make sure it does not move or fall off.
4. Fill the paper bowl about halfway full with water.
5. Place the cork, clay, and needle in the water. It will float. Give it a minute to settle and stop moving.
6. Use another compass to locate north. Look to see if your magnet is pointing north as well.

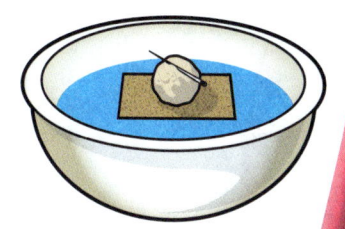

Does your compass point north?

_____

Does the North Pole attract or repulse the needle?

_____

Play a compass game like Tyler and Kayla! Hide treasures for your friends to seek. Let them use your compass to help find them.

The Sun

Directions: Read about the Sun. Answer the questions below. Then, use the passage to help you complete the crossword puzzle on page 133.

> The Sun is a star. It is the center of our solar system. The planets travel around the Sun. The Sun is made up of gases. Hydrogen makes up most of the Sun, but it also contains a lot of helium.
>
> The Sun makes its own light. The Sun shines and makes plants grow. Many living things need the Sun to survive. Even if we cannot see the Sun through clouds, it is there!
>
> The Sun also gives off heat. It keeps us warm. It is the nearest star to Earth. We could not live without the Sun.

1. Name two gases that make up part of the Sun.

   _____

2. What is the nearest star to Earth? _____

3. Name two things we need the Sun to do.

   _____

The Sun

Directions: Complete the puzzle. Use page 132 to help. One is done for you.

Across

3. The Sun is the center of the ____ system.
4. The Sun is mostly made of ____.
6. The Sun also contains ____.

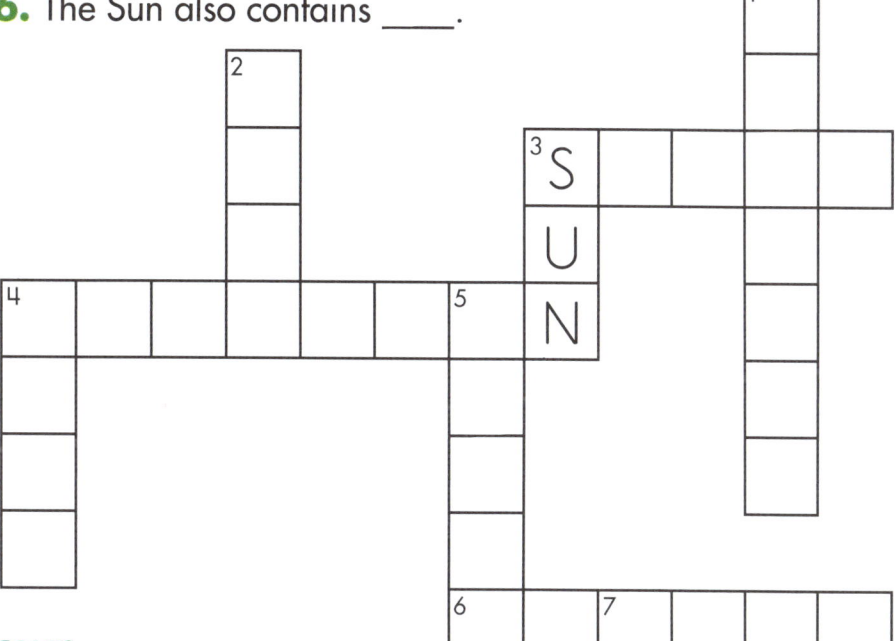

Down

1. The ____ travel around the Sun.
2. The Sun is a ____.
3. We could not live without the ____.
4. The Sun gives off ____.
5. The Sun is the nearest star to ____.
7. The Sun makes its own ____.

Moon Facts

Kayla created a secret code for Tyler. She wrote a fun fact about the Moon. The Moon is Earth's **satellite**, which means it follows Earth around its orbit. Can you help Tyler solve the code and learn a fun fact about the Moon?

Directions: Use the key to solve the code.

A	B	C	D	E	F	G	H	I	J	K	L	M
1	2	3	4	5	6	7	8	9	10	11	12	13

N	O	P	Q	R	S	T	U	V	W	X	Y	Z
14	15	16	17	18	19	20	21	22	23	24	25	26

O N E   D A Y   O N   T H E
15 14 5   4 1 25   15 14   20 8 5

M O O N   I S   _ _ _
13 15 15 14   9 19   2 7 G

D A Y S,   _   _ _ _ _ _,
4 1 25 19   7   8 15 21 18 19
            G

_ _ _   _ _   _ _ _ _ _ _ _.
1 14 4   4 3.2   13 9 14 21 20 5 19

The Moon: Phases

Directions: Read the passage. Answer the questions.

The Moon lights up the night sky. Sometimes, the Moon looks narrow. Sometimes, it looks round. The way it looks to us has to do with the position of the Moon. When the Moon is between the Sun and Earth, it looks black. This is called a **new moon**. When Earth is between the Sun and Moon, it looks bright and round. This is called a **full moon**. In the middle of these periods, when half of the Moon is lit and getting brighter, this is called **waxing**. Then, when the other half is dark and narrow it is called **waning**. It takes one month for the Moon to finish the entire cycle.

What is the main idea of this passage?

    The Moon can look thin or fat.
    The Moon travels around Earth.
    The Moon looks different throughout the month.

What makes the Moon's appearance change? _____
_____

When does a new moon happen? _____
_____

When does a full moon happen? _____
_____

Marshmallow Moons

Charting the Moon's cycle has never been tastier! Use marshmallows and scientific observation to learn all about the phases of the Moon. This project takes a month to complete, but it is simple and fun.

What you'll need:
- Bag of marshmallows
- Glue
- Construction paper
- Crayons

What to do:

1. Read about the Moon's four phases on page 135. Start observing the Moon every night at the beginning of the month.

2. Each night, go outside and look at the Moon.

3. Go back inside and take a bite out of a marshmallow to match the shape of the Moon you observed.

4. Glue the rest of the marshmallow to the piece of construction paper.

5. Use a crayon to write the date below it.

6. Continue this process every night for a month. If you miss a night, make your best guess at the size of the Moon.

What patterns did you notice? _____

_____

_____

Earth Scramble

Kayla and Tyler are on another field trip. They are reading about Earth at the science museum. They notice some of the words are scrambled up! Help them unscramble the words.

Directions: Read about Earth. Unscramble the words.

The third _____ **lpneta** from the Sun is our planet Earth. Earth is at the right distance from the Sun to have the _____ **trwae** necessary to support life. The planets Mercury and _____ **sVneu** are too hot because they are so close to the Sun. The other planets are too far from the Sun.

_____ **rEtha** has a lot of water. Most living things need water. Water helps control Earth's _____ **eathwre** and climate. Water also breaks rock into soil, which _____ **tpalsn** need to grow.

Earth is a special planet!

Earth's Layers

The planet Earth has three layers. The **core** is the inner layer. It is the hardest and hottest part. Around the core is the **mantle**, it is the largest layer. It is also hot and rocky. The **crust** is the outer layer of Earth. It is the thinnest layer, but it is very hard. We live on the crust.

Directions: Find the core. Color it **black**. Color the mantle **red**. Color the crust **green** and **blue**. The land should be **green** and the oceans should be **blue**.

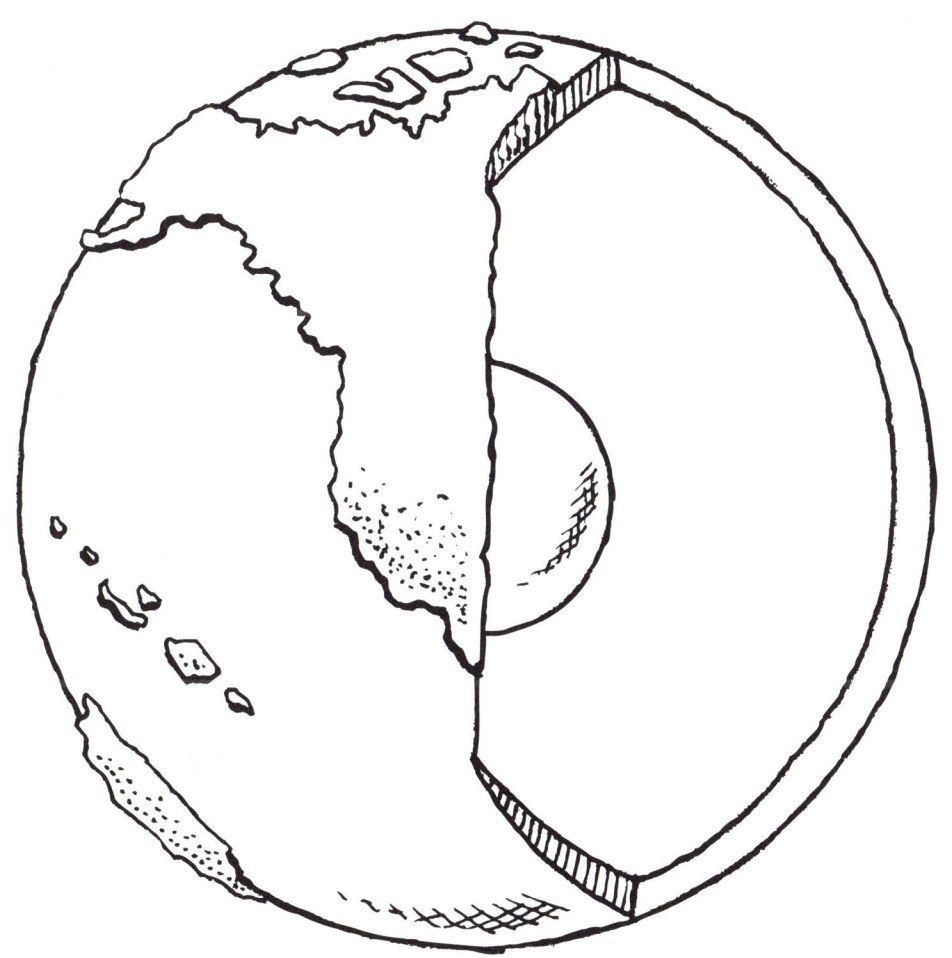

Super Sediment

Earth's crust is filled with **sediment**, which is matter that settles to the bottom of a liquid. Sediment is usually found in oceans, lakes, and streams. Use this experiment to find out what sinks to the bottom of a river first—soil, sand, or pebbles?

What you'll need:
- Three paper cups
- Sand
- Funnel
- Soda bottle (2-liter with cap)
- Soil
- Pebbles
- Water

What to do:

1. Fill one paper cup with soil, one with sand, and one with pebbles. These will be the sediment.
2. Use the funnel to pour the soil, sand, and pebbles into the bottle.
3. Pour water into the bottle until it is almost full. Close the cap tightly.
4. Shake the bottle until everything is mixed well.
5. Place the bottle on a table. On a separate sheet of paper, draw a picture of what you see in the bottle.
6. Check the bottle after 15–30 minutes. Draw what you see.
7. Check the bottle again after 24 hours. Draw what you see.

Directions: Circle your answer.

Which one settled to the bottom the fastest?

soil   sand   pebbles

Which one was the last to settle to the bottom?

soil   sand   pebbles

What happened?

In the bottle you created a small body of water with a lot of sediment. The larger pieces of sediment settle to the bottom more quickly. The smaller pieces of sediment are more likely to float in the water longer and settle to the bottom more slowly.

Weather

Look outside, what is the weather like today? No matter what the weather looks like, there is always water in the air. Sometimes, the water is a gas called **water vapor**. Other times, it is a liquid—like raindrops. Or, it is a solid—like snow or ice.

Clouds are also an important part of observing weather. Each cloud is different. Clouds can tell you if you should bring an umbrella or if it is going to be a nice day outside.

Directions: Read about each cloud. Then, follow the directions.

Cirrus clouds are high in the sky. They are white and feathery and contain ice crystals. Paint white streaks below. Sprinkle glitter on the wet paint. The glitter represents the ice crystals.

Cumulus clouds are low in the sky. They are puffy and white, like cotton balls. Glue different sized cotton balls below.

Stratus clouds are low in the sky. They are wide, often gray, and bring snow and rain. Glue dryer lint or gray flannel below.

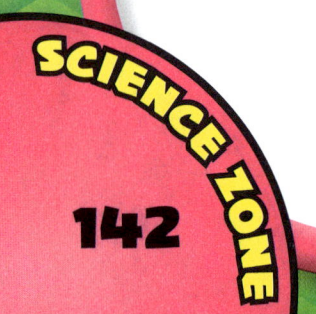

Weather Chart

Good scientists make good observations. Practice observing the weather for one week.

Directions: Fill out the chart below.

Day of the Week	Types of Clouds	Draw the Weather Today
Sunday		
Monday		
Tuesday		
Wednesday		
Thursday		
Friday		
Saturday		

The Water Cycle

Directions: Read the passage. Answer the questions.

> Water starts out in oceans, lakes, and streams. When the Sun heats the water, drops of water rise into the air. Water in this form is called *water vapor*, it is a gas. As the air cools, water droplets form clouds. When the clouds become too heavy with water, they produce rain, sleet, hail, or snow. The water falls back to Earth. Some of the water goes into the soil, where plants grow. Some falls back into the oceans, lakes, and streams. Then, the water cycle begins again.

Where does the water cycle begin? _____

Is water vapor a liquid or a gas? _____

What happens when the clouds become too heavy with water?

_____

_____

Where does the rain go after it falls back to Earth?

_____

_____

Water Cycle Word Search

Directions: Find the water cycle words hidden in the word search. Words can be up, down, across, diagonal, or backward.

rain	oceans	lakes	streams
water vapor	cycle	sleet	sun
clouds	snow	hail	

```
l  l  c  l  w  t  l  l  s  e
y  p  v  o  w  a  t  s  a  w
e  o  s  h  a  c  r  s  t  s
a  s  c  l  a  e  r  m  n  u
w  s  n  o  w  i  s  a  c  n
n  d  l  c  y  c  l  e  i  e
e  u  l  e  r  t  e  r  l  n
r  o  p  a  v  r  e  t  a  w
k  l  e  n  o  s  t  s  y  s
e  c  t  s  e  k  a  l  a  o
```

Evaporation: A Disappearing Act

Evaporation is part of the water cycle described on page 144. When the liquid water is heated by the Sun and changes into a water vapor, this is evaporation. Evaporation is a vanishing act. Sometimes, minerals are left behind after evaporation. If you try this experiment, the process of evaporation will make your water disappear!

What you'll need:
- Masking tape
- Two pie tins
- Drinking glass
- 1 tablespoon of salt
- Measuring cup
- Pencil
- Water
- Spoon

water drops become heavy

rain falls

clouds form

water vapor rises

water flows back into ocean

What to do:

1. Use the masking tape and a pencil to label the outside of the pie tins. Label the first pie tin *salt water*. Label the second pie tin *tap water*.

2. Use the measuring cup to pour 4 ounces of warm water into a drinking glass.

3. Add one tablespoon of salt to the water. Stir the water until the salt dissolves.

4. Add salt until no more will dissolve. Pour the salt water into the pie tin labeled *salt water*.

5. Use the measuring cup to pour 4 ounces of tap water into the pie tin labeled *tap water*.

6. Put the pie tins side-by-side in a safe place. Record your observations each day until the water in both pie tins has evaporated.

Look at the *tap water* pan, what is left after evaporation?

_____

Look at the *salt water* pan, what is left after evaporation?

_____

What Happened?
Because salt is a mineral, it stays in the pan after evaporation. Only water is evaporated. All the sediment in the oceans, lakes, and streams stays behind during evaporation.

Plants

All plants begin from **seeds**. The **roots** are in the ground and suck up water. The plant's **stem** is above the ground. **Leaves** grow off of the stem. Sometimes, a plant has a **flower** on top of the stem. **Buds** are small flowers that have not finished growing yet. Most plants need water and sunlight to survive.

Directions: Create your own flower. Make sure you draw the roots, stem, leaves, and buds. Give your flower a name.

Parts of a Plant

Kayla is growing flowers in her garden. She wants to label the parts of the flowers, but she keeps mixing them up! Can you help her unscramble the words and label the flower?

Directions: Unscramble each word, then write the word on the line. Write the correct number to label the parts of the plant. Use the information on page 148 if you need help.

1. efla _____

2. refolw _____

3. eeds _____

4. mtes _____

5. toros _____

Leafy Collection

Explore nature around your home. Collect leaves and practice classifying them. Use the chart on page 151 to help you study your leaves.

What you'll need:
- A plastic bag
- Glue
- Different types of trees and bushes
- An adult

What to do:

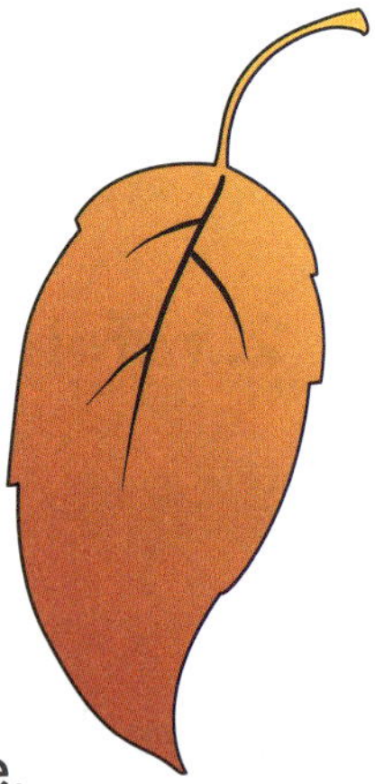

1. Ask an adult to take you for a walk around your neighborhood.

2. Carefully, collect many different types of leaves off of trees and bushes.

3. Place the leaves in a bag until you get home.

4. Once you are home, lay all the leaves out on the table.

5. You can sort the leaves by size, shape, color, texture, or any way you want.

6. Then, choose your favorite leaves to glue to your observation chart on page 151.

Leafy Collection

Directions: Use the chart below to compare and contrast the leaves you found. Glue a leaf in each box. Then, fill in your observations about each leaf.

The Leaf	Color	Size

Birds

Look outside. Do you see any birds? Birds come in many shapes, sizes, and colors. They also have many habitats. A **habitat** is an animal's natural home. Some birds live in rainforests, while others live in the desert. Some birds even live in the snow! A bird's color, beak, and feet tell us a lot about where it lives.

Directions: Label the parts of a bird below. Use the words in the word box to help you.

| beak | feet | wing | eye | tail |

Bird Watching

Bird watching is peaceful and fun. You never know how many birds are around your house until you write them all down!

What you'll need:
- Paper
- Pencils
- Bird feeder—see Craft Zone pages 38–39 (optional)

What to do:

1. Choose a quiet spot to sit. If you have a bird feeder, sit somewhere you can see it clearly.

2. Patiently wait for different birds to come to the feeder or near the spot you are sitting. Make a list of how many different birds you see.

3. Observe the shape of each bird. Write down the size of the beak—is it long or short?

4. Write down each bird's habits—does it walk or fly? Or does it sit in the trees or on the ground?

5. Write down each bird's flight pattern in the sky—is it a wavy path or a straight line?

6. Observe each bird's voice. Every bird has a unique song, try to remember the songs of different birds.

Insects

Learn all about insects! You will become a bug expert after you complete these next few pages. Remember, the best way to learn about science is to observe it.

Every insect has three body parts. The first part is the **head**. The middle of an insect is the **thorax**. Then, the **abdomen** is the last part. An insect always has six **legs**. Insects have **eyes**, but not like our eyes, their eyes are compound so they can see many things at once. Insects do not have noses, instead they have two **antennae** they use to feel the world around them. Some insects also have **wings** they use to fly around and collect pollen and food.

Directions: Create a colorful insect. Follow the directions and color the correct parts of the insect.

Color the head **green**.

Color the thorax **orange**.

Color the abdomen **blue**.

Color the six legs **brown**.

Point to the eyes.

Color the antennae **purple**.

Draw wings for this insect.

Create Your Own Insect

Use your imagination and knowledge about insects to create your own!

Directions: Draw your insect below. Use the words in the word box to correctly label your insect.

| eyes | thorax | wings |
| head | abdomen | legs |

Check out pages 42 and 43 in the Craft Zone to make your own nature picture! You can make your new insect!

SCIENCE ZONE
155

Insect Collection

Tyler has a really big insect collection! He needs six more insects to complete it. Help Tyler search for the insects. Don't worry, he always lets them go after he observes them!

What you'll need:
- One glass jar with a lid (remember to poke holes on the top of the lid)
- Net
- Pencil
- An adult to go outside or to the park with

What to do:

1. Go outside and look around bushes, grass, and flowers for different insects.

2. When you see an insect you like, carefully use the net or your jar to trap it.

3. Place the insect in the jar and put the lid on tightly. Collect one insect at a time and observe it in your jar.

4. Use the observation charts on pages 157 and 158 to write your observations about each insect.

5. When you are finished observing the insect, carefully release it back where you found it.

6. Then, catch another one! See if you can catch all the insects on pages 157 and 158.

Insect Chart

Directions: Each time you find one of the insects below, fill out the chart.

Insect	My observations: (colors, wings, body parts)	What kind of insect is it?	How do I know? (wing patterns, size, jumping legs, colors)

SCIENCE ZONE
157

Insect Chart

Directions: Each time you find one of the insects below, fill out the chart.

Insect	My observations: (colors, wings, body parts)	What kind of insect is it?	How do I know? (wing patterns, size, jumping legs, colors)

Game Zone

Maze

Directions: Chase Flash through the maze. Draw a line through the maze.

Start

End

GAME ZONE

Crack The Code

Tyler and Kayla created a secret language! Use the code to solve riddles and jokes in the Game Zone!

Directions: Use Tyler and Kayla's secret code to unlock the answer to a joke.

Why can't you play basketball with pigs?

BECAUSE THEY HOG THE BALL.

GAME ZONE

161

Hidden Picture

Directions: There are six things hidden in the picture. Find and circle them.

basketball	pizza	sign
clock	present	umbrella

GAME ZONE

162

Word Search

Directions: Find the nature words from the word box. Words can be across, down, diagonal, or backward.

flower	seeds	birds	rain
water cycle	insects	habitat	
soil	clouds	evaporation	

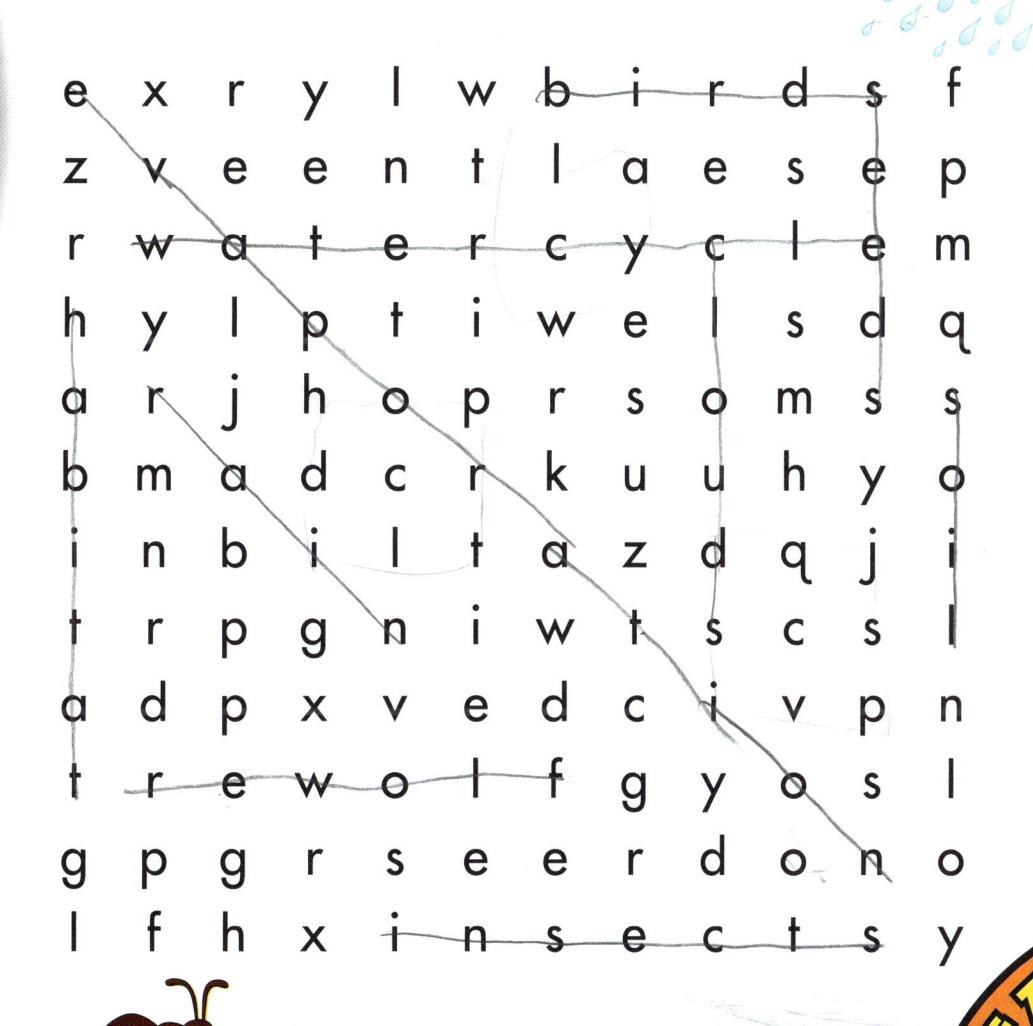

e x r y l w b i r d s f
z v e e n t l a e s e p
r w a t e r c y c l e m
h y l p t i w e l s d q
a r j h o p r s o m s s
b m a d c r k u u h y o
i n b i l t a z d q j i
t r p g n i w t s c s l
a d p x v e d c i v p n
t r e w o l f g y o s l
g p g r s e e r d o n o
l f h x i n s e c t s y

163

Sudoku

Directions: Complete the Sudoku puzzle. Every row and column must contain the numbers **5**, **6**, **7**, and **8**. Do not repeat the same number twice in any row or column.

5			7
	8	6	
	5	7	
6			8

Picture Puzzle

Directions: Cut out the pieces and mix them up. Then, see how fast you can put them back together.

Grid Art

Learn how to draw Kayla! Follow the directions below.

Directions: Finish drawing the picture by using the grid as a guide. Then, color it.

GAME ZONE

167

Crossword Puzzle

Directions: Write the correct opposite into the crossword.

Across

1. If something is small, it is not _____.
4. opposite of over
6. _____ is the opposite of in.

Down

2. If you are _____ then you are not near.
3. _____ is the opposite of loud.
5. opposite of up
6. opposite of new

Maze: Flash's Riddle

Directions: Help Flash answer a riddle. Draw a line through the maze to find the answer.

What is **orange** and sounds like a parrot?

Start

End

GAME ZONE

169

Snow Day!

Directions: Fill in the nouns, adjectives, and verbs below. Then, write them in the story to create your own fun and silly Tyler and Kayla adventure.

Adjective (describing word) _____

Noun (person, place, or thing) _____

Verb (action word) _____

Verb (action word) _____

Adjective (describing word) _____

Verb (action word) _____

Tyler looked out the window, it had snowed! "No school today!" Tyler said. Tyler went outside to play in the _____ snow. Kayla met him
           adjective
outside. "Let's build a _____!"
                              noun
she said. Kayla _____ in the
                     verb
snow. Tyler _____ in it. They
                  verb
finished their _____ creation.
                    adjective
"Let's go get some hot chocolate now!" Kayla said. They _____ inside.
        verb

GAME ZONE
170

Tic-Tac-Toe

Directions: Play with a friend. Take turns writing **X**s and **O**s. Three in a row wins the game!

Which Is Different?

Directions: Look at the two pictures. There are five things different in **Picture 2**. Find and circle the five things that are different in **Picture 2**.

Picture 1

Picture 2

GAME ZONE

172

Tongue Twisters

Directions: Read the tongue twisters below out loud. Can you say them fast three times? Share them with your friends and family.

She sells sea shells by the sea shore

Mad bunny, bad money

Mary made more mango muffins

Black background, **brown** background

Rolling **red** wagons

Black back bat

Six slimy snails sailed silently

Crack The Code

Directions: Use Tyler and Kayla's secret code to discover a silly but true fact.

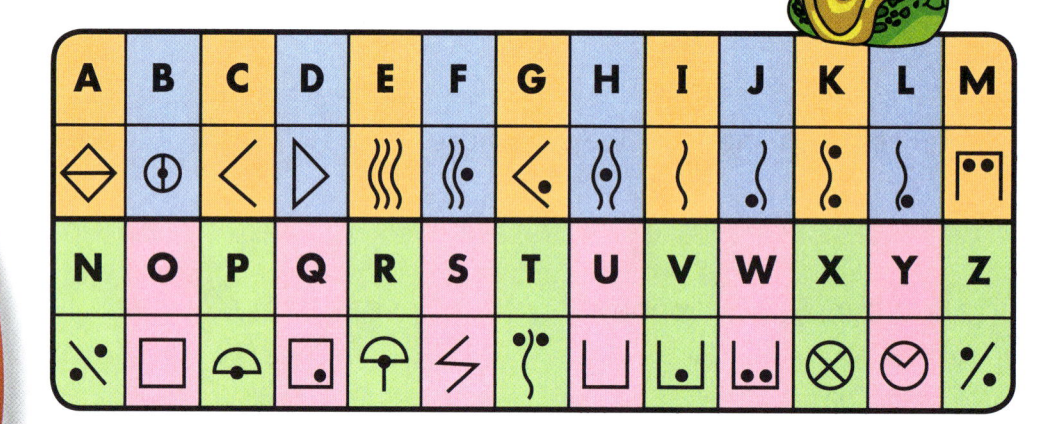

Word Search

Tyler is pretending to visit Mars! He wrote some words to describe it, then hid them in a puzzle. Can you find them below?

Directions: Find the Mars words from the word box. Words can be across, down, diagonal, or backward.

```
v o l c a n o e s c y
r e d k m n a h e r a
b v r w i h e a u a l
i x y d n i w r f t i
t t p l l k p r c e f
y k s u d g o d g r e
s g c s r z n v l s l
h l r s e r e s c c e
m o u n t a i n o u s
a a m v u h r r h l s
```

red	dusky	craters
windy	lifeless	volcanoes
dry	mountainous	frozen

What do you think Mars is like based on these words?

175

Animal Riddles

Directions: Draw a line from the riddle to the correct answer.

I love to walk in the snow and slide on the ice.
What am I?

I slither on the ground because I have no arms or legs.
What am I?

I save lots of bones and bury them in the yard.
What am I?

I hop on lily pads in a pond with my webbed feet.
What am I?

I am very big and I live in the ocean.
What am I?

Finish The Picture

Directions: Draw and color the other half of the ladybug.

Word Scramble

Directions: Look at the pictures and words. The words are all scrambled up! Write the word correctly on the lines.

mclea _____

bltae _____

wrinoab _____

ttrebyulf _____

ovclona _____

Picture Puzzle

Directions: Cut out the pieces and mix them up. Then, see how fast you can put them back together.

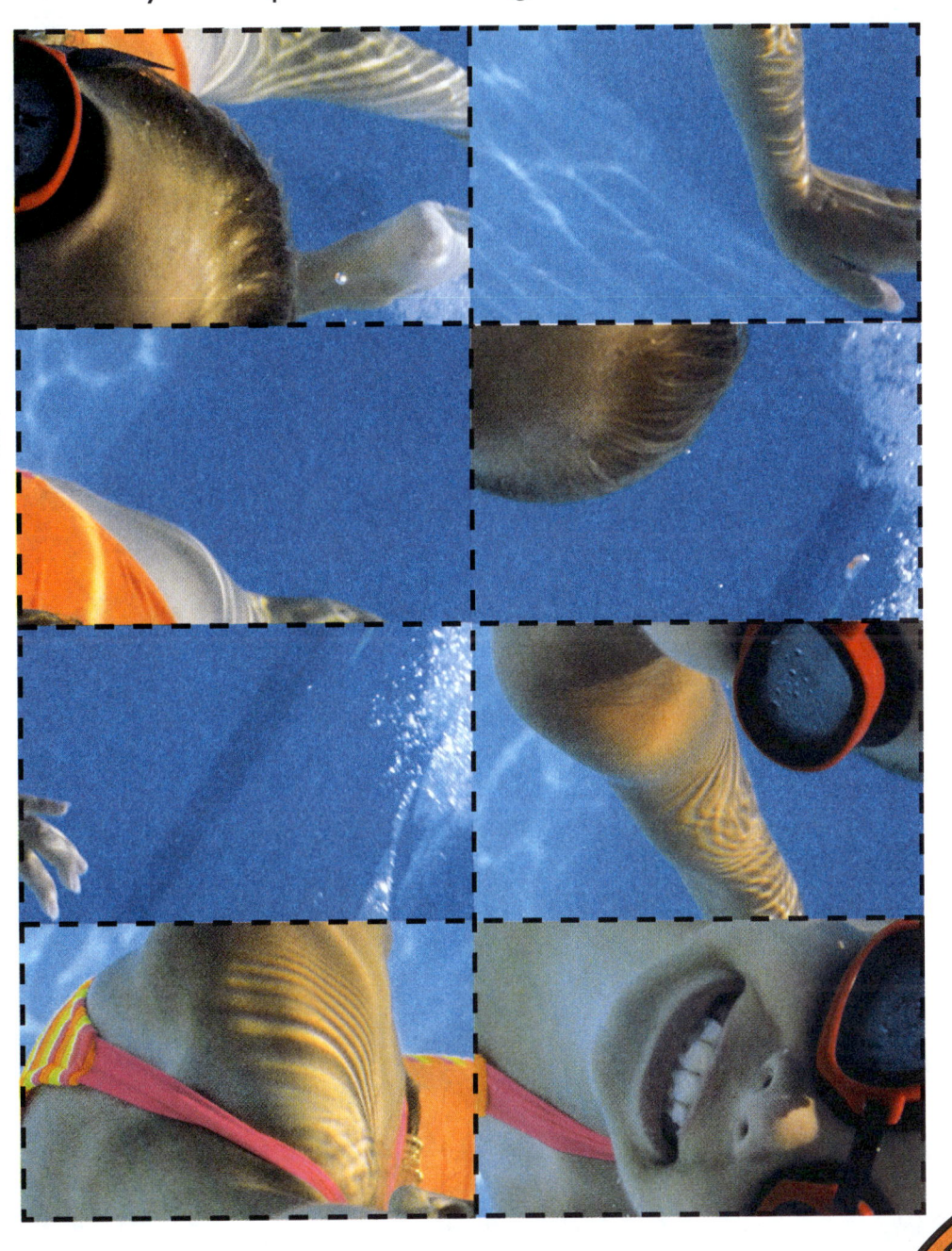

GAME ZONE

179

Crack The Code

Directions: Use Tyler and Kayla's secret code to unlock the answer to a joke.

Why did the banana go to the doctor?

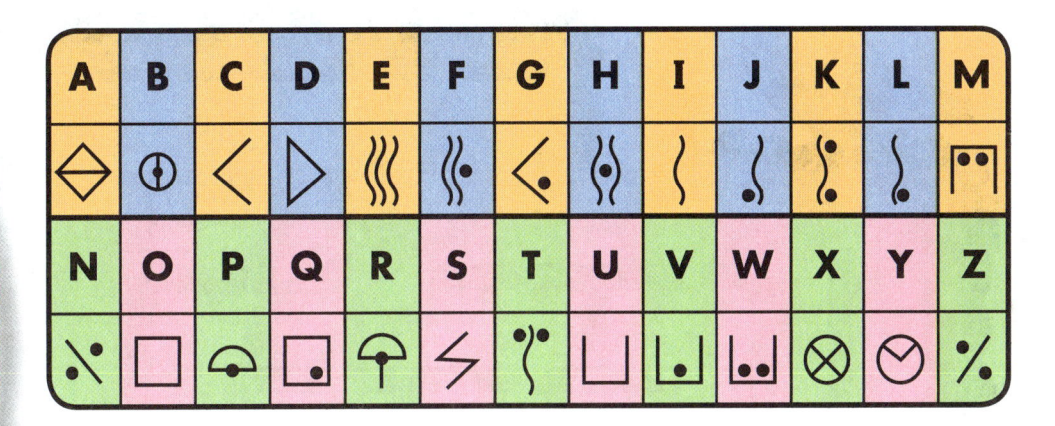

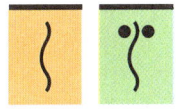

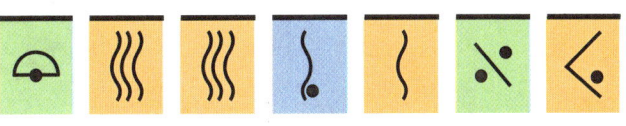

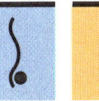

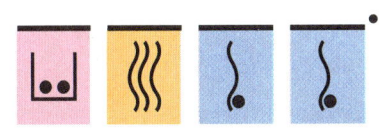

Maze

Directions: Help the bird find the feeder. Draw a line through the maze.

Start

End

Hidden Picture

Directions: There are eight things hidden in the picture. Find and circle them.

bow	lime	marble	soccer ball
flower	lock	pepper	tennis ball

GAME ZONE

Word Search

Directions: Find the number words from the word box. Words can be across or down.

```
t e a z w z x a b i g t e n
o l z r b e r e v e d l a j
t w e l v e a b o n e c d z
i a r p q d p s u j x e i w
c f o p l s c k i q u i i o
m s t f v i o e t t f g h d
t n u w u x g z w h g h r o
n i n e k f d f o u r t j f
a s g l q c w k o s n v m i
n y c e b o n h h p o m p v
b e x v s s e v e n w e n e
t h r e e r t a l j k x q z
m o a n e n i m u t w a y x
```

zero	three	six	nine	twelve
one	four	seven	ten	
two	five	eight	eleven	

Find The Same

Tyler's dog loves to play! He has four pictures of his dog, but two are the same. Can you spot them?

Directions: Circle the two pictures that are the same.

Shape Sudoku

Directions: Complete the Sudoku puzzle. Every row and column must contain a ♥, ■, ●, and ▲. Do not repeat the same shape twice in any row or column.

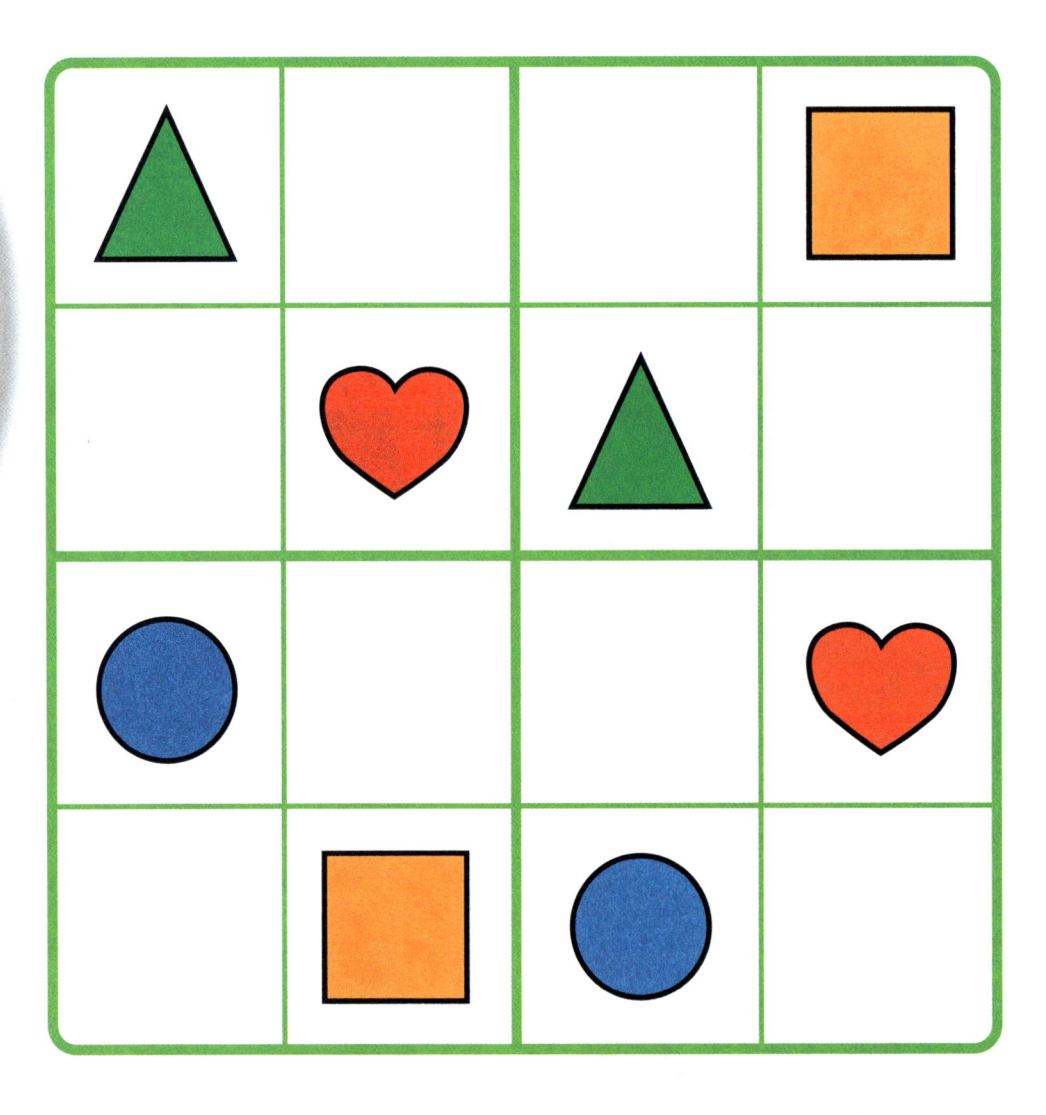

Grid Art

Learn how to draw Tyler! Follow the directions below.

Directions: Finish drawing the picture by using the grid as a guide. Then, color it.

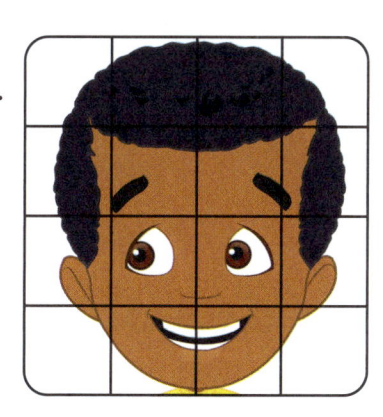

GAME ZONE

187

Finish The Picture

Directions: Draw and color the other half of the sailboat.

Hidden Picture

Kayla lost some items in her room. Can you help her find them?

Directions: There are six things hidden in the picture. Find and circle them.

shoe	apple	flower
soccer ball	clock	hat

GAME ZONE

189

Sudoku

Directions: Complete the Sudoku puzzle. Every row and column must contain the numbers 1, 2, 3, and 4. Do not repeat the same number twice in any row or column.

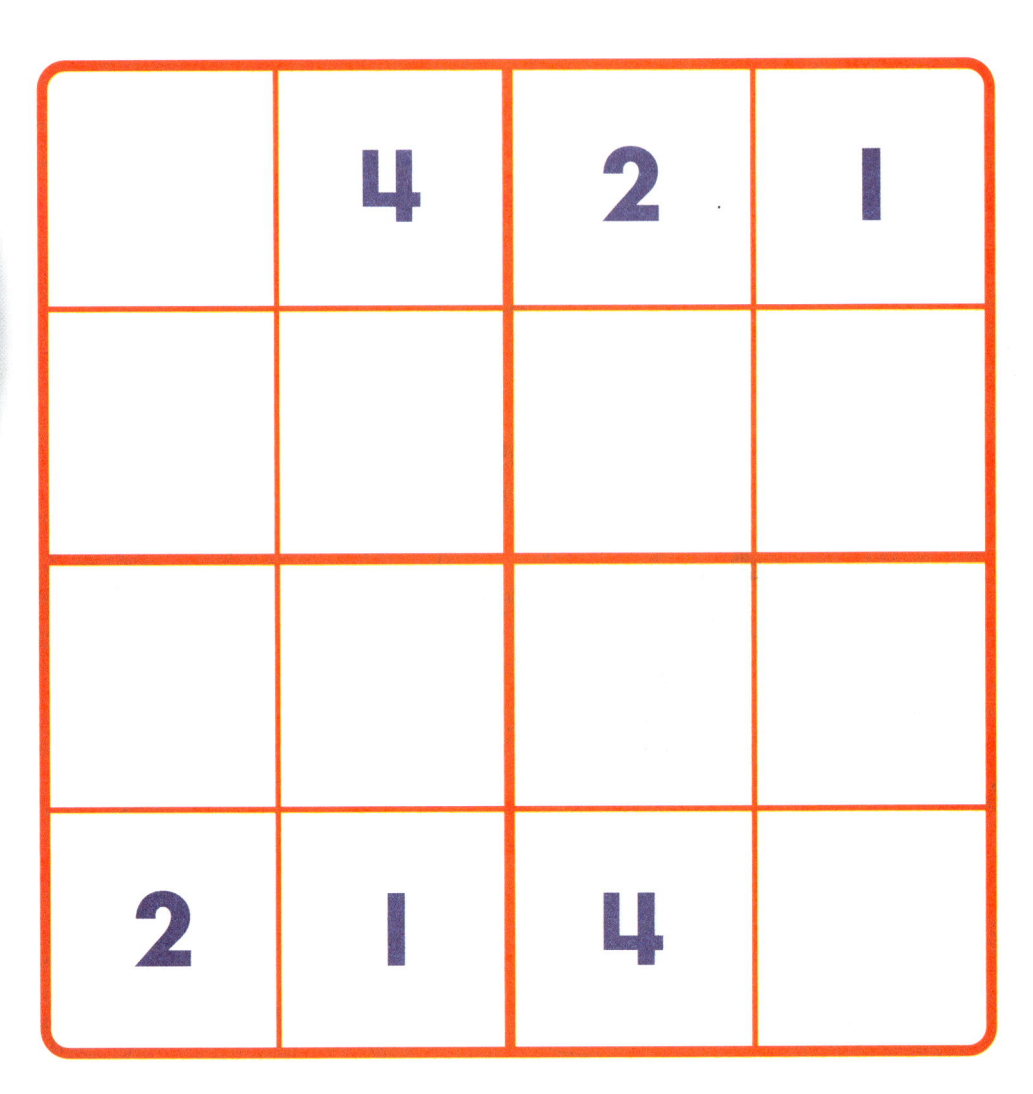

	4	2	1
2	1	4	

Picture Puzzle

Directions: Cut out the pieces and mix them up. Then, see how fast you can put them back together.

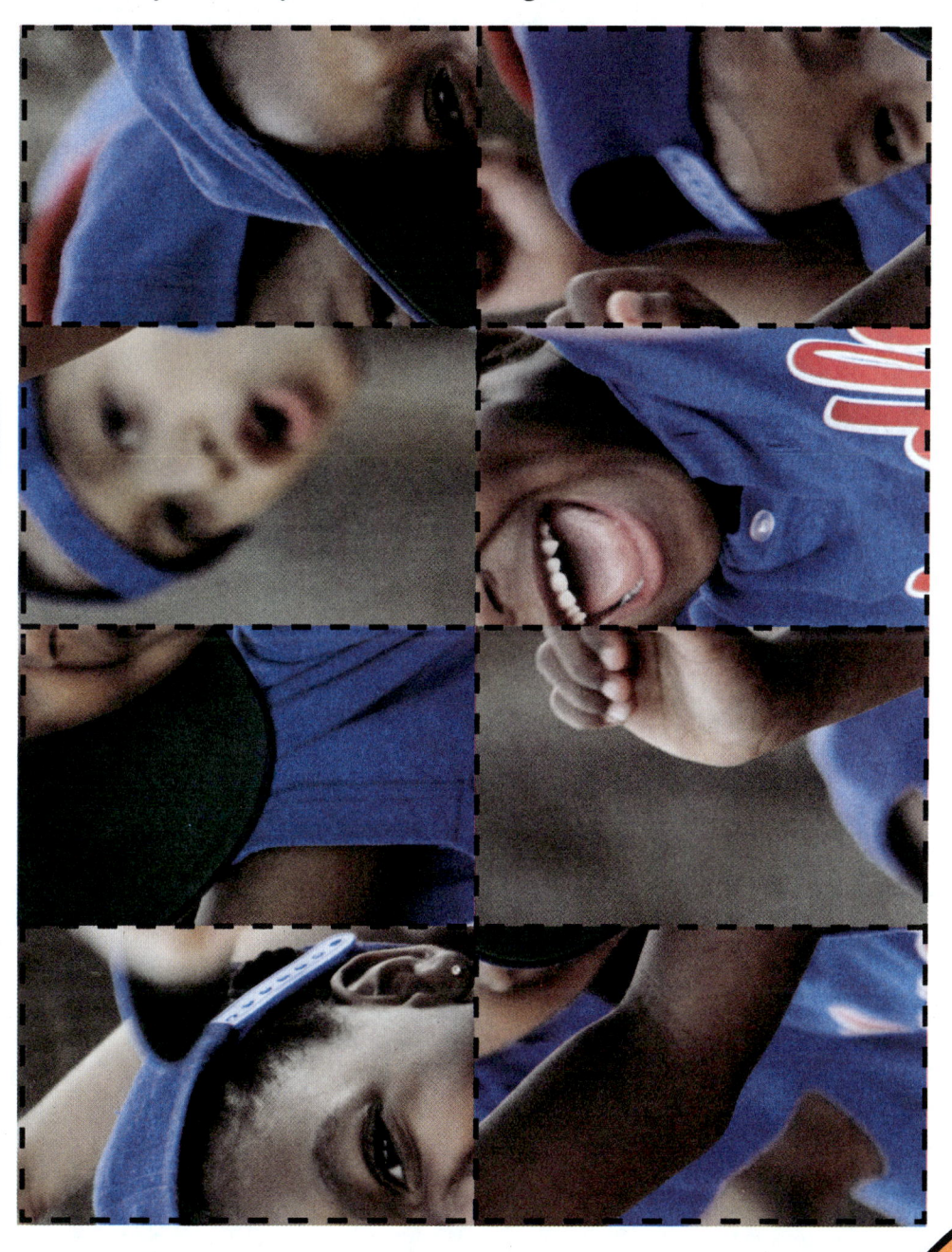

GAME ZONE

191

Crack The Code

Directions: Use Tyler and Kayla's secret code to discover a silly but true fact.

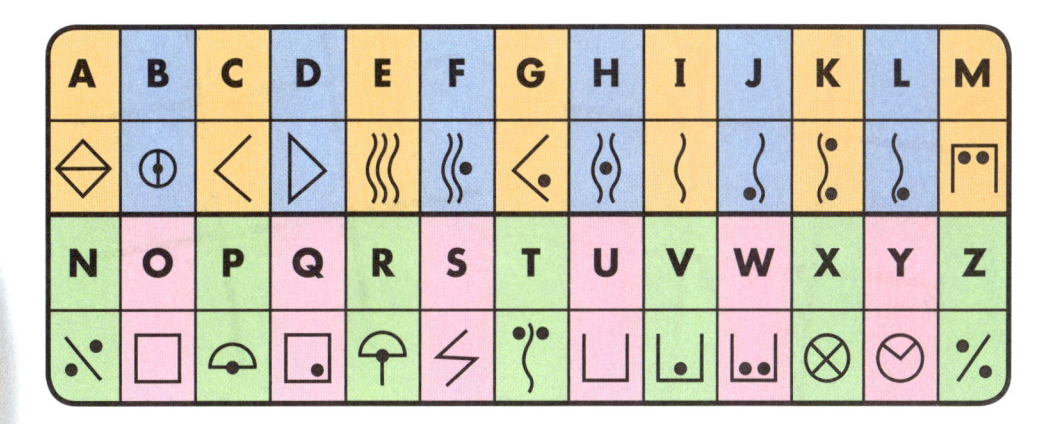

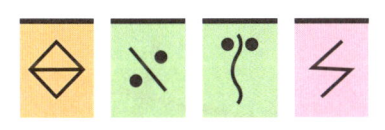

Tic-Tac-Toe

Directions: Play with a friend. Take turns writing **X**s and **O**s. Three in a row wins the game!

What Is Different?

Directions: Look at the pictures. Find and circle the picture that is different.

GAME ZONE

195

Word Scramble

Directions: Look at the pictures and words. The words are all scrambled up! Write the word correctly on the lines.

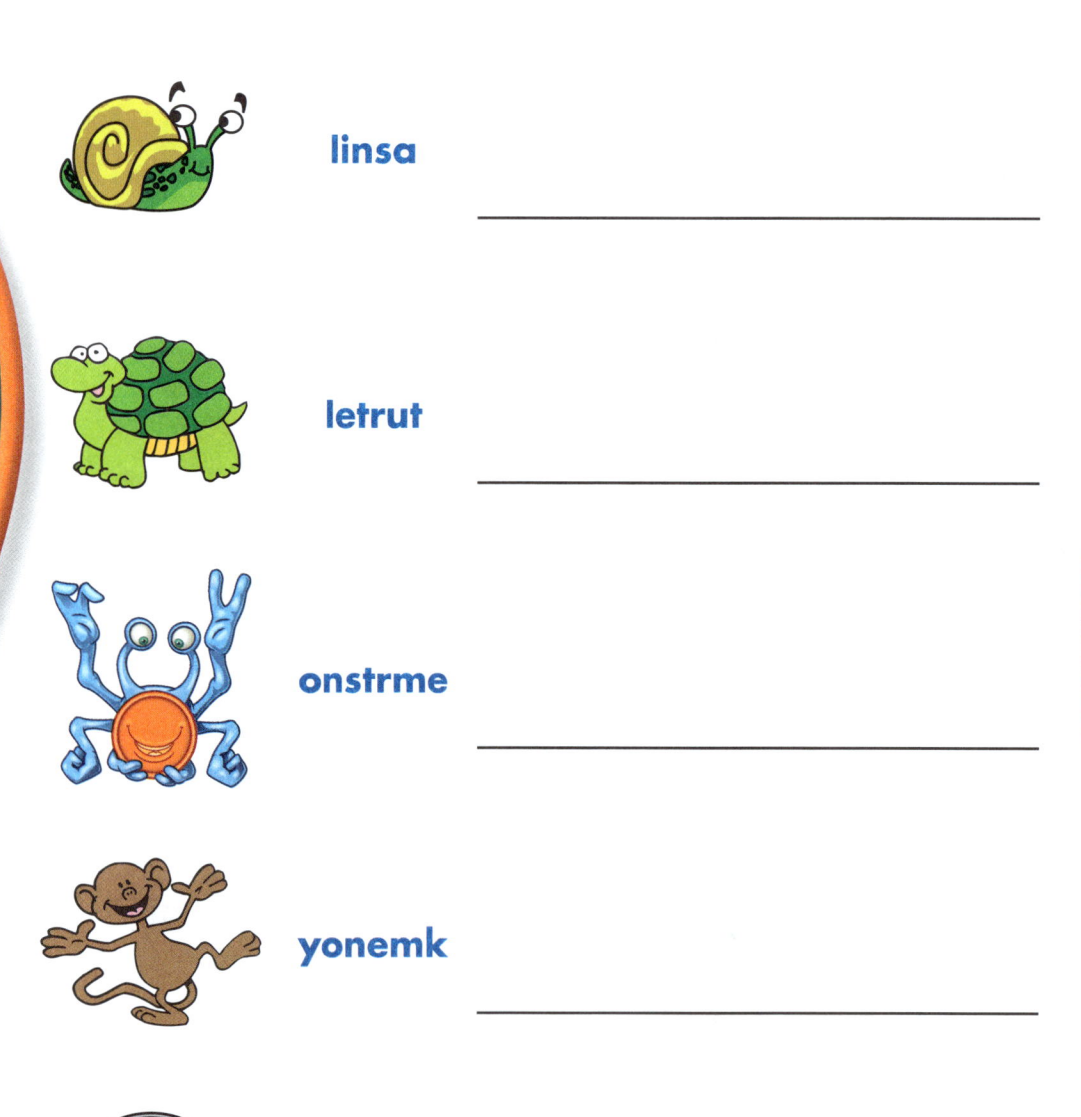

linsa

_____

letrut

_____

onstrme

_____

yonemk

_____

ruqrtea

_____

Maze

Directions: Help Tyler answer a riddle. Draw a line through the maze to find the answer.

What kind of key will not open a door?

Word Search

Directions: Use a **red** crayon to circle the names of three animals that would make good pets. Use a **blue** crayon to circle the names of three wild animals. Use an **orange** crayon to circle two animals that live on a farm. Words can be across or down.

bear	lion	bird	cow
cat	sheep	dog	tiger

```
a  m  e  o  w  w  n  l  i  o  n
b  m  d  o  g  g  x  i  i  s  o
a  b  e  a  r  r  v  l  m  h  r
r  m  r  m  o  o  u  s  e  e  k
k  c  a  b  b  i  r  d  s  e  m
i  o  t  t  i  g  e  r  m  p  q
b  w  n  o  w  w  r  q  n  e  n
d  n  c  p  h  h  i  d  u  d  n
f  k  c  a  t  t  r  o  a  r  m
```

Picture Puzzle

Directions: Cut out the pieces and mix them up. Then, see how fast you can put them back together.

Grid Art

Learn how to draw a monster! Follow the directions below.

Directions: Finish drawing the picture by using the grid as a guide. Then, color it.

GAME ZONE
201

On The Playground

Directions: Fill in the nouns, adjectives, and verbs below. Then, write them in the story to create your own fun and silly Tyler and Kayla adventure.

Noun (person, place, or thing) _____

Verb (action word) _____

Adjective (describing word) _____

Noun (person or thing) _____

Verb (action word) _____

Finally, the recess bell rings! Tyler goes straight

to the _____ to play. Kayla
          noun

_____ to the swings. Next, Kayla's
  verb +s

_____ friends want to play a game
    adjective

of kickball. Tyler grabs a _____ so
                              noun

he can play, too. He rolls the ball straight to Kayla. She

_____ the ball high in the air.
  verb +s

Hidden Picture

Tyler needs to find six insects. Can you help him find them?

Directions: There are six insects hidden in the picture. Find and circle them.

ant	grasshopper	ladybug
butterfly	dragonfly	bumblebee

GAME ZONE

203

Crack The Code

Directions: Use Tyler and Kayla's secret code to unlock the answer to a joke.

Why was the baby ant confused?

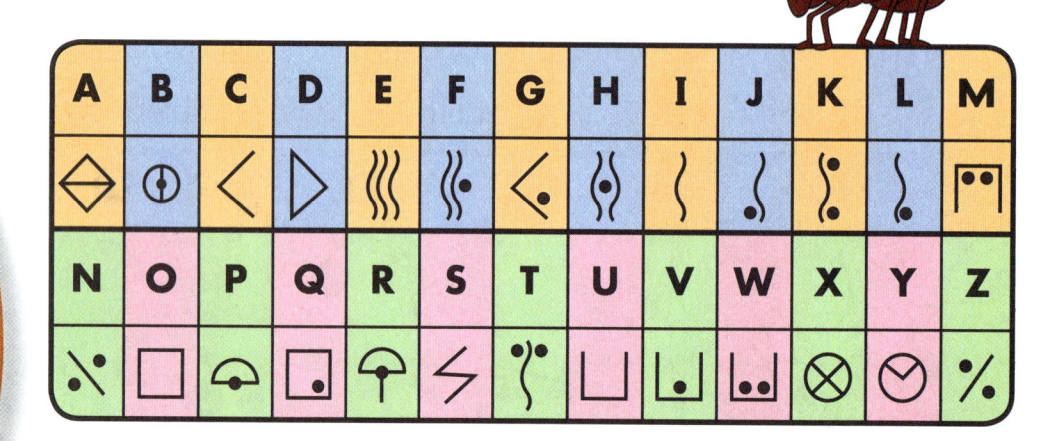

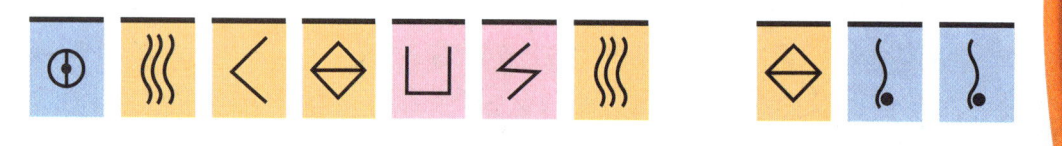

Maze

Directions: Chase Flash through the maze. Draw a line to the finish.

Start

End

GAME ZONE
205

Sudoku

Directions: Complete the Sudoku puzzle. Every row and column must contain the numbers 1, 2, 3, and 4. Do not repeat the same number twice in any row or column.

	1	4	
4			2
1			4
	4	2	

Find The Same

Directions: Circle the two pictures that are the same.

GAME ZONE

207

Color Code

Directions: Solve the subtraction problems. Then, color the spaces according to the answers.

Color Code:

1 = white　　4 = green　　7 = pink　　10 = red
2 = purple　　5 = yellow　　8 = gray
3 = black　　6 = blue　　9 = orange

Crack The Code

Directions: Use Tyler and Kayla's secret code to unlock the answer to a joke.

Who is bigger, Mr. Bigger or Mr. Bigger's baby?

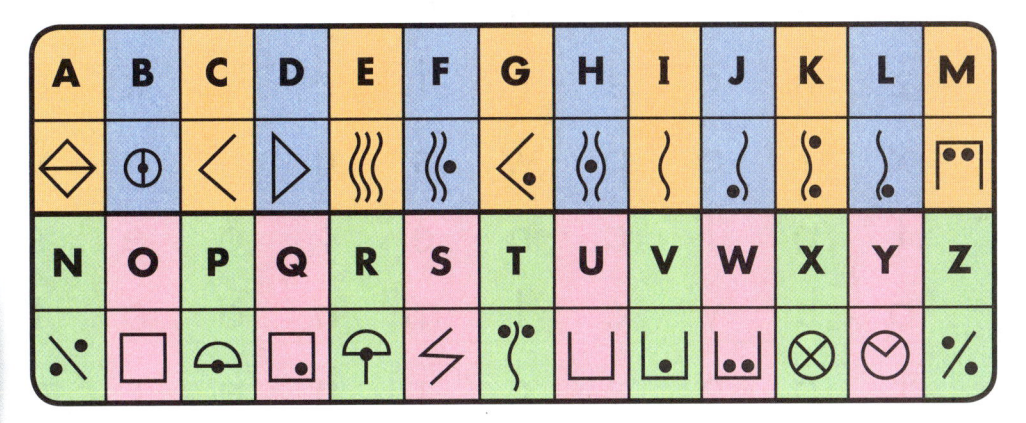

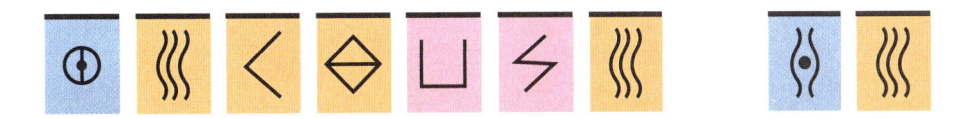

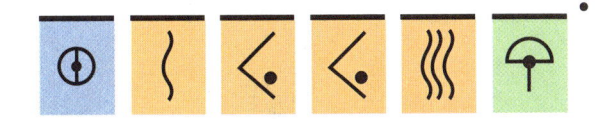

A	B	C	D	E	F	G	H	I	J	K	L	M
N	O	P	Q	R	S	T	U	V	W	X	Y	Z

The baby, because he is a little Bigger.

Word Search

Directions: Find the out-of-this-world space words from the word box. Words can be across, down, or diagonal.

c s t b n o j r p i
z h c s k i e s k d
x i g p w s u h n v
t p l a n e t q e s
o u y c l m n a a t
r a a e c i h e r o
b w e c s r e j t s
i e u r s l k n h u
t v r l w d g f a l
c x g m a r s n r a

space	alien	ship
orbit	earth	planet
skies	stars	mars

GAME ZONE
210

Tic-Tac-Toe

Directions: Play with a friend. Take turns writing **X**s and **O**s. Three in a row wins the game!

Hidden Picture

Directions: There are five things hidden in the picture. Find and circle them.

caterpillar	drums	soccer ball
dog	pear	

GAME ZONE
212

Grid Art

Learn how to draw Flash! Follow the directions below.

Directions: Finish drawing the picture by using the grid as a guide. Then, color it.

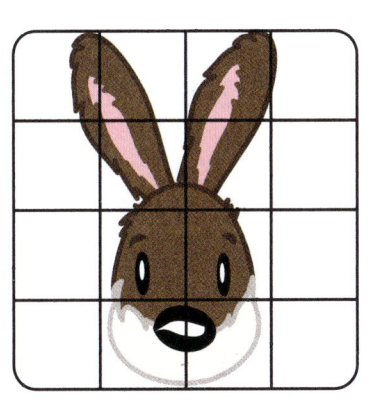

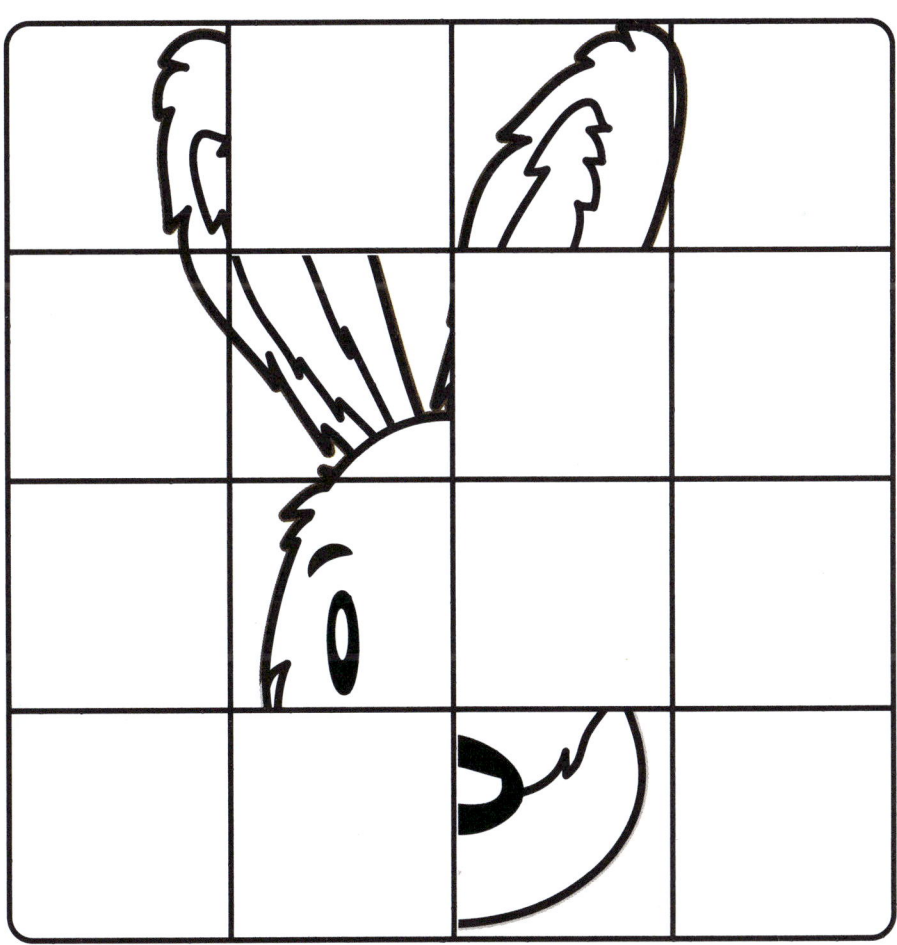

GAME ZONE

213

Space Riddles

Directions: Read each riddle. Write the answer using one of the scrambled words from the word box.

| srast | nuS | erscrat |
| rMas | rEath | nruSat |

This huge star lights the day. ___ ___ ___

These shine at night. ___ ___ ___ ___ ___

These are on the moon. ___ ___ ___ ___ ___ ___ ___

This is our home planet. ___ ___ ___ ___ ___

This planet is red. ___ ___ ___ ___

This planet has rings. ___ ___ ___ ___ ___ ___

Number Search

Directions: Find the hidden numbers from the box below. They may be hidden across or down.

16177	33899	46437
37269	16396	77468
89448	97987	76373

4 6 4 3 7 1 6 3 9 6
1 3 2 5 7 8 2 6 4 1
0 3 5 1 4 2 3 9 0 8
4 8 7 1 6 1 7 7 6 2
2 9 1 7 8 3 2 8 5 7
5 9 4 9 0 2 6 1 4 6
3 1 7 3 9 7 9 8 7 3
5 2 0 2 1 4 2 6 3 7
7 8 9 4 4 8 3 4 5 3
0 4 1 6 2 3 9 2 7 1

Tongue Twisters

Directions: Read the tongue twisters below out loud. Can you say them fast three times? Share them with your friends and family.

We shall surely see the sun shine soon

Twelve twins twirled twelve twigs

Big bad bugs bit Bitsy's back

The rich wicked witch wished a wicked wish

Red leather, yellow leather

Unique New York

The blue bird blinks

Word Scramble

Directions: Look at the pictures and words. The words are all scrambled up! Write the word correctly on the lines.

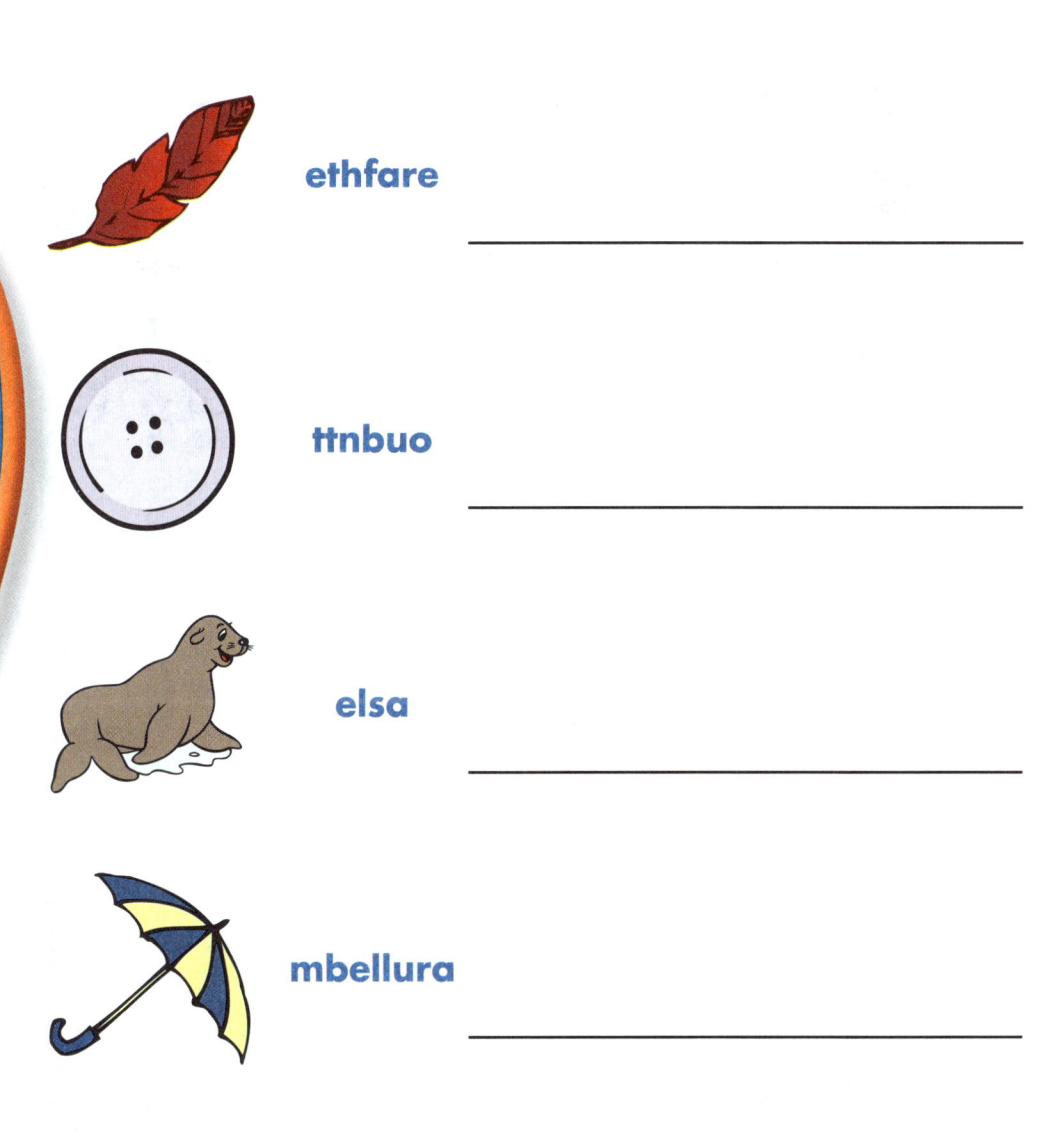

ethfare _____

ttnbuo _____

elsa _____

mbellura _____

gloio _____

GAME ZONE

217

Maze

Kayla has a riddle for you! See if you can find the answer.

Directions: Solve Kayla's riddle. Draw a line through the maze to find the answer.

What has bark, but no bite?

Start

End

Picture Puzzle

Directions: Cut out the pieces and mix them up. Then, see how fast you can put them back together.

GAME ZONE

219

Crack The Code

Directions: Use Tyler and Kayla's secret code to unlock a silly but true fact.

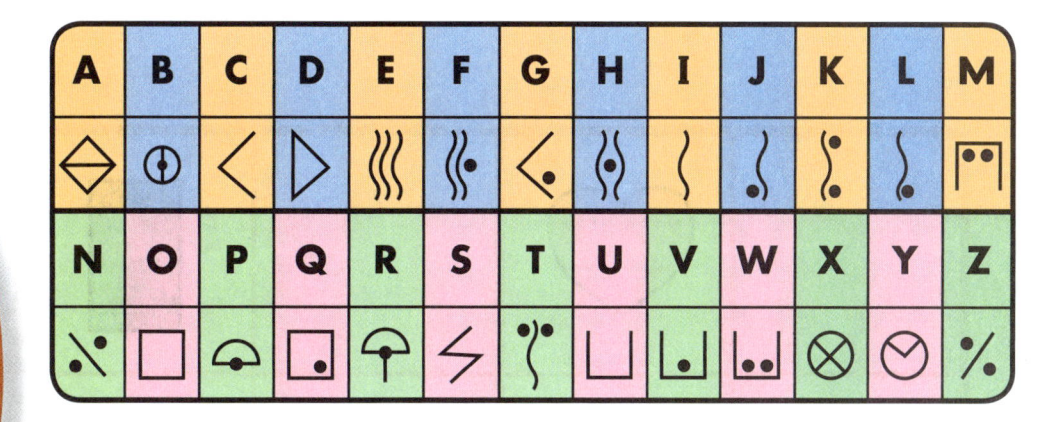

A	B	C	D	E	F	G	H	I	J	K	L	M
◇	⊕	<	▷	≋	⸱⸱	<⸱	⸱⸱	﹜	﹜⸱	﹜⸱	⁑

N	O	P	Q	R	S	T	U	V	W	X	Y	Z
⁂	□	⌓	□⸱	⌒	⚡	⸴	⊔	⊔⸱	⊔⸱⸱	⊗	⊙	%

CAMELS HAVE THREE EYELIDS.

Shape Sudoku

Directions: Complete the Sudoku puzzle. Every row and column must contain a △, ▪, ♥, and ●. Do not repeat the same shape twice in any row or column.

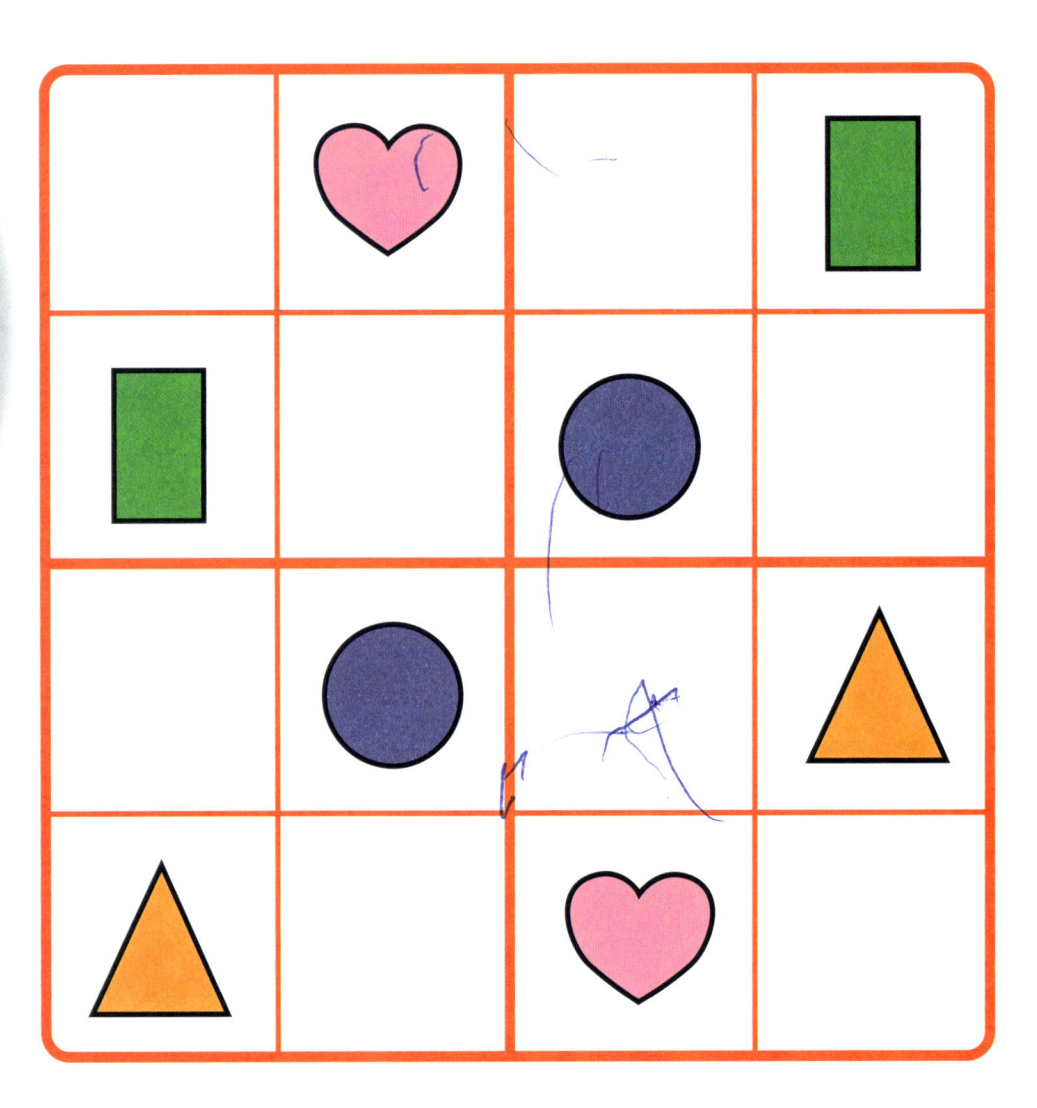

Hidden Picture

Flash and his friends are hiding in Tyler and Kayla's classroom. Can you help find them?

Directions: There are six rabbits hiding. Find and circle them.

A New Invention

Directions: Fill in the nouns, adjectives, and verbs below. Then, write them in the story to create your own fun and silly Tyler and Kayla adventure.

Noun (a thing) _____

Adjective (describing word) _____

Verb (action word) _____

Adjective (describing word) _____

Verb (action word) _____

Tyler is at it again! He made a new invention for

the _____. Kayla came
      noun

over to try Tyler's _____
                    adjective

invention. "This is great Ty," Kayla said. "It

even _____." Tyler's
     verb +s

_____ sister can use it. She
   adjective

likes to _____ over it.
         verb

GAME ZONE

What Is Different?

Directions: Look at the pictures. Find and circle the picture that is different.

GAME ZONE

225

Create Your Own Message

Tyler and Kayla want you to write a secret message! Give your message to a friend.

Directions: Use Tyler and Kayla's code key to create your own secret message in the space below.

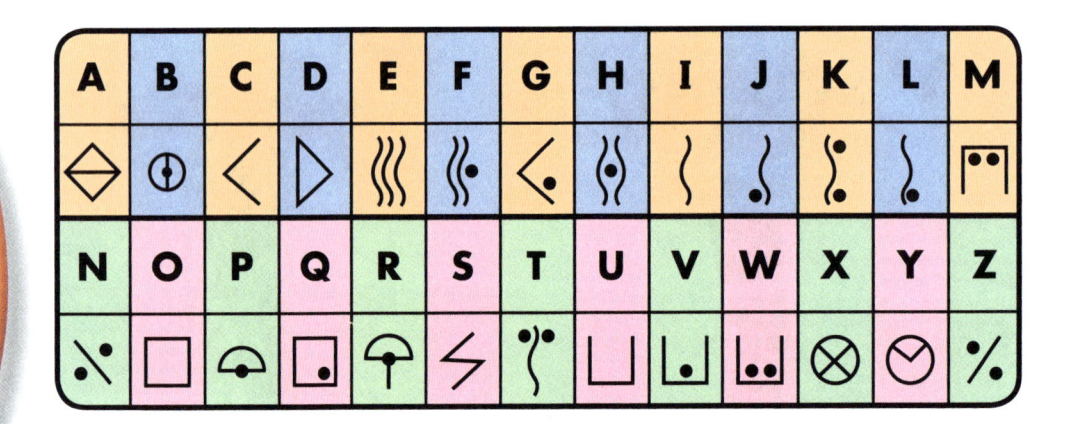

Answer Zone

Number Recognition: Dot-to-Dot Fun

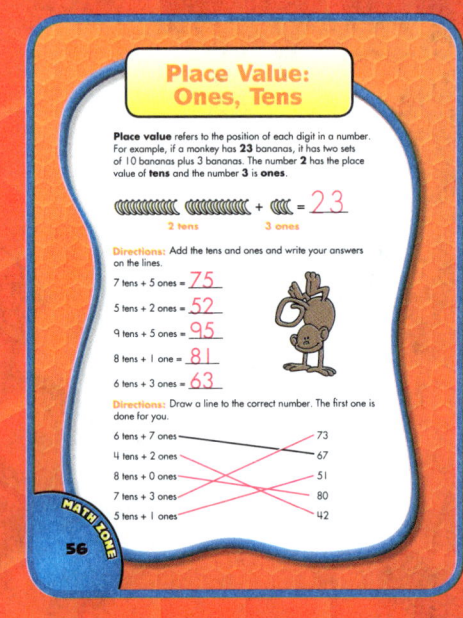

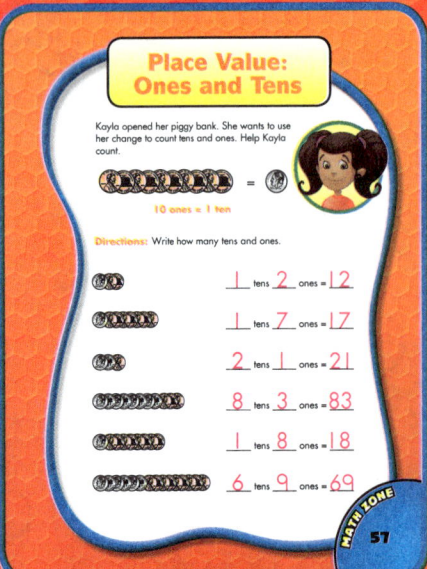

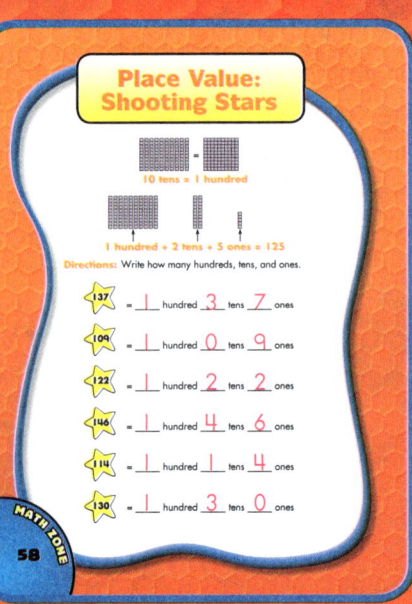

Directions: Connect the dots from **1** to **50**. Color the picture.

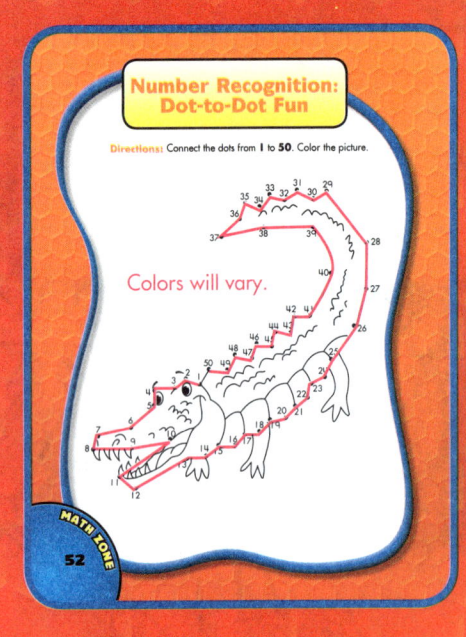

Colors will vary.

52

Number Recognition: Matching Game

Directions: Cut out the pictures and number words below. Mix them up and match them.

one	two
three	four
five	six
seven	eight
nine	ten

53

Ordinal Numbers: Tyler's Toy Chest

Directions: Count Tyler's toys. Write your answers.

Where are the teddy bears?
eighth
seventeenth

Where are the dinosaurs?
sixth
tenth
twentieth

Underline the **seventh** toy.
Circle the **thirteenth** toy.
Which toy do you think is Tyler's favorite? Draw it below.

Drawings will vary.

55

Place Value: Ones, Tens

Place value refers to the position of each digit in a number. For example, if a monkey has **23** bananas, it has two sets of 10 bananas plus 3 bananas. The number **2** has the place value of **tens** and the number **3** is **ones**.

2 tens + 3 ones = 23

Directions: Add the tens and ones and write your answers on the lines.

7 tens + 5 ones = 75
5 tens + 2 ones = 52
9 tens + 5 ones = 95
8 tens + 1 one = 81
6 tens + 3 ones = 63

Directions: Draw a line to the correct number. The first one is done for you.

6 tens + 7 ones — 73
4 tens + 2 ones — 67
8 tens + 0 ones — 51
7 tens + 3 ones — 80
5 tens + 1 ones — 42

56

Place Value: Ones and Tens

Kayla opened her piggy bank. She wants to use her change to count tens and ones. Help Kayla count.

10 ones = 1 ten

Directions: Write how many tens and ones.

1 tens 2 ones = 12
1 tens 7 ones = 17
2 tens 1 ones = 21
8 tens 3 ones = 83
1 tens 8 ones = 18
6 tens 9 ones = 69

57

Place Value: Shooting Stars

10 tens = 1 hundred

1 hundred + 2 tens + 5 ones = 125

Directions: Write how many hundreds, tens, and ones.

137 = 1 hundred 3 tens 7 ones
109 = 1 hundred 0 tens 9 ones
122 = 1 hundred 2 tens 2 ones
146 = 1 hundred 4 tens 6 ones
114 = 1 hundred 1 tens 4 ones
130 = 1 hundred 3 tens 0 ones

58

ANSWER ZONE

228

Place Value: Up, Up, and Away

Directions: Use the code to color the balloons.

Color Code:
- 7 hundreds = red
- 6 hundreds = green
- 5 hundreds = orange
- 8 tens = yellow
- 3 ones = brown

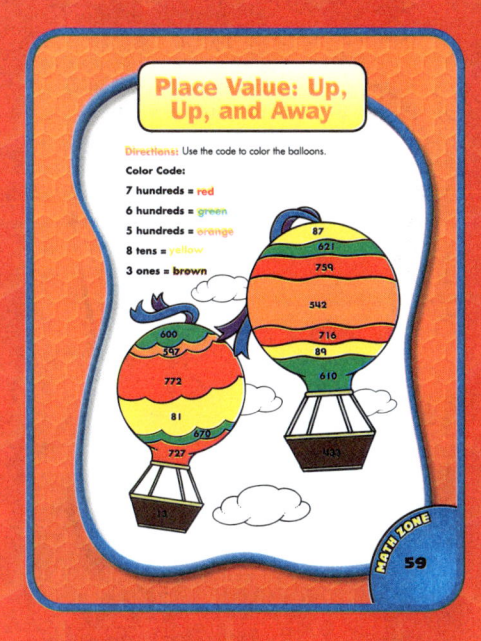

Balloon numbers: 87, 621, 759, 542, 716, 89, 610, 600, 597, 772, 81, 670, 727, 13, 433

Addition: Apple Picking

Directions: Add the numbers. Write the answer on the apples.

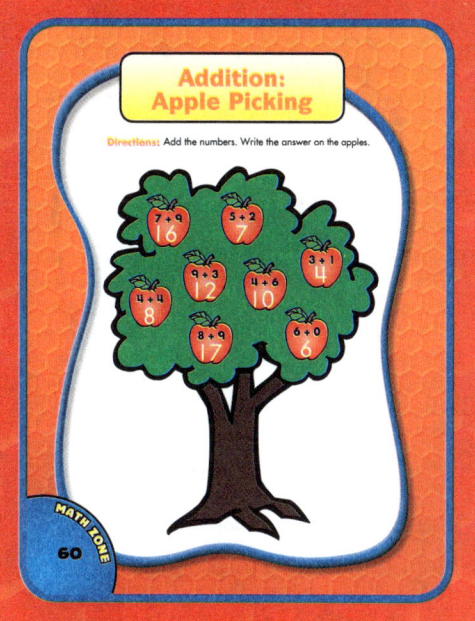

- 7 + 9 = 16
- 5 + 2 = 7
- 4 + 4 = 8
- 9 + 3 = 12
- 4 + 6 = 10
- 3 + 1 = 4
- 8 + 9 = 17
- 6 + 0 = 6

Addition: Solve the Riddle

Directions: Add to find the sums. Use the code to answer the riddle. One is done for you.

11	18	3	9	13	10	12	6	14	7	20
E	U	H	A	S	F	D	T	R	Y	L	W

Why are teddy bears never hungry?

8+4=12 (T), 1+2=3 (H), 5+6=11 (E), 8+7=14 (Y), 4+4 (A), 5+1=6 (R), 9+2=11 (E)

7+2=9 (A), 4+3=7 (L), 10+10=20 (W), 6+3=9 (A), 11+3=14 (Y), 7+6=13 (S)

10+3=13 (S), 9+3=12 (T), 9+9=18 (U), 5+5=10 (F), 6+4=10 (F), 11+0=11 (E), 2+2=4 (D)

Addition: 2-Digit

Kayla wrote some 2-digit addition problems for Tyler! Help Tyler solve them. Look at the example. Then, follow the directions.

Example:

Step 1: Add the ones.
25
+43
  8

Step 2: Add the tens.
25
+43
sum = 68

Directions: Add to find the sum.

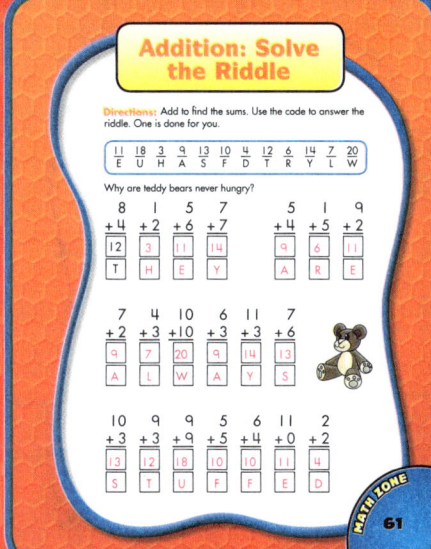

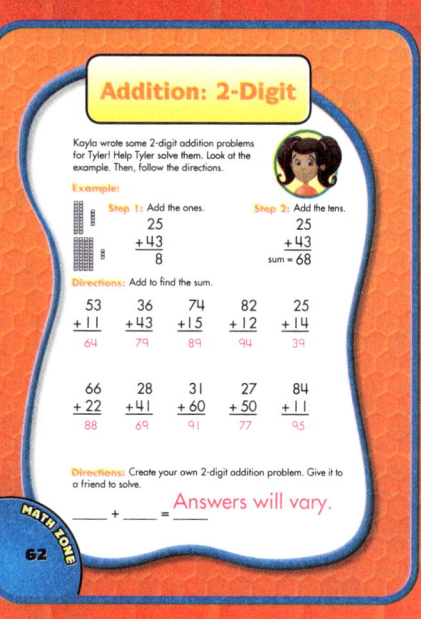

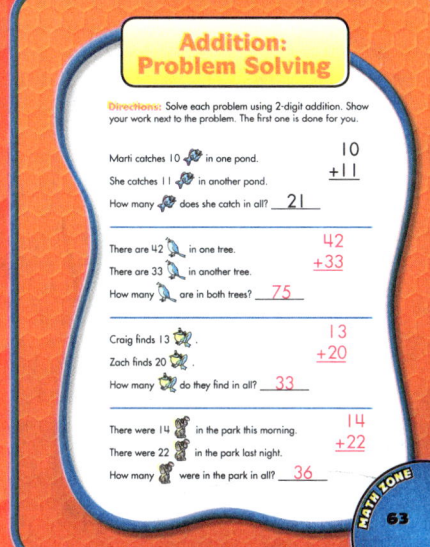

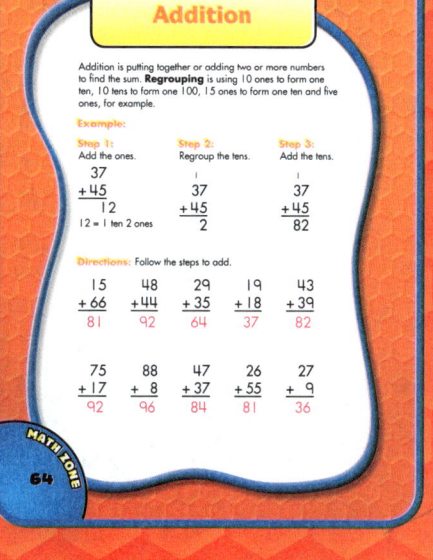

- 53 + 11 = 64
- 36 + 43 = 79
- 74 + 15 = 89
- 82 + 12 = 94
- 25 + 14 = 39

- 66 + 22 = 88
- 28 + 41 = 69
- 31 + 60 = 91
- 27 + 50 = 77
- 84 + 11 = 95

Directions: Create your own 2-digit addition problem. Give it to a friend to solve.

___ + ___ = Answers will vary.

Addition: Problem Solving

Directions: Solve each problem using 2-digit addition. Show your work next to the problem. The first one is done for you.

Marti catches 10 in one pond. She catches 11 in another pond. How many does she catch in all? **21**
10 + 11

There are 42 in one tree. There are 33 in another tree. How many are in both trees? **75**
42 + 33

Craig finds 13. Zach finds 20. How many do they find in all? **33**
13 + 20

There were 14 in the park this morning. There were 22 in the park last night. How many were in the park in all? **36**
14 + 22

Addition

Addition is putting together or adding two or more numbers to find the sum. **Regrouping** is using 10 ones to form one ten, 10 tens to form one 100, 15 ones to form one ten and five ones, for example.

Example:

Step 1: Add the ones.
37
+45
12
12 = 1 ten 2 ones

Step 2: Regroup the tens.
 1
37
+45
 2

Step 3: Add the tens.
 1
37
+45
82

Directions: Follow the steps to add.

- 15 + 66 = 81
- 48 + 44 = 92
- 29 + 35 = 64
- 19 + 18 = 37
- 43 + 39 = 82

- 75 + 17 = 92
- 88 + 8 = 96
- 47 + 37 = 84
- 26 + 55 = 81
- 27 + 9 = 36

ANSWER ZONE

229

Addition: Follow the Path (65)

Directions: Write each sum. Connect the sums of **83** to make a road for the truck.

| 17 +66 **83** | 48 +26 **74** | 42 +19 **61** |

| 28 +38 **66** | 64 +19 **83** | 26 +57 **83** | 58 +25 **83** | 17 +75 **92** | 65 +29 **94** |

| 37 +39 **76** | 48 +35 **83** | 58 +37 **95** | 65 +16 **81** | 38 +25 **63** | 39 +59 **98** |

| 59 +27 **86** | 55 +28 **83** | 39 +44 **83** |

Subtraction: Hidden Differences (66)

Directions: Circle the pairs that have a difference of **3**. One is done for you.

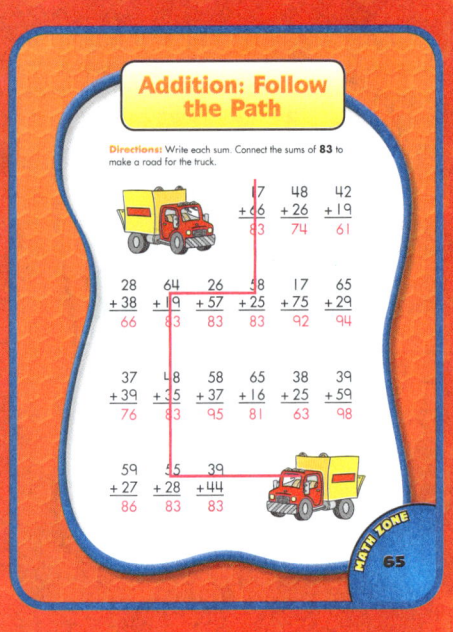

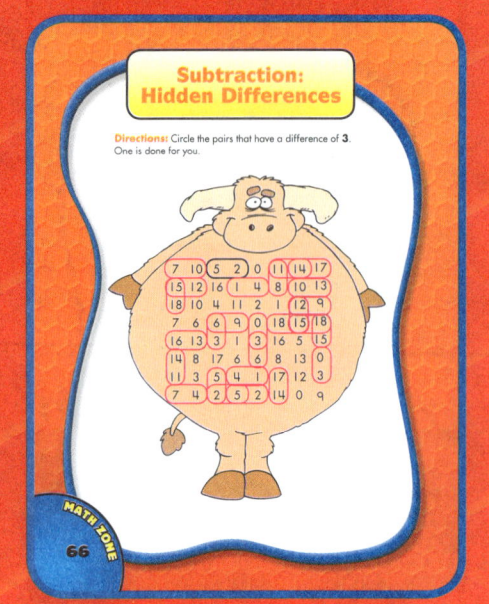

Subtraction (67)

Tyler wrote some subtraction problems for Kayla. Help Kayla solve the problems!

Directions: Subtract to find the difference.

| 13 -4 **9** | 7 -1 **6** | 4 -2 **2** | 14 -8 **6** | 10 -9 **1** | 5 -0 **5** |

| 11 -4 **7** | 15 -6 **9** | 6 -6 **0** | 17 -8 **9** | 8 -2 **6** | 12 -5 **7** |

Directions: Create your own subtraction problem. Give it to a friend to solve.

___ − ___ = ___

Answers will vary.

Subtraction: 2-Digit Numbers (68)

Example:
Step 1: Subtract the ones.
77 −26 = 1

Step 2: Subtract the tens.
77 −26, difference = 51

Directions: Subtract to find the difference. Write the answers on the clouds. Use the color code to color the clouds.

Color Code:
12 = gray
21 = black
24 = purple
33 = blue

36 −24 **12**
74 −50 **24**
65 −32 **33**
59 −38 **21**
78 −66 **12**
86 −62 **24**
82 −61 **21**
35 −11 **24**

Subtraction: Color Code (69)

Directions: Solve the subtraction problems. Use the code to color the picture.

Color Code:
25 = blue   57 = green
31 = yellow   14 = orange
21 = brown   11 = red

52 −21 **31**
47 −22 **25**
25 −11 **14**
62 −31 **31**
77 −20 **57**
51 −40 **11**
85 −84 **21** (?)
69 −12 **57**
98 −41 **57**

Subtraction: Regrouping (70)

Subtraction is taking away or subtracting one number from another to find the difference. **Regrouping** is using one ten to form 10 ones, one 100 to form 10 tens, for example.

Example:
Step 1: Regroup.
33 −19

Step 2: Subtract the ones.
33 −19 = 4

Step 3: Subtract the tens.
33 −19, difference = 14

3 tens 3 ones =
2 tens 13 ones

Directions: Follow the steps to subtract.

| 36 −17 **19** | 51 −39 **12** | 44 −15 **29** | 84 −47 **37** | 72 −65 **7** |

| 76 −19 **57** | 90 −78 **12** | 53 −26 **27** | 94 −85 **9** | 75 −18 **57** |

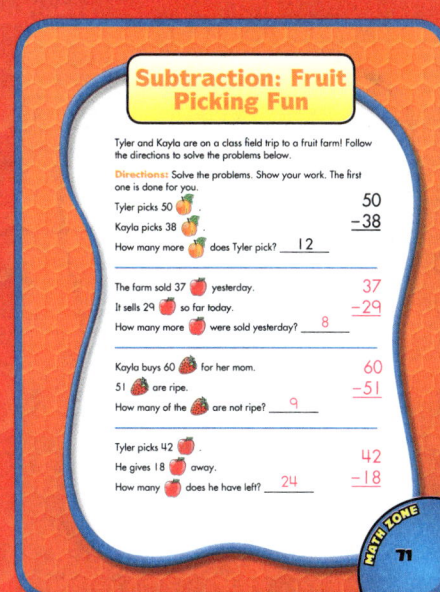

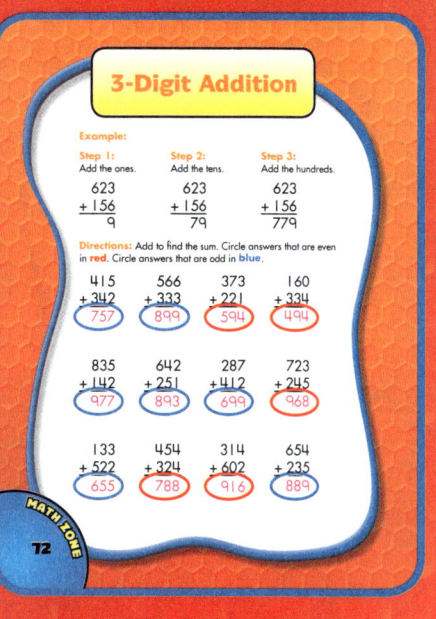

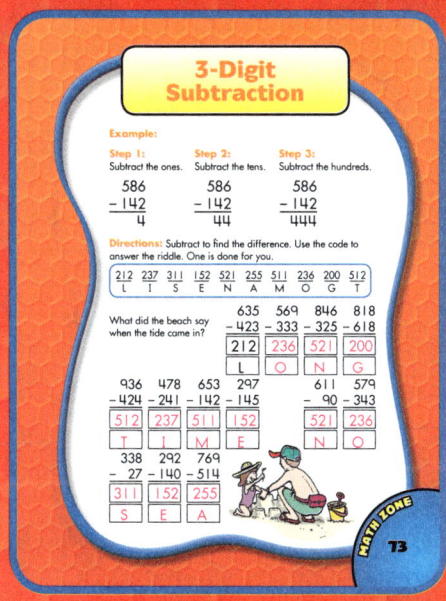

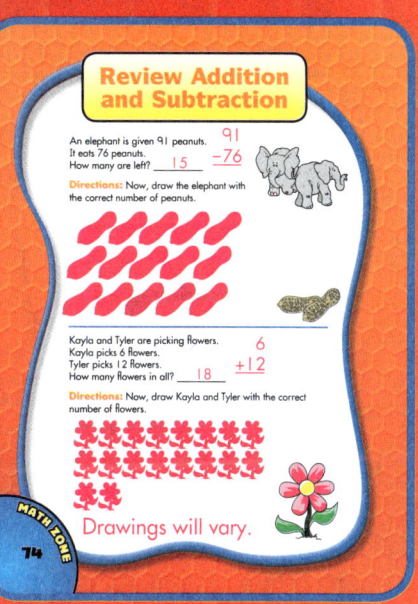

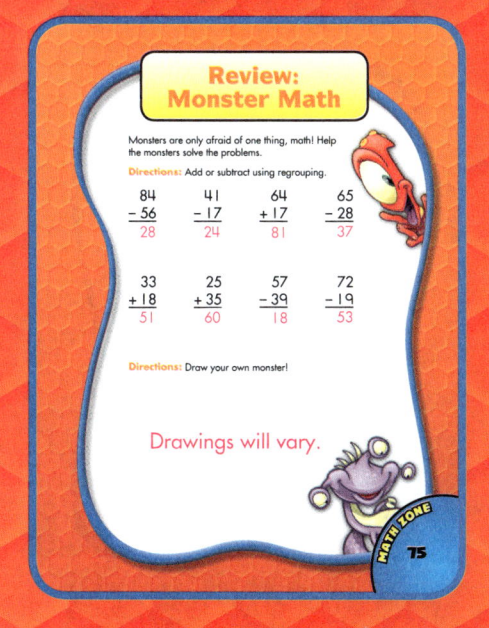

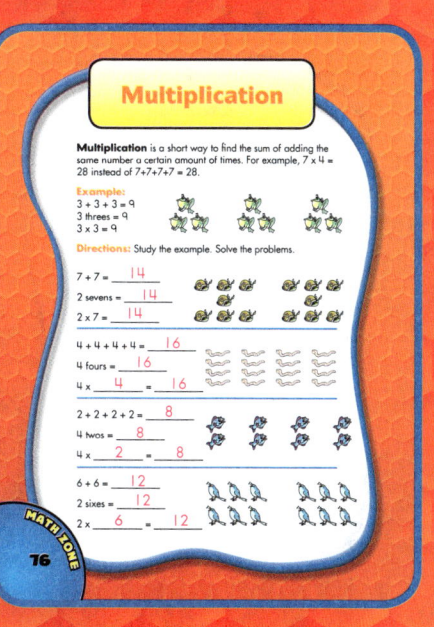

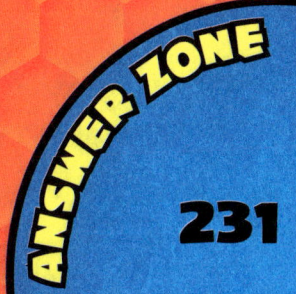

Subtraction: Fruit Picking Fun

Tyler and Kayla are on a class field trip to a fruit farm! Follow the directions to solve the problems below.

Directions: Solve the problems. Show your work. The first one is done for you.

Tyler picks 50.
Kayla picks 38.
How many more does Tyler pick? __12__

$$50 \\ -38$$

The farm sold 37 yesterday.
It sells 29 so far today.
How many more were sold yesterday? __8__

$$37 \\ -29$$

Kayla buys 60 for her mom.
51 are ripe.
How many of the are not ripe? __9__

$$60 \\ -51$$

Tyler picks 42.
He gives 18 away.
How many does he have left? __24__

$$42 \\ -18$$

71

3-Digit Addition

Example:
Step 1: Add the ones.
Step 2: Add the tens.
Step 3: Add the hundreds.

623 + 156 = 779

Directions: Add to find the sum. Circle answers that are even in red. Circle answers that are odd in blue.

415 + 342 = **757**
566 + 333 = **899**
373 + 221 = **594**
160 + 334 = **494**

835 + 142 = **977**
642 + 251 = **893**
287 + 412 = **699**
723 + 245 = **968**

133 + 522 = **655**
454 + 324 = **788**
314 + 602 = **916**
654 + 235 = **889**

72

3-Digit Subtraction

Example:
Step 1: Subtract the ones.
Step 2: Subtract the tens.
Step 3: Subtract the hundreds.

586 − 142 = 444

Directions: Subtract to find the difference. Use the code to answer the riddle. One is done for you.

212	237	311	152	521	255	511	236	200	512
L	I	S	E	N	A	M	O	G	T

What did the beach say when the tide came in?

635 − 423 = **212** L
569 − 333 = **236** O
846 − 325 = **521** N
818 − 618 = **200** G

936 − 424 = **512** T
478 − 241 = **237** I
653 − 142 = **511** M
297 − 145 = **152** E

611 − 90 = **521** N
579 − 343 = **236** O

338 − 27 = **311** S
292 − 140 = **152** E
769 − 514 = **255** A

73

Review Addition and Subtraction

An elephant is given 91 peanuts.
It eats 76 peanuts.
How many are left? __15__

$$91 \\ -76$$

Directions: Now, draw the elephant with the correct number of peanuts.

Kayla and Tyler are picking flowers.
Kayla picks 6 flowers.
Tyler picks 12 flowers.
How many flowers in all? __18__

$$6 \\ +12$$

Directions: Now, draw Kayla and Tyler with the correct number of flowers.

Drawings will vary.

74

Review: Monster Math

Monsters are only afraid of one thing, math! Help the monsters solve the problems.

Directions: Add or subtract using regrouping.

84 − 56 = **28**
41 − 17 = **24**
64 + 17 = **81**
65 − 28 = **37**

33 + 18 = **51**
25 + 35 = **60**
57 − 39 = **18**
72 − 19 = **53**

Directions: Draw your own monster!

Drawings will vary.

75

Multiplication

Multiplication is a short way to find the sum of adding the same number a certain amount of times. For example, 7 × 4 = 28 instead of 7+7+7+7 = 28.

Example:
3 + 3 + 3 = 9
3 threes = 9
3 × 3 = 9

Directions: Study the example. Solve the problems.

7 + 7 = __14__
2 sevens = __14__
2 × 7 = __14__

4 + 4 + 4 + 4 = __16__
4 fours = __16__
4 × __4__ = __16__

2 + 2 + 2 + 2 = __8__
4 twos = __8__
4 × __2__ = __8__

6 + 6 = __12__
2 sixes = __12__
2 × __6__ = __12__

76

ANSWER ZONE

231

Multiplication

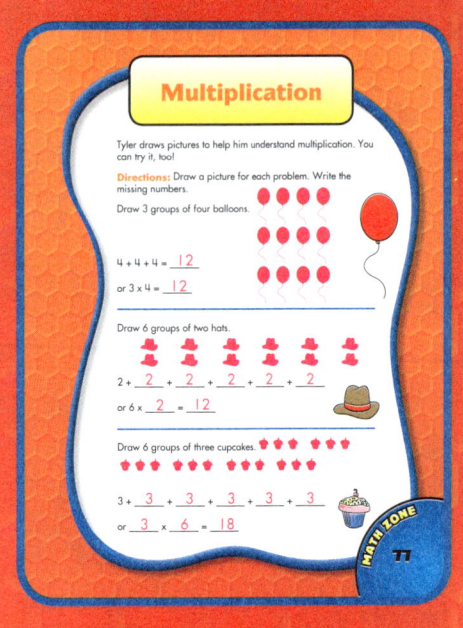

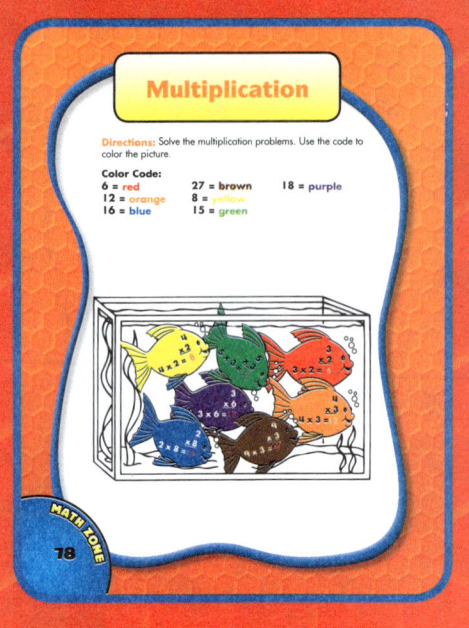

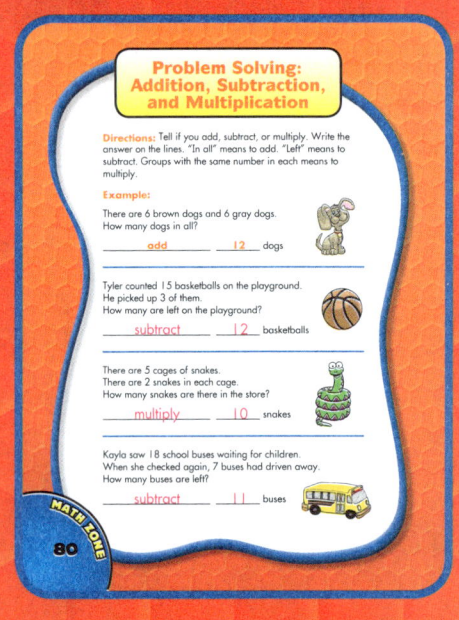

Tyler draws pictures to help him understand multiplication. You can try it, too!

Directions: Draw a picture for each problem. Write the missing numbers.

Draw 3 groups of four balloons.

$4 + 4 + 4 = \underline{12}$

or $3 \times 4 = \underline{12}$

Draw 6 groups of two hats.

$2 + \underline{2} + \underline{2} + \underline{2} + \underline{2} + \underline{2} = \underline{12}$

or $6 \times \underline{2} = \underline{12}$

Draw 6 groups of three cupcakes.

$3 + \underline{3} + \underline{3} + \underline{3} + \underline{3} + \underline{3} = \underline{18}$

or $\underline{3} \times \underline{6} = \underline{18}$

77

Multiplication

Directions: Solve the multiplication problems. Use the code to color the picture.

Color Code:
6 = red   27 = brown   18 = purple
12 = orange   8 = yellow
16 = blue   15 = green

78

Multiplication

Directions: Solve the multiplication problems. Use the code to color the picture.

Color Code:
6 = green   16 = pink   25 = orange
8 = purple   18 = white   27 = blue
9 = red   21 = brown

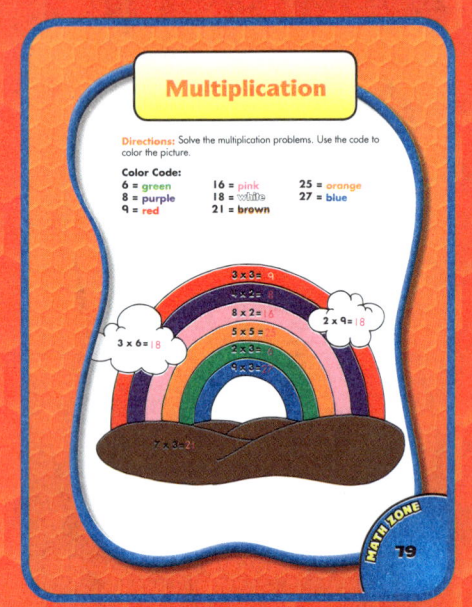

$3 \times 3 = 9$
$4 \times 2 = 8$
$8 \times 2 = 16$
$2 \times 9 = 18$
$3 \times 6 = 18$
$5 \times 5 = 25$
$2 \times 3 = 6$
$3 \times 7 = 21$
$7 \times 3 = 21$

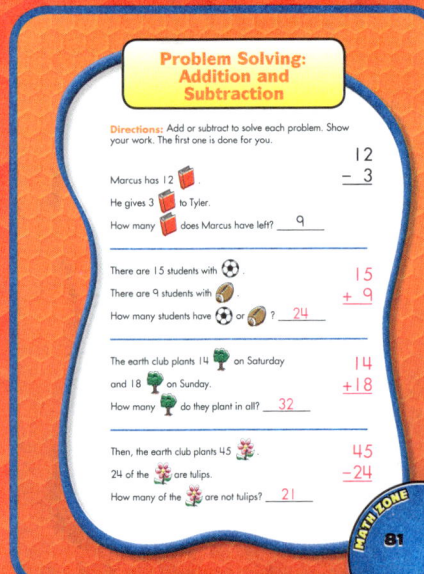

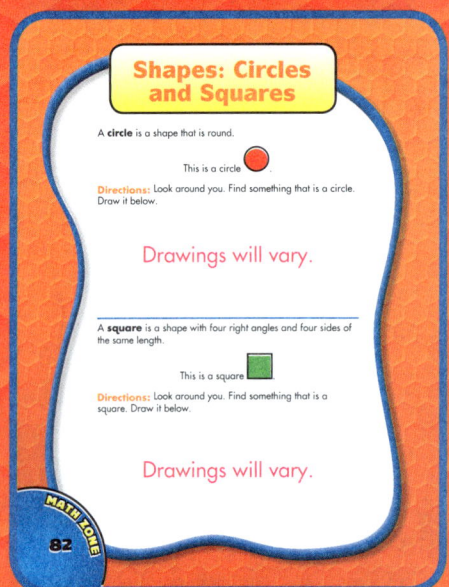

79

Problem Solving: Addition, Subtraction, and Multiplication

Directions: Tell if you add, subtract, or multiply. Write the answer on the lines. "In all" means to add. "Left" means to subtract. Groups with the same number in each means to multiply.

Example:
There are 6 brown dogs and 6 gray dogs. How many dogs in all?
   <u>add</u>   <u>12</u> dogs

Tyler counted 15 basketballs on the playground. He picked up 3 of them. How many are left on the playground?
   <u>subtract</u>   <u>12</u> basketballs

There are 5 cages of snakes. There are 2 snakes in each cage. How many snakes are there in the store?
   <u>multiply</u>   <u>10</u> snakes

Kayla saw 18 school buses waiting for children. When she checked again, 7 buses had driven away. How many buses are left?
   <u>subtract</u>   <u>11</u> buses

80

Problem Solving: Addition and Subtraction

Directions: Add or subtract to solve each problem. Show your work. The first one is done for you.

Marcus has 12 📕.
He gives 3 📕 to Tyler.
How many 📕 does Marcus have left?   <u>9</u>

12
-3

There are 15 students with ⚽.
There are 9 students with 🏈.
How many students have ⚽ or 🏈?   <u>24</u>

15
$+9$

The earth club plants 14 🌳 on Saturday and 18 🌳 on Sunday.
How many 🌳 do they plant in all?   <u>32</u>

14
$+18$

Then, the earth club plants 45 🌷.
24 of the 🌷 are tulips.
How many of the 🌷 are not tulips?   <u>21</u>

45
-24

81

Shapes: Circles and Squares

A **circle** is a shape that is round.

This is a circle 🔴

Directions: Look around you. Find something that is a circle. Draw it below.

Drawings will vary.

A **square** is a shape with four right angles and four sides of the same length.

This is a square 🟩

Directions: Look around you. Find something that is a square. Draw it below.

Drawings will vary.

82

ANSWER ZONE

232

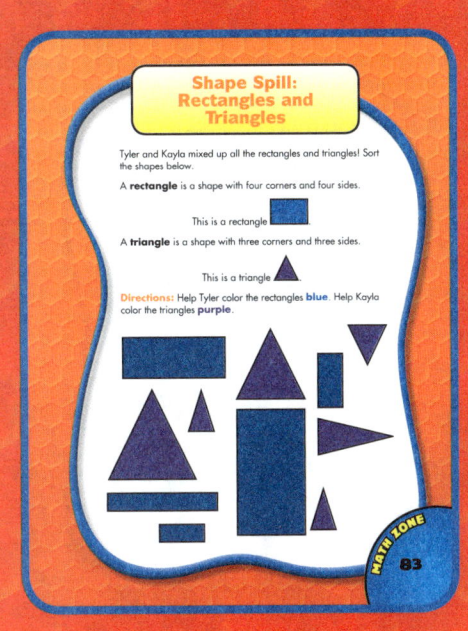

Shape Spill: Rectangles and Triangles

Tyler and Kayla mixed up all the rectangles and triangles! Sort the shapes below.

A **rectangle** is a shape with four corners and four sides.

This is a rectangle ▬

A **triangle** is a shape with three corners and three sides.

This is a triangle ▲

Directions: Help Tyler color the rectangles **blue**. Help Kayla color the triangles **purple**.

83

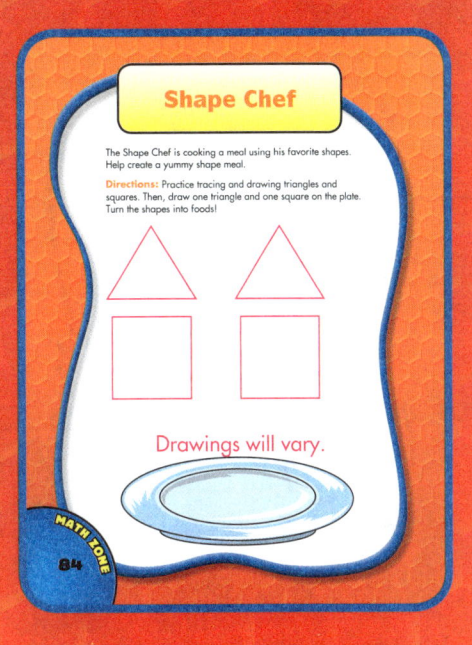

Shape Chef

The Shape Chef is cooking a meal using his favorite shapes. Help create a yummy shape meal.

Directions: Practice tracing and drawing triangles and squares. Then, draw one triangle and one square on the plate. Turn the shapes into foods!

Drawings will vary.

84

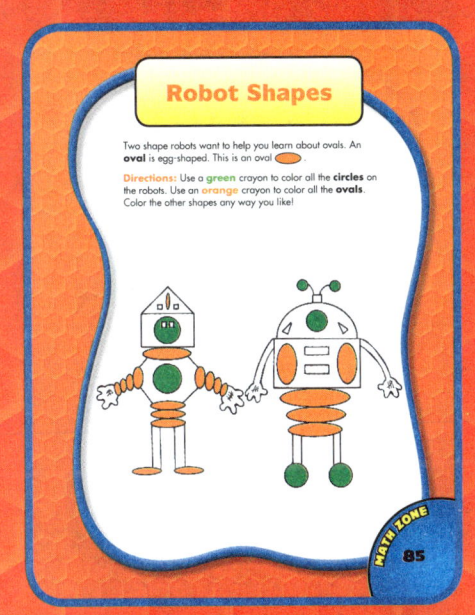

Robot Shapes

Two shape robots want to help you learn about ovals. An **oval** is egg-shaped. This is an oval ⬭.

Directions: Use a **green** crayon to color all the **circles** on the robots. Use an **orange** crayon to color all the **ovals**. Color the other shapes any way you like!

85

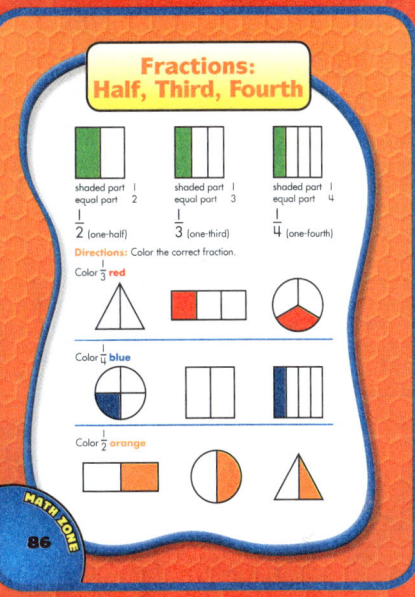

Fractions: Half, Third, Fourth

shaded part 1 shaded part 1 shaded part 1
equal part 2   equal part 3   equal part 4

$\frac{1}{2}$ (one-half) $\frac{1}{3}$ (one-third) $\frac{1}{4}$ (one-fourth)

Directions: Color the correct fraction.

Color $\frac{1}{3}$ **red**

Color $\frac{1}{4}$ **blue**

Color $\frac{1}{2}$ **orange**

86

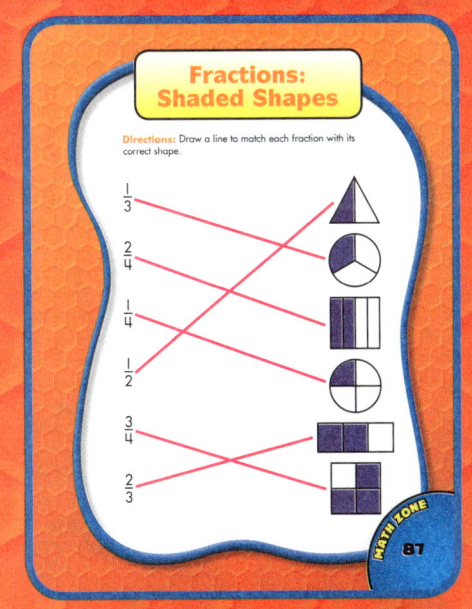

Fractions: Shaded Shapes

Directions: Draw a line to match each fraction with its correct shape.

$\frac{1}{3}$
$\frac{2}{4}$
$\frac{1}{4}$
$\frac{1}{2}$
$\frac{3}{4}$
$\frac{2}{3}$

87

Time: Time to the Hour and Half Hour

Hour: **Half Hour:**
4 o'clock   Half past 4
4:00   4:30

Directions: Write the time two ways.

 7 o'clock   9 o'clock
 7 : 00   9 : 00

 6:30

Half past 6   Half past 1
 6 : 30   1 : 30

Half past 3   12 o'clock
 3 : 30   12 : 00

88

ANSWER ZONE

233

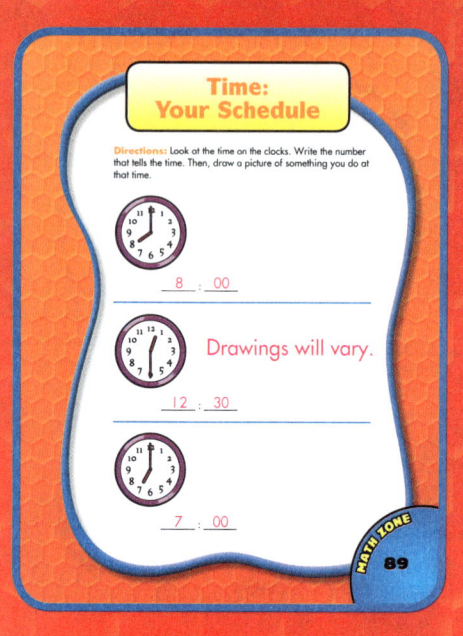

Time: Your Schedule

Directions: Look at the time on the clocks. Write the number that tells the time. Then, draw a picture of something you do at that time.

8 : 00

Drawings will vary.

12 : 30

7 : 00

89

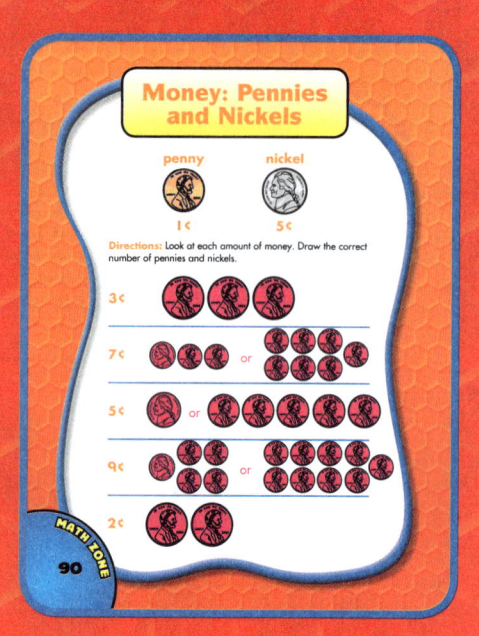

Money: Pennies and Nickels

penny 1¢   nickel 5¢

Directions: Look at each amount of money. Draw the correct number of pennies and nickels.

3¢

7¢ ... or ...

5¢ ... or ...

9¢ ... or ...

2¢

90

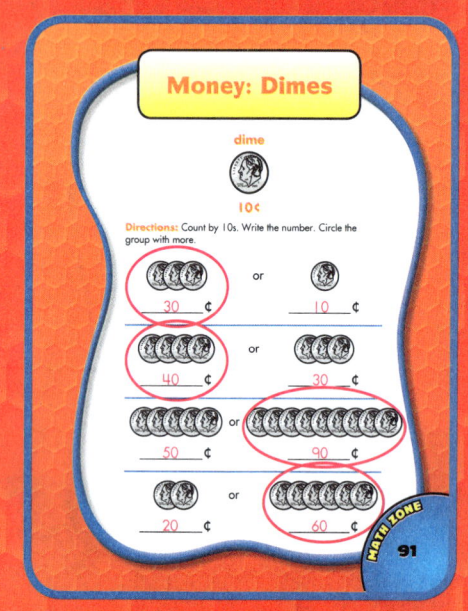

Money: Dimes

dime 10¢

Directions: Count by 10s. Write the number. Circle the group with more.

30 ¢   10 ¢

40 ¢   30 ¢

50 ¢   **90** ¢

20 ¢   **60** ¢

91

Money: Quarters

Kayla is counting the quarters she has in her piggy bank! Help Kayla count the quarters.

quarter 25¢

Directions: Count the quarters. Write the answer on the line.

50 ¢

75 ¢

25 ¢

Make your own piggy bank in the Craft Zone! Check it out on pages 40 and 41.

What should Kayla buy with her quarters? Draw it below.

Drawings will vary.

92

Money: Counting Change

Directions: Elephants never forget how much change they have! Draw a line from the change to the elephant with the correct number.

27¢
32¢
15¢
76¢
55¢

93

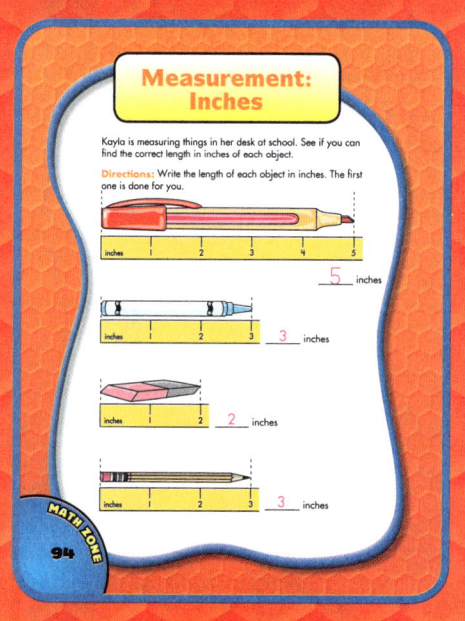

Measurement: Inches

Kayla is measuring things in her desk at school. See if you can find the correct length in inches of each object.

Directions: Write the length of each object in inches. The first one is done for you.

5 inches

3 inches

2 inches

3 inches

94

ANSWER ZONE

234

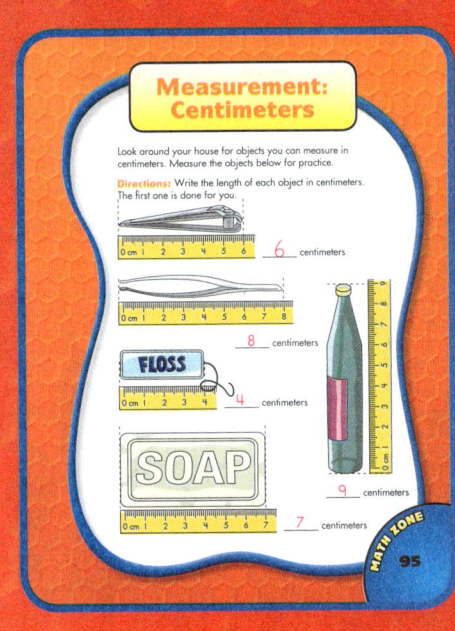

Measurement: Centimeters

Look around your house for objects you can measure in centimeters. Measure the objects below for practice.

Directions: Write the length of each object in centimeters. The first one is done for you.

- 6 centimeters
- 8 centimeters
- 4 centimeters
- 9 centimeters
- 7 centimeters

95

Measurement

Directions: Use a centimeter ruler to measure the distance each animal has to travel to reach the watering hole. Write the answer on each line.

- 4 cm
- 6 cm
- 7 cm
- 3 cm
- 11 cm
- 12 cm

96

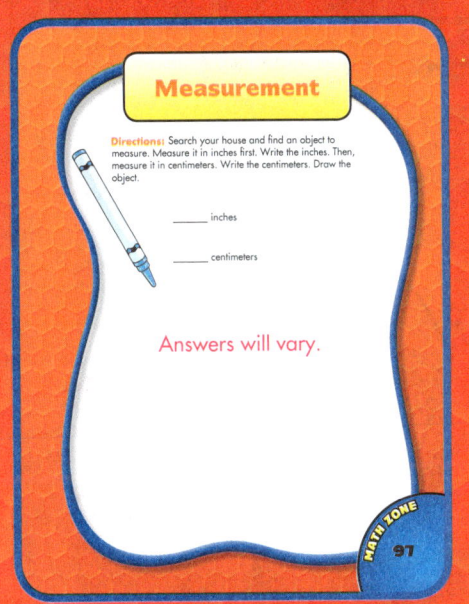

Measurement

Directions: Search your house and find an object to measure. Measure it in inches first. Write the inches. Then, measure it in centimeters. Write the centimeters. Draw the object.

____ inches

____ centimeters

Answers will vary.

97

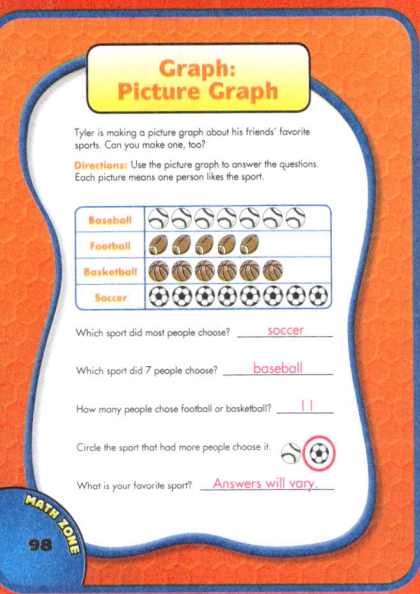

Graph: Picture Graph

Tyler is making a picture graph about his friends' favorite sports. Can you make one, too?

Directions: Use the picture graph to answer the questions. Each picture means one person likes the sport.

Which sport did most people choose? __soccer__

Which sport did 7 people choose? __baseball__

How many people chose football or basketball? __11__

Circle the sport that had more people choose it.

What is your favorite sport? __Answers will vary.__

98

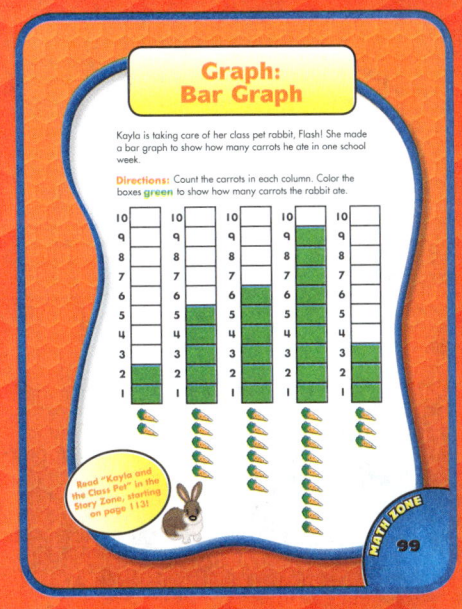

Graph: Bar Graph

Kayla is taking care of her class pet rabbit, Flash! She made a bar graph to show how many carrots he ate in one school week.

Directions: Count the carrots in each column. Color the boxes green to show how many carrots the rabbit ate.

99

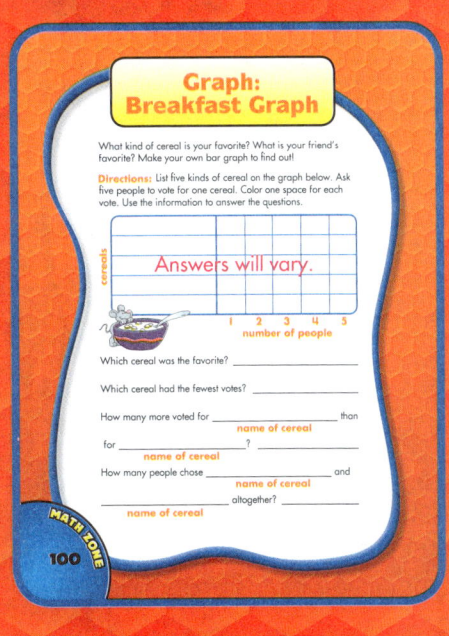

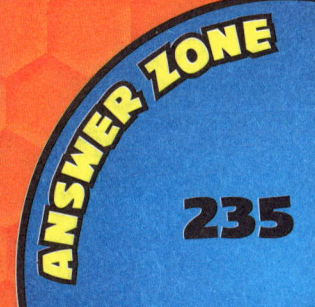

Graph: Breakfast Graph

What kind of cereal is your favorite? What is your friend's favorite? Make your own bar graph to find out!

Directions: List five kinds of cereal on the graph below. Ask five people to vote for one cereal. Color one space for each vote. Use the information to answer the questions.

Answers will vary.

Which cereal was the favorite? _____

Which cereal had the fewest votes? _____

How many more voted for _____ name of cereal than for _____ name of cereal?

How many people chose _____ name of cereal and _____ name of cereal altogether?

100

ANSWER ZONE 235

102

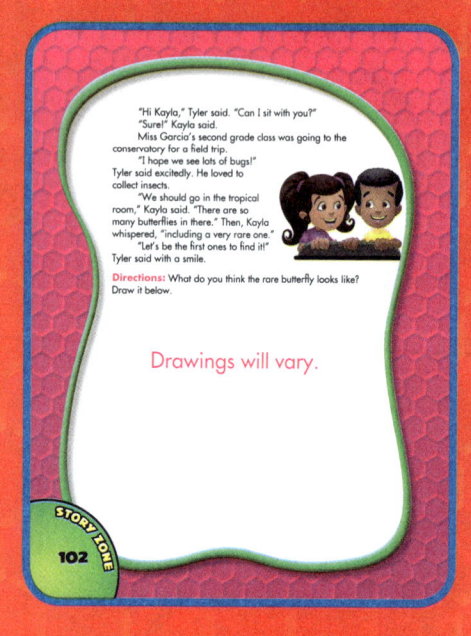

"Hi Kayla," Tyler said. "Can I sit with you?"
"Sure!" Kayla said.
Miss Garcia's second grade class was going to the conservatory for a field trip.
"I hope we see lots of bugs!" Tyler said excitedly. He loved to collect insects.
"We should go in the tropical room," Kayla said. "There are so many butterflies in there." Then, Kayla whispered, "including a very rare one."
"Let's be the first ones to find it!" Tyler said with a smile.

Directions: What do you think the rare butterfly looks like? Draw it below.

Drawings will vary.

103

Soon, Miss Garcia's class was in the tropical room.
"Listen closely everyone," Miss Garcia said. "Explore the tropical room and fill out your worksheets. We will meet again in a half hour."
"If you are lucky," Miss Garcia said with a smile. "You might see a rare orange and blue butterfly called the Pipevine Swallowtail."
"Let's go Ty!" Kayla said. Kayla and Tyler began their search.
"Don't worry Kayla. I'm the best at hide and seek," Tyler said. "I'll find it."

Directions: Help Kayla and Tyler fill out their worksheets. Fill in the blanks below. Use the words from the word box to help.

Butterfly Conservatory Worksheet
Miss Garcia's Class

| blue | insect | colors | egg |

A butterfly is an ___insect___.

A butterfly's life cycle is ___egg___, larva, pupa, and adult.

Butterflies come in many different ___colors___.

The Pipevine Swallowtail is orange and ___blue___.

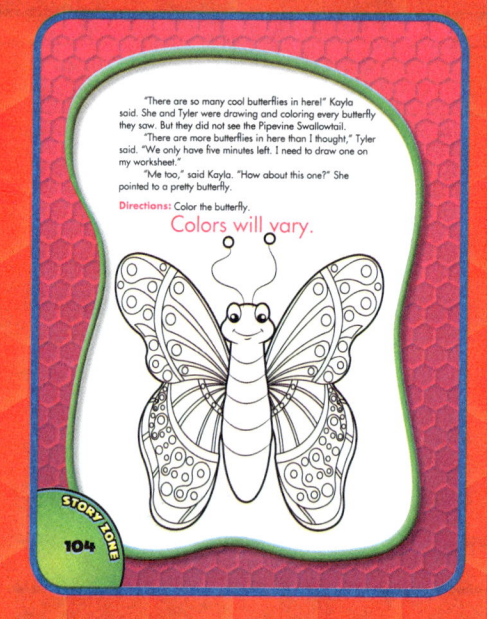

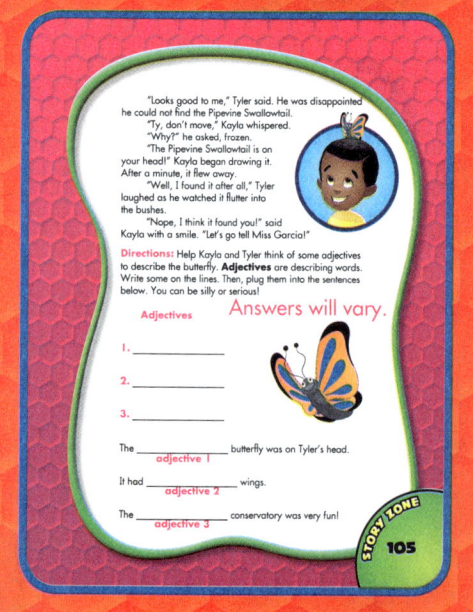

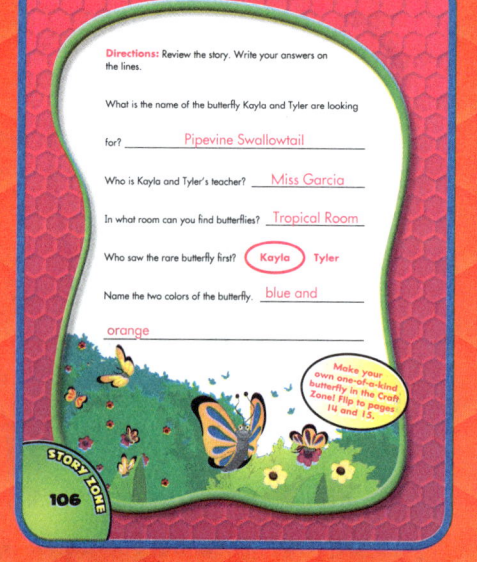

104

"There are so many cool butterflies in here!" Kayla said. She and Tyler were drawing and coloring every butterfly they saw. But they did not see the Pipevine Swallowtail.
"There are more butterflies in here than I thought," Tyler said. "We only have five minutes left. I need to draw one on my worksheet."
"Me too," said Kayla. "How about this one?" She pointed to a pretty butterfly.

Directions: Color the butterfly.

Colors will vary.

105

"Looks good to me," Tyler said. He was disappointed he could not find the Pipevine Swallowtail.
"Ty, don't move," Kayla whispered.
"Why?" he asked, frozen.
"The Pipevine Swallowtail is on your head!" Kayla began drawing it. After a minute, it flew away.
"Well, I found it after all," Tyler laughed as he watched it flutter into the bushes.
"Nope, I think it found you!" said Kayla with a smile. "Let's go tell Miss Garcia!"

Directions: Help Kayla and Tyler think of some adjectives to describe the butterfly. **Adjectives** are describing words. Write some on the lines. Then, plug them into the sentences below. You can be silly or serious!

Adjectives — *Answers will vary.*

1. _____
2. _____
3. _____

The ___adjective 1___ butterfly was on Tyler's head.

It had ___adjective 2___ wings.

The ___adjective 3___ conservatory was very fun!

106

Directions: Review the story. Write your answers on the lines.

What is the name of the butterfly Kayla and Tyler are looking for? ___Pipevine Swallowtail___

Who is Kayla and Tyler's teacher? ___Miss Garcia___

In what room can you find butterflies? ___Tropical Room___

Who saw the rare butterfly first? (**Kayla**) Tyler

Name the two colors of the butterfly. ___blue and orange___

Make your own one-of-a-kind butterfly in the Craft Zone! Flip to pages 14 and 15.

ANSWER ZONE
236

108

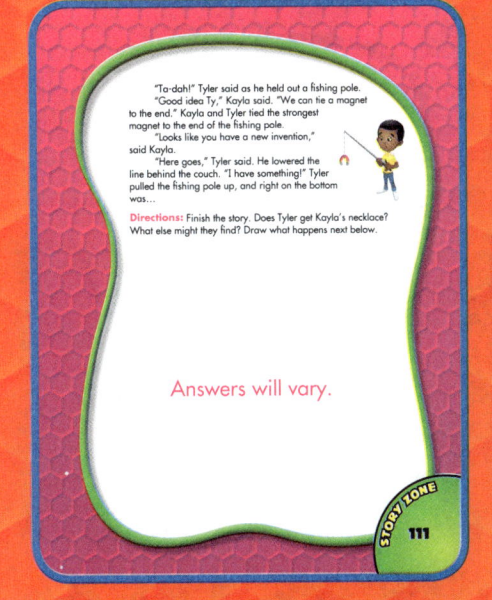

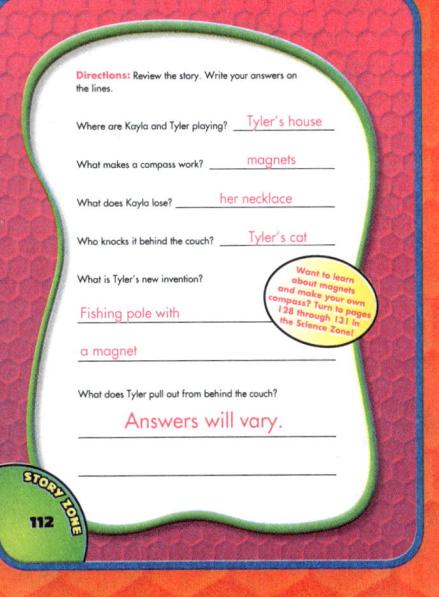

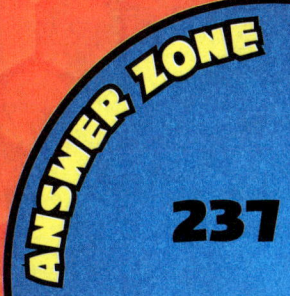

Ding-dong. The doorbell rang and Tyler opened the door.
"Hi Ty," Kayla said. "Thanks for letting me come over."
"No problem," said Tyler. "I have a fun game for us to try." Tyler handed Kayla a compass.
"What's this?" Kayla asked.
"A compass, you use it to find north," Tyler said. "Okay, I hid five things in the living room. Use the compass to help you find them!" Tyler said.

Directions: Help Kayla find the hidden objects. Follow the directions below. Circle the objects when you find them.

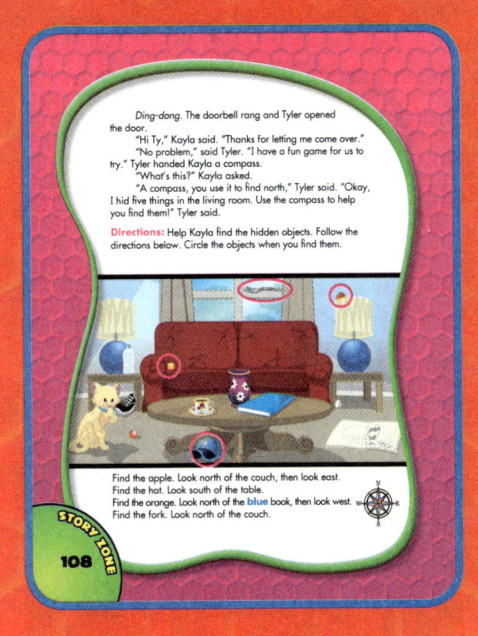

Find the apple. Look north of the couch, then look east.
Find the hat. Look south of the table.
Find the orange. Look north of the **blue** book, then look west.
Find the fork. Look north of the couch.

109

"Good job!" Tyler said. "Do you know what makes a compass work?"
"What?" asked Kayla.
"Magnets," Tyler said. "My dad just gave me some to make my inventions with." Tyler loved to make his own wacky inventions.
"Let's see what we can find that is magnetic," Kayla suggested.
They tested magnetic objects like coins and paperclips and non-magnetic ones like wood and plastic.
"Let's try this," Kayla said as she took off her necklace.

Directions: What do you know about magnets? Draw things you think are magnetic below. Test them out!

Drawings will vary.

110

"It works," Tyler said holding up Kayla's necklace with the magnet.
"Cool," said Kyla with a smile. She set the necklace on top of the couch.
"Let's get a snack," Tyler said. They went into the kitchen. They came back twenty minutes later.
"I almost forgot!" Kayla said reaching for her necklace. But it was gone. "Oh no! I lost it," Kayla said. Tyler looked behind the couch.
"I see it, but I can't reach it," he said. "Don't worry, I have an idea!"

Directions: How did Kayla's necklace fall? Use the context clues to fill in the blank below. **Context clues** can help you figure out a missing word just by looking at the other words in the sentence.

Tyler's ___**cat**___ jumped on the couch. It loves to take a nap on top of the couch. Its tail pushed the necklace behind the couch.

mom   **cat**   goat   magnets

Directions: Draw a picture of how Kayla's necklace fell behind the couch.

Drawings will vary.

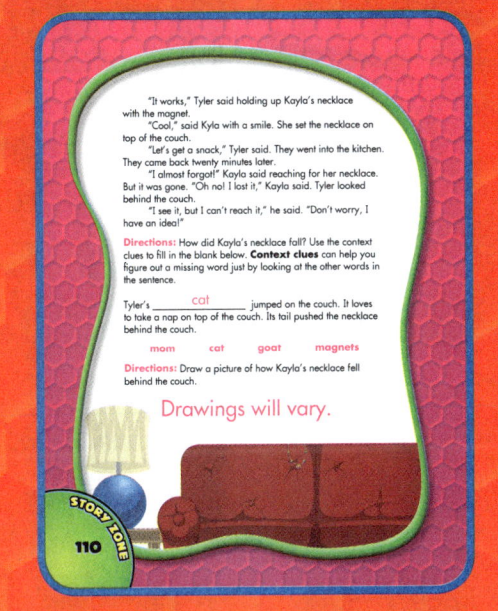

111

"Ta-dah!" Tyler said as he held out a fishing pole.
"Good idea Ty," Kayla said. "We can tie a magnet to the end." Kayla and Tyler tied the strongest magnet to the end of the fishing pole.
"Looks like you have a new invention," said Kayla.
"Here goes," Tyler said. He lowered the line behind the couch. "I have something!" Tyler pulled the fishing pole up, and right on the bottom was...

Directions: Finish the story. Does Tyler get Kayla's necklace? What else might they find? Draw what happens next below.

Answers will vary.

112

Directions: Review the story. Write your answers on the lines.

Where are Kayla and Tyler playing? __Tyler's house__

What makes a compass work? __magnets__

What does Kayla lose? __her necklace__

Who knocks it behind the couch? __Tyler's cat__

What is Tyler's new invention? __Fishing pole with a magnet__

Want to learn about magnets and make your own compass? Turn to pages 128 through 131 in the Science Zone!

What does Tyler pull out from behind the couch?
__Answers will vary.__

ANSWER ZONE

237

Page 114

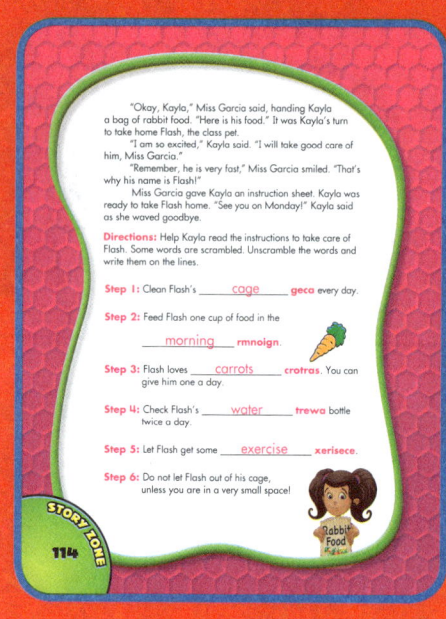

"Okay, Kayla," Miss Garcia said, handing Kayla a bag of rabbit food. "Here is his food." It was Kayla's turn to take home Flash, the class pet.

"I am so excited," Kayla said. "I will take good care of him, Miss Garcia."

"Remember, he is very fast," Miss Garcia smiled. "That's why his name is Flash!"

Miss Garcia gave Kayla an instruction sheet. Kayla was ready to take Flash home. "See you on Monday!" Kayla said as she waved goodbye.

Directions: Help Kayla read the instructions to take care of Flash. Some words are scrambled. Unscramble the words and write them on the lines.

Step 1: Clean Flash's ___cage___ geca every day.

Step 2: Feed Flash one cup of food in the ___morning___ rnnoign.

Step 3: Flash loves ___carrots___ crotras. You can give him one a day.

Step 4: Check Flash's ___water___ trewa bottle twice a day.

Step 5: Let Flash get some ___exercise___ xerisece.

Step 6: Do not let Flash out of his cage, unless you are in a very small space!

Page 115

Kayla set up a spot for Flash's cage in her room. The doorbell rang. "Tyler must be here," Kayla said as she walked to the door.

"Hi Kayla," Tyler said. "Can I play with Flash?"

"Sure, he is in my room," Kayla said. "Go ahead and see him, I need to put my backpack away." Tyler went into Kayla's room. When Kayla walked in she did not see Flash in his cage.

"Wow, he is fast!" Tyler exclaimed.

Directions: Color Flash below. If you had a rabbit, what would you name it?

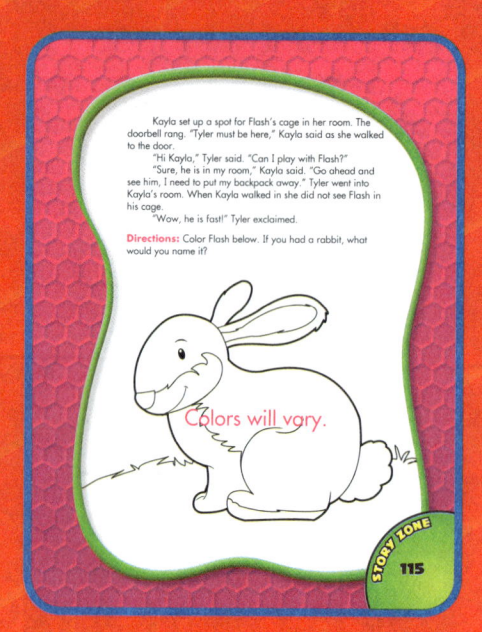

Colors will vary.

Page 116

"Uh oh," Kayla said. "Did he get out of my room?"
"No," Tyler said, "but he is hiding!"
"Ty!" Kayla said. "We are not supposed to let him out of the cage unless we are in a smaller room."
"Sorry," Tyler said. "I will help you catch him though."
Suddenly, Flash ran past them.
"It's okay," Kayla said. "At least he is getting his exercise, but where is he now?"

Directions: Find and circle Flash.

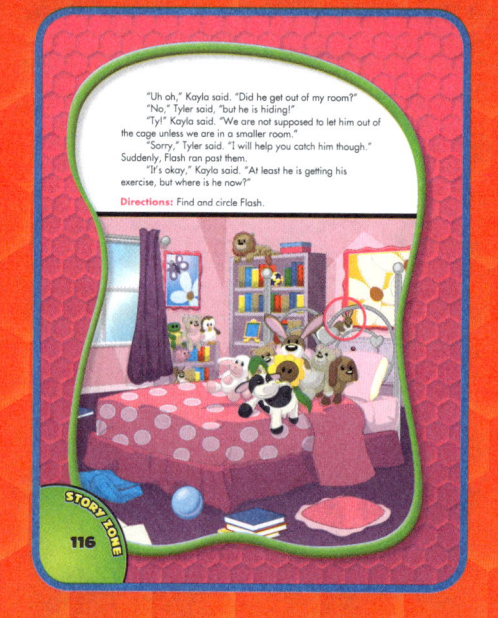

Page 117

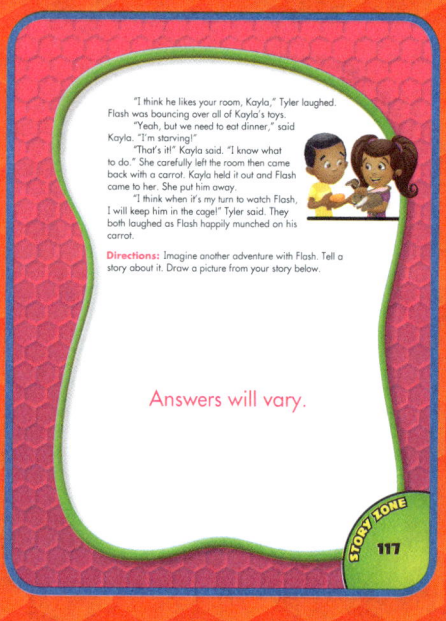

"I think he likes your room, Kayla," Tyler laughed. Flash was bouncing over all of Kayla's toys.
"Yeah, but we need to eat dinner," said Kayla. "I'm starving!"
"That's it!" Kayla said. "I know what to do." She carefully left the room then came back with a carrot. Kayla held it out and Flash came to her. She put him away.
"I think when it's my turn to watch Flash, I will keep him in the cage!" Tyler said. They both laughed as Flash happily munched on his carrot.

Directions: Imagine another adventure with Flash. Tell a story about it. Draw a picture from your story below.

Answers will vary.

Page 118

Directions: Review the story. Write your answers on the lines.

Why is the rabbit named Flash? ___It is fast.___

Name two things from the instruction sheet Kayla needs to do.

___Answers may include: clean his cage,___
___feed him in the morning, give him carrots,___
___check his water, give him exercise___

What is Flash's favorite food? ___carrots___

Where is Flash hiding? ___In Kayla's room.___

Who let Flash out of his cage? ___Tyler___

What will Tyler do when he watches Flash?

___Keep him in the cage.___

Chase Flash through mazes in the Game Zone! Try the maze on page 160.

ANSWER ZONE

238

States of Matter: Liquids

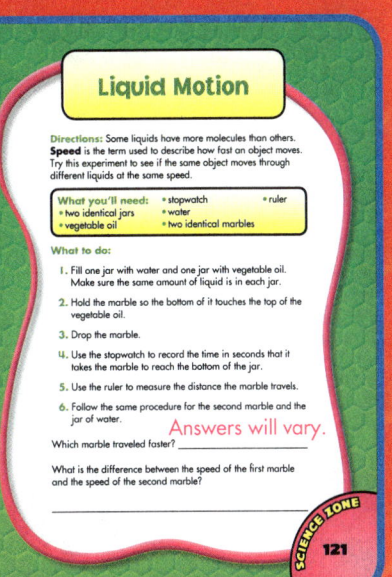

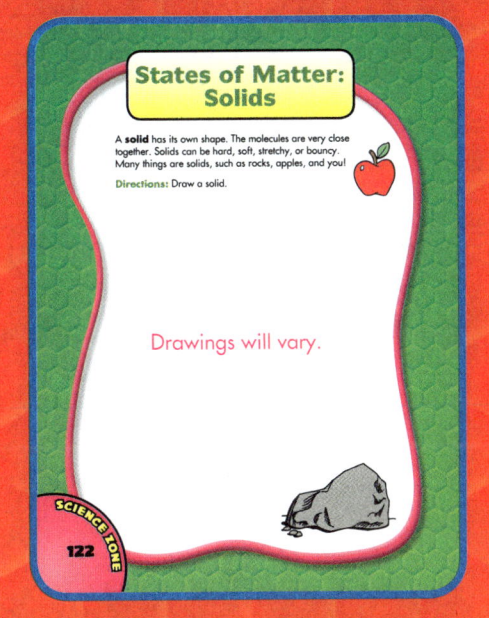

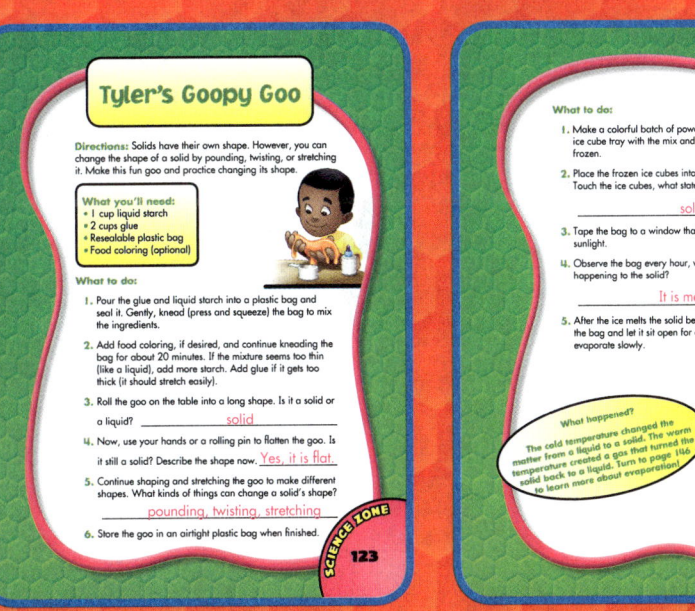

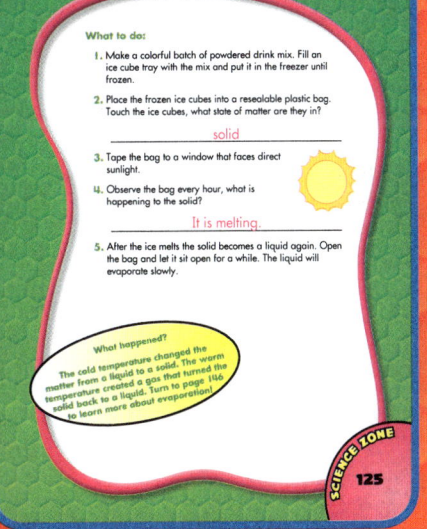

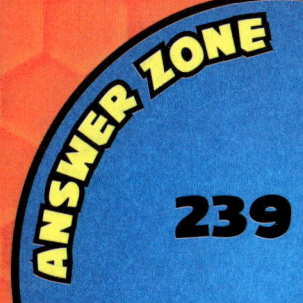

Matter is everywhere. Everything on Earth is made of matter. All matter takes up space. There are three types of matter: liquids, solids, and gases. Each type of matter is made of tiny **molecules**.

A **liquid** does not have a shape. Molecules move around easily in liquid. Liquids take the shape of the container they are in. Water is a liquid. If you pour water in a glass, it takes the shape of the glass.

Directions: Circle the liquids below. Can you think of another liquid? Draw it.

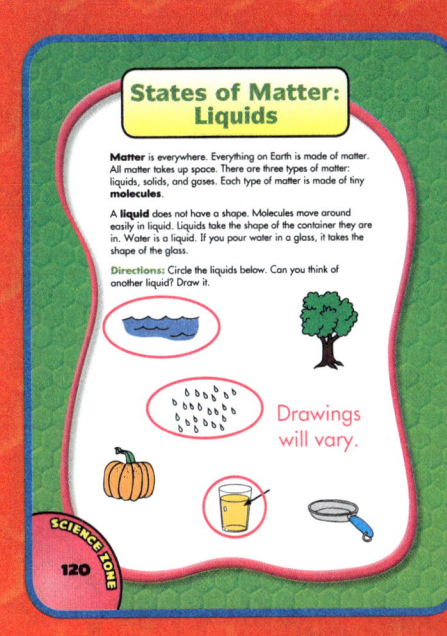

Drawings will vary.

Liquid Motion

Directions: Some liquids have more molecules than others. **Speed** is the term used to describe how fast an object moves. Try this experiment to see if the same object moves through different liquids at the same speed.

What you'll need:	• stopwatch	• ruler
• two identical jars	• water	
• vegetable oil	• two identical marbles	

What to do:
1. Fill one jar with water and one jar with vegetable oil. Make sure the same amount of liquid is in each jar.
2. Hold the marble so the bottom of it touches the top of the vegetable oil.
3. Drop the marble.
4. Use the stopwatch to record the time in seconds that it takes the marble to reach the bottom of the jar.
5. Use the ruler to measure the distance the marble travels.
6. Follow the same procedure for the second marble and the jar of water.

Which marble traveled faster? **Answers will vary.**

What is the difference between the speed of the first marble and the speed of the second marble?

States of Matter: Solids

A **solid** has its own shape. The molecules are very close together. Solids can be hard, soft, stretchy, or bouncy. Many things are solids, such as rocks, apples, and you!

Directions: Draw a solid.

Drawings will vary.

Tyler's Goopy Goo

Directions: Solids have their own shape. However, you can change the shape of a solid by pounding, twisting, or stretching it. Make this fun goo and practice changing its shape.

What you'll need:
- 1 cup liquid starch
- 2 cups glue
- Resealable plastic bag
- Food coloring (optional)

What to do:
1. Pour the glue and liquid starch into a plastic bag and seal it. Gently, knead (press and squeeze) the bag to mix the ingredients.
2. Add food coloring, if desired, and continue kneading the bag for about 20 minutes. If the mixture seems too thin (like a liquid), add more starch. Add glue if it gets too thick (it should stretch easily).
3. Roll the goo on the table into a long shape. Is it a solid or a liquid? __solid__
4. Now, use your hands or a rolling pin to flatten the goo. Is it still a solid? Describe the shape now. __Yes, it is flat.__
5. Continue shaping and stretching the goo to make different shapes. What kinds of things can change a solid's shape? __pounding, twisting, stretching__
6. Store the goo in an airtight plastic bag when finished.

What to do:
1. Make a colorful batch of powdered drink mix. Fill an ice cube tray with the mix and put it in the freezer until frozen.
2. Place the frozen ice cubes into a resealable plastic bag. Touch the ice cubes, what state of matter are they in? __solid__
3. Tape the bag to a window that faces direct sunlight.
4. Observe the bag every hour, what is happening to the solid? __It is melting.__
5. After the ice melts the solid becomes a liquid again. Open the bag and let it sit open for a while. The liquid will evaporate slowly.

What happened? The cold temperature changed the matter from a liquid to a solid. The warm temperature created a gas that turned the solid back to a liquid. Turn to page 146 to learn more about evaporation!

ANSWER ZONE
239

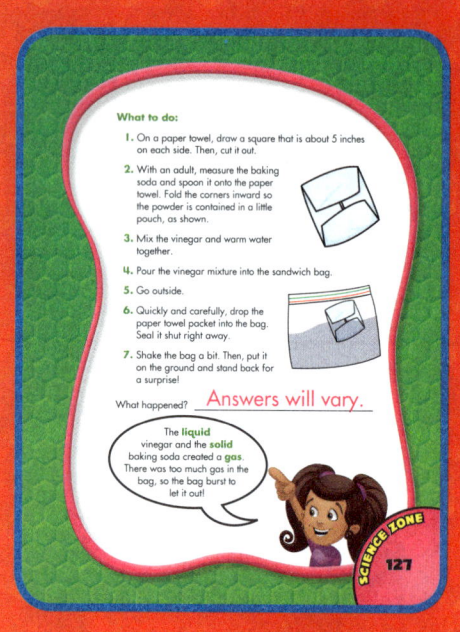

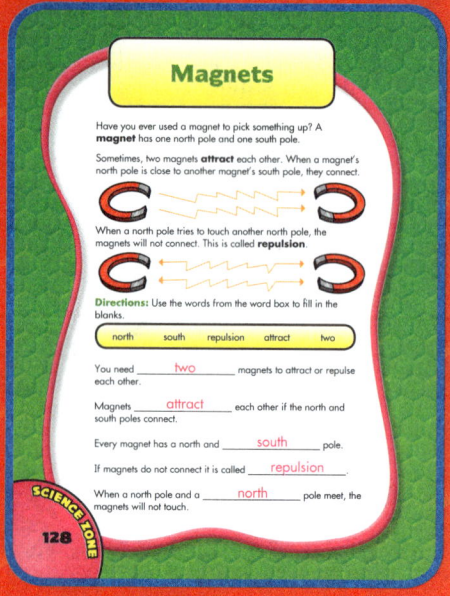

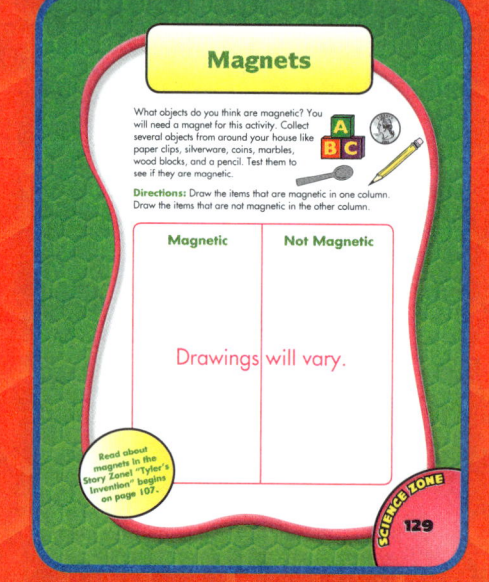

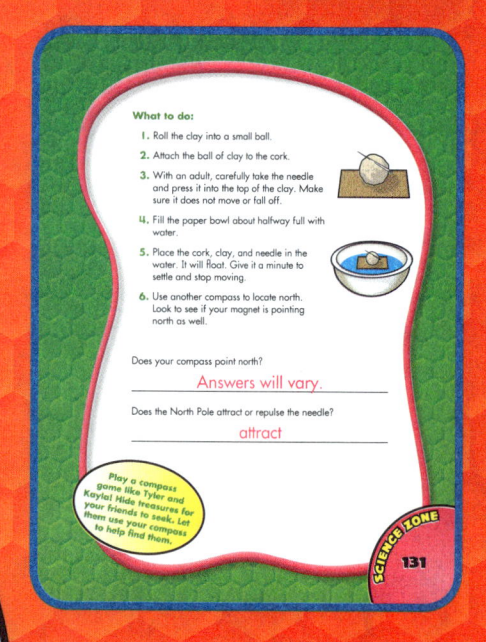

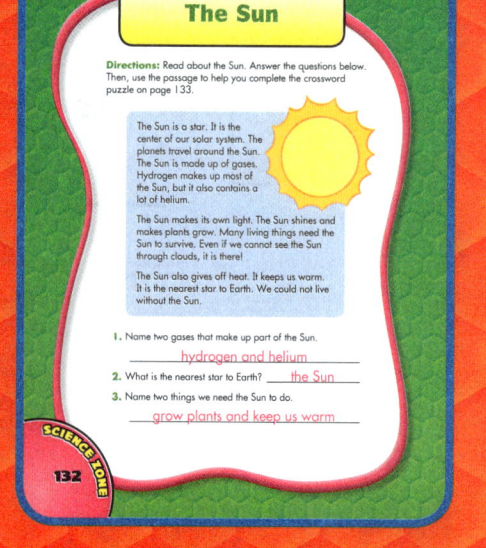

What to do:
1. On a paper towel, draw a square that is about 5 inches on each side. Then, cut it out.
2. With an adult, measure the baking soda and spoon it onto the paper towel. Fold the corners inward so the powder is contained in a little pouch, as shown.
3. Mix the vinegar and warm water together.
4. Pour the vinegar mixture into the sandwich bag.
5. Go outside.
6. Quickly and carefully, drop the paper towel packet into the bag. Seal it shut right away.
7. Shake the bag a bit. Then, put it on the ground and stand back for a surprise!

What happened? **Answers will vary.**

The **liquid** vinegar and the **solid** baking soda created a **gas**. There was too much gas in the bag, so the bag burst to let it out!

127

Magnets

Have you ever used a magnet to pick something up? A **magnet** has one north pole and one south pole.

Sometimes, two magnets **attract** each other. When a magnet's north pole is close to another magnet's south pole, they connect.

When a north pole tries to touch another north pole, the magnets will not connect. This is called **repulsion**.

Directions: Use the words from the word box to fill in the blanks.

| north | south | repulsion | attract | two |

You need __two__ magnets to attract or repulse each other.

Magnets __attract__ each other if the north and south poles connect.

Every magnet has a north and __south__ pole.

If magnets do not connect it is called __repulsion__.

When a north pole and a __north__ pole meet, the magnets will not touch.

128

Magnets

What objects do you think are magnetic? You will need a magnet for this activity. Collect several objects from around your house like paper clips, silverware, coins, marbles, wood blocks, and a pencil. Test them to see if they are magnetic.

Directions: Draw the items that are magnetic in one column. Draw the items that are not magnetic in the other column.

Magnetic	Not Magnetic

Drawings will vary.

Read about magnets in the Story Zone! "Tyler's Invention" begins on page 107.

129

What to do:
1. Roll the clay into a small ball.
2. Attach the ball of clay to the cork.
3. With an adult, carefully take the needle and press it into the top of the clay. Make sure it does not move or fall off.
4. Fill the paper bowl about halfway full with water.
5. Place the cork, clay, and needle in the water. It will float. Give it a minute to settle and stop moving.
6. Use another compass to locate north. Look to see if your magnet is pointing north as well.

Does your compass point north?
__Answers will vary.__

Does the North Pole attract or repulse the needle?
__attract__

Play a compass game like Tyler and Kayla! Hide treasures for your friends to seek. Let them use your compass to help find them.

131

The Sun

Directions: Read about the Sun. Answer the questions below. Then, use the passage to help you complete the crossword puzzle on page 133.

The Sun is a star. It is the center of our solar system. The planets travel around the Sun. The Sun is made up of gases. Hydrogen makes up most of the Sun, but it also contains a lot of helium.

The Sun makes its own light. The Sun shines and makes plants grow. Many living things need the Sun to survive. Even if we cannot see the Sun through clouds, it is there!

The Sun also gives off heat. It keeps us warm. It is the nearest star to Earth. We could not live without the Sun.

1. Name two gases that make up part of the Sun.
   __hydrogen and helium__
2. What is the nearest star to Earth? __the Sun__
3. Name two things we need the Sun to do.
   __grow plants and keep us warm__

132

ANSWER ZONE
240

The Sun

Directions: Complete the puzzle. Use page 132 to help. One is done for you.

Across
3. The Sun is the center of the ____ system.
4. The Sun is mostly made of ____.
6. The Sun also contains ____.

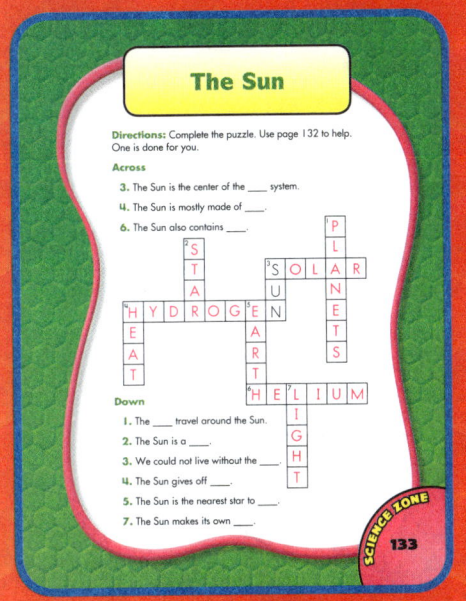

Crossword answers:
- 1 down: PLANETS
- 2 down: STAR
- 3 across: SOLAR
- 3 down: SUN
- 4 across: HYDROGEN
- 4 down: EARTH
- 5 down: LIGHT
- 6 across: HELIUM

Down
1. The ____ travel around the Sun.
2. The Sun is a ____.
3. We could not live without the ____.
4. The Sun gives off ____.
5. The Sun is the nearest star to ____.
7. The Sun makes its own ____.

133

Moon Facts

Kayla created a secret code for Tyler. She wrote a fun fact about the Moon. The Moon is Earth's **satellite**, which means it follows Earth around its orbit. Can you help Tyler solve the code and learn a fun fact about the Moon?

Directions: Use the key to solve the code.

A	B	C	D	E	F	G	H	I	J	K	L	M
1	2	3	4	5	6	7	8	9	10	11	12	13

N	O	P	Q	R	S	T	U	V	W	X	Y	Z
14	15	16	17	18	19	20	21	22	23	24	25	26

O N E   D A Y   O N   T H E
15 14 5 4 1 25 15 14 20 8 5

M O O N   I S   2 7
13 15 15 14 9 19

D A Y S,   7   H O U R S,
4 1 25 19   8 15 21 18 19

A N D   4 3.2   M I N U T E S.
1 14 4   13 9 14 21 20 5 19

134

The Moon: Phases

Directions: Read the passage. Answer the questions.

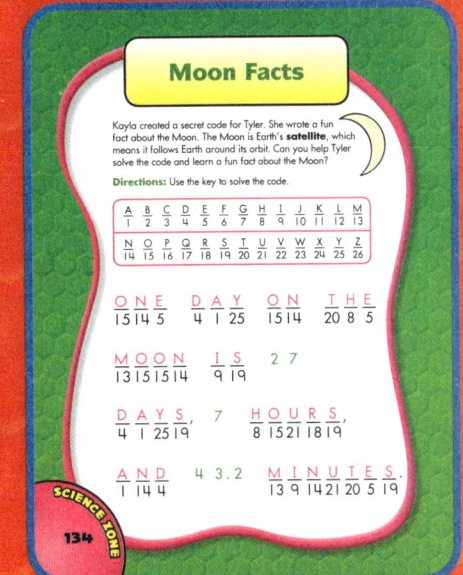

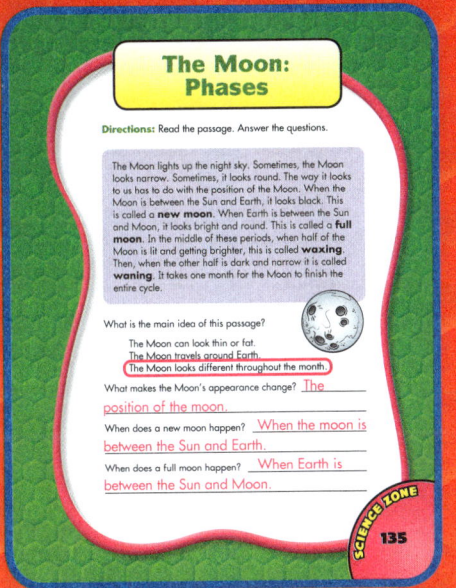

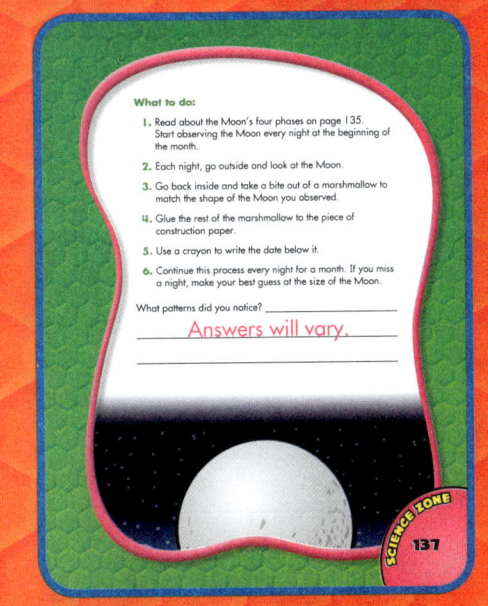

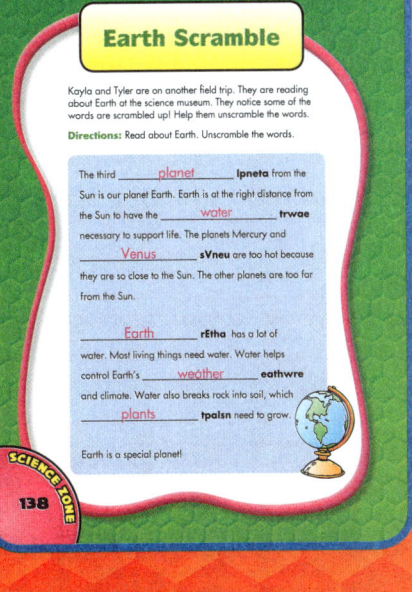

The Moon lights up the night sky. Sometimes, the Moon looks narrow. Sometimes, it looks round. The way it looks to us has to do with the position of the Moon. When the Moon is between the Sun and Earth, it looks black. This is called a **new moon**. When Earth is between the Sun and Moon, it looks bright and round. This is called a **full moon**. In the middle of these periods, when half of the Moon is lit and getting brighter, this is called **waxing**. Then, when the other half is dark and narrow it is called **waning**. It takes one month for the Moon to finish the entire cycle.

What is the main idea of this passage?
- The Moon can look thin or fat.
- The Moon travels around Earth.
- **The Moon looks different throughout the month.**

What makes the Moon's appearance change? _The position of the moon._

When does a new moon happen? _When the moon is between the Sun and Earth._

When does a full moon happen? _When Earth is between the Sun and Moon._

135

What to do:

1. Read about the Moon's four phases on page 135. Start observing the Moon every night at the beginning of the month.
2. Each night, go outside and look at the Moon.
3. Go back inside and take a bite out of a marshmallow to match the shape of the Moon you observed.
4. Glue the rest of the marshmallow to the piece of construction paper.
5. Use a crayon to write the date below it.
6. Continue this process every night for a month. If you miss a night, make your best guess at the size of the Moon.

What patterns did you notice? _Answers will vary._

137

Earth Scramble

Kayla and Tyler are on another field trip. They are reading about Earth at the science museum. They notice some of the words are scrambled up! Help them unscramble the words.

Directions: Read about Earth. Unscramble the words.

The third _planet_ **lpneta** from the Sun is our planet Earth. Earth is at the right distance from the Sun to have the _water_ **trwae** necessary to support life. The planets Mercury and _Venus_ **sVneu** are too hot because they are so close to the Sun. The other planets are too far from the Sun.

Earth **rEtha** has a lot of water. Most living things need water. Water helps control Earth's _weather_ **eathwre** and climate. Water also breaks rock into soil, which _plants_ **tpalsn** need to grow.

Earth is a special planet!

138

ANSWER ZONE

241

Earth's Layers

The planet Earth has three layers. The **core** is the inner layer. It is the hardest and hottest part. Around the core is the **mantle**. It is the largest layer. It is also hot and rocky. The **crust** is the outer layer of Earth. It is the thinnest layer, but it is very hard. We live on the crust.

Directions: Find the core. Color it **black**. Color the mantle **red**. Color the crust **green** and **blue**. The land should be **green** and the oceans should be **blue**.

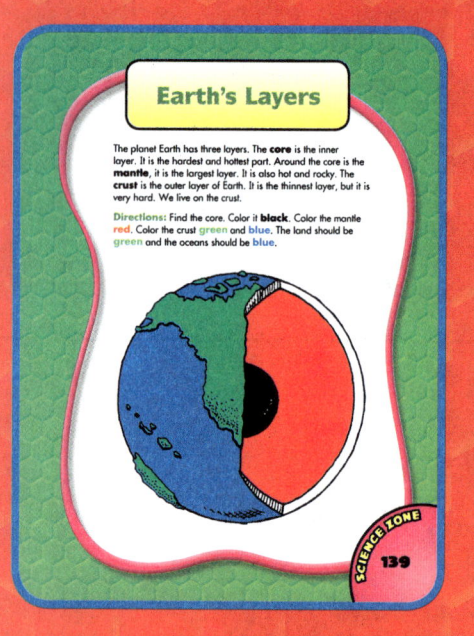

139

What to do:

1. Fill one paper cup with soil, one with sand, and one with pebbles. These will be the sediment.
2. Use the funnel to pour the soil, sand, and pebbles into the bottle.
3. Pour water into the bottle until it is almost full. Close the cap tightly.
4. Shake the bottle until everything is mixed well.
5. Place the bottle on a table. On a separate sheet of paper, draw a picture of what you see in the bottle.
6. Check the bottle after 15–30 minutes. Draw what you see.
7. Check the bottle again after 24 hours. Draw what you see.

Directions: Circle your answer.
Which one settled to the bottom the fastest?
soil   sand   (pebbles)
Which one was the last to settle to the bottom?
soil   (sand)   pebbles

What happened?
In the bottle you created a small body of water with a lot of sediment. The larger pieces of sediment settle to the bottom more quickly. The smaller pieces of sediment are more likely to float in the water longer and settle to the bottom more slowly.

141

Weather

Look outside, what is the weather like today? No matter what the weather looks like, there is always water in the air. Sometimes, the water is a gas called **water vapor**. Other times, it is a liquid—like raindrops. Or, it is a solid—like snow or ice.

Clouds are also an important part of observing weather. Each cloud is different. Clouds can tell you if you should bring an umbrella or if it is going to be a nice day outside.

Directions: Read about each cloud. Then, follow the directions.

Cirrus clouds are high in the sky. They are white and feathery and contain ice crystals. Paint white streaks below. Sprinkle glitter on the wet paint. The glitter represents the ice crystals.

Answers will vary.

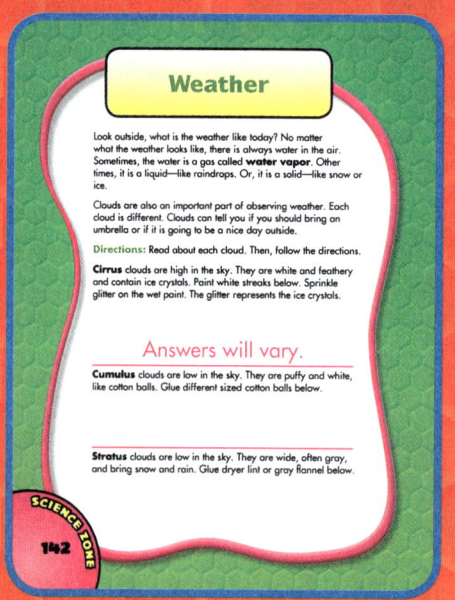

Cumulus clouds are low in the sky. They are puffy and white, like cotton balls. Glue different sized cotton balls below.

Stratus clouds are low in the sky. They are wide, often gray, and bring snow and rain. Glue dryer lint or gray flannel below.

142

Weather Chart

Good scientists make good observations. Practice observing the weather for one week.

Directions: Fill out the chart below.

Day of the Week	Types of Clouds	Draw the Weather Today
Sunday		
Monday		
Tuesday		
Wednesday	Answers	will vary.
Thursday		
Friday		
Saturday		

143

The Water Cycle

Directions: Read the passage. Answer the questions.

Water starts out in oceans, lakes, and streams. When the Sun heats the water, drops of water rise into the air. Water in this form is called water vapor, it is a gas. As the air cools, water droplets form clouds. When the clouds become too heavy with water, they produce rain, sleet, hail, or snow. The water falls back to Earth. Some of the water goes into the soil, where plants grow. Some falls back into the oceans, lakes, and streams. Then, the water cycle begins again.

Where does the water cycle begin? _oceans, lakes, and streams_
Is water vapor a liquid or a gas? _gas_
What happens when the clouds become too heavy with water?
They produce rain, sleet, hail, or snow.

Where does the rain go after it falls back to Earth?
the soil or the oceans, lakes, and streams

144

ANSWER ZONE

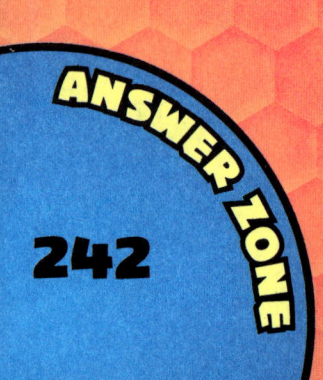

242

Water Cycle Word Search

Directions: Find the water cycle words hidden in the word search. Words can be up, down, across, diagonal, or backward.

rain	oceans	lakes	streams
water vapor	cycle	sleet	sun
clouds	snow	hail	

```
l c l w t l l s e
y p v o w a t s a w
e o s h a c r s t s
a s c l a e m n e
w n o w i s a c i n
d l c y c u e l
e u l e r t e r w
r o p a v r e t a w
k l e n o s t s y s
e c t s e k a l a o
```

145

What to do:

1. Use the masking tape and a pencil to label the outside of the pie tins. Label the first pie tin *salt water*. Label the second pie tin *tap water*.
2. Use the measuring cup to pour 4 ounces of warm water into a drinking glass.
3. Add one tablespoon of salt to the water. Stir the water until the salt dissolves.
4. Add salt until no more will dissolve. Pour the salt water into the pie tin labeled *salt water*.
5. Use the measuring cup to pour 4 ounces of tap water into the pie tin labeled *tap water*.
6. Put the pie tins side-by-side in a safe place. Record your observations each day until the water in both pie tins has evaporated.

Look at the *tap* water pan, what is left after evaporation? __nothing__

Look at the *salt* water pan, what is left after evaporation? __salt__

What Happened? Because salt is a mineral, it stays in the pan after evaporation. Only water is evaporated. All the sediment in the oceans, lakes, and streams stays behind during evaporation.

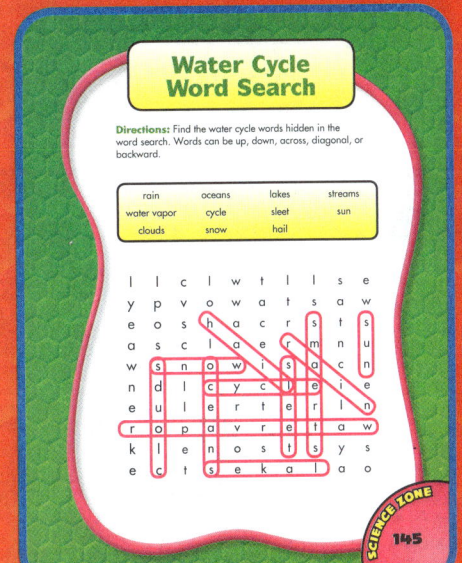

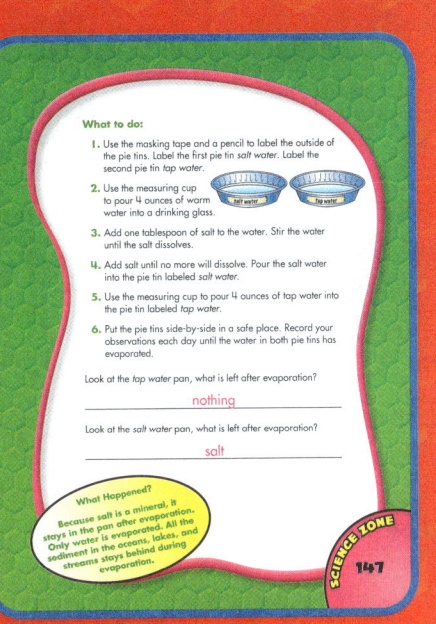

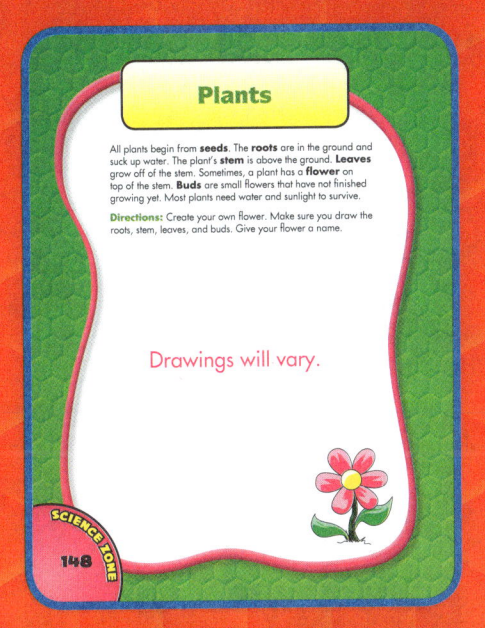

147

Plants

All plants begin from **seeds**. The **roots** are in the ground and suck up water. The plant's **stem** is above the ground. **Leaves** grow off of the stem. Sometimes, a plant has a **flower** on top of the stem. **Buds** are small flowers that have not finished growing yet. Most plants need water and sunlight to survive.

Directions: Create your own flower. Make sure you draw the roots, stem, leaves, and buds. Give your flower a name.

Drawings will vary.

148

Parts of a Plant

Kayla is growing flowers in her garden. She wants to label the parts of the flowers, but she keeps mixing them up! Can you help her unscramble the words and label the flower?

Directions: Unscramble each word, then write the word on the line. Write the correct number to label the parts of the plant. Use the information on page 148 if you need help.

1. efla ____leaf____
2. refotw ____flower____
3. eeds ____seeds____
4. mtes ____stem____
5. toros ____roots____

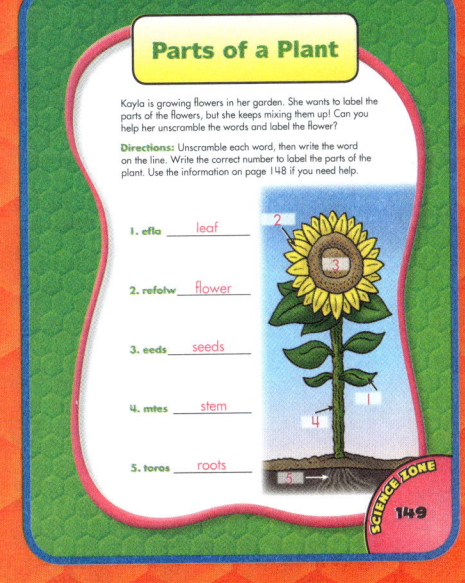

149

Leafy Collection

Directions: Use the chart below to compare and contrast the leaves you found. Glue a leaf in each box. Then, fill in your observations about each leaf.

The Leaf	Color	Size
	Answers will vary.	

151

ANSWER ZONE

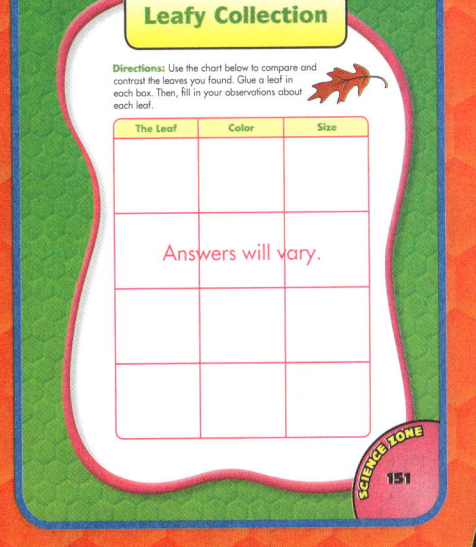

243

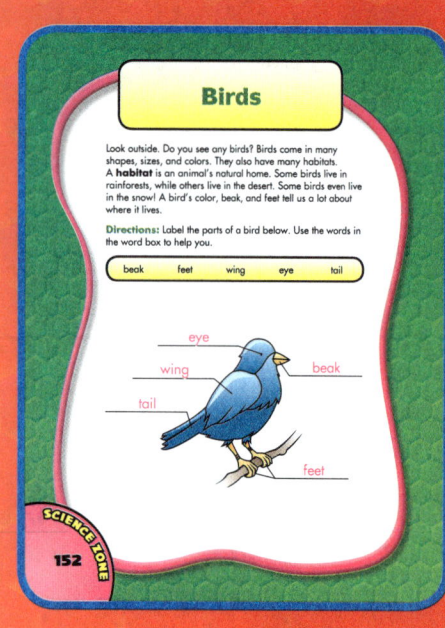

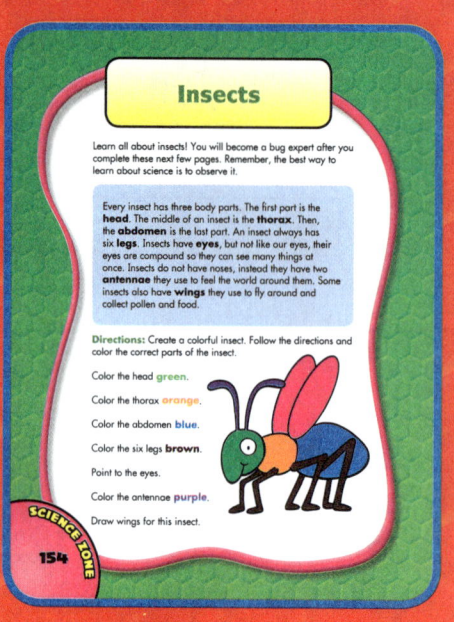

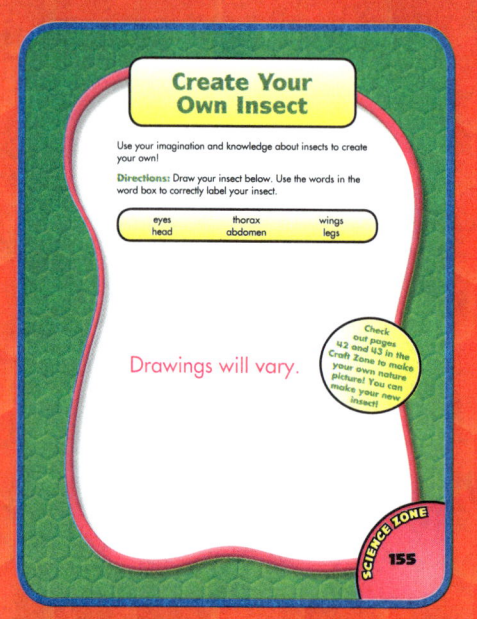

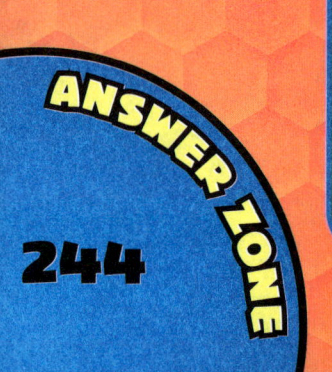

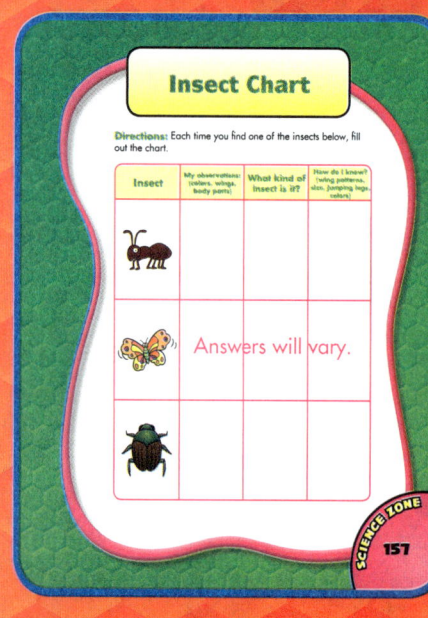

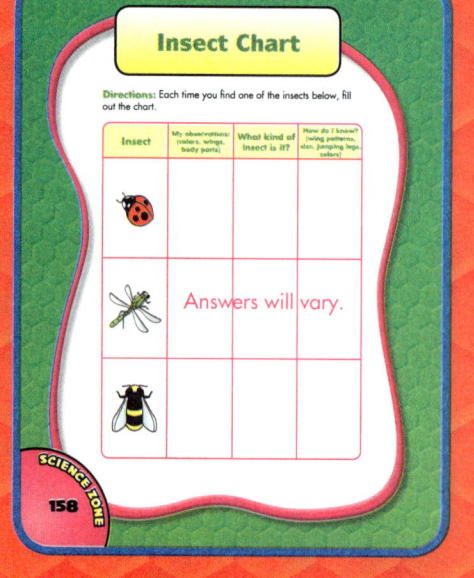

Birds

Look outside. Do you see any birds? Birds come in many shapes, sizes, and colors. They also have many habitats. A **habitat** is an animal's natural home. Some birds live in rainforests, while others live in the desert. Some birds even live in the snow! A bird's color, beak, and feet tell us a lot about where it lives.

Directions: Label the parts of a bird below. Use the words in the word box to help you.

| beak | feet | wing | eye | tail |

- eye
- wing
- beak
- tail
- feet

152

Insects

Learn all about insects! You will become a bug expert after you complete these next few pages. Remember, the best way to learn about science is to observe it.

Every insect has three body parts. The first part is the **head**. The middle of an insect is the **thorax**. Then, the **abdomen** is the last part. An insect always has six **legs**. Insects have **eyes**, but not like our eyes, their eyes are compound so they can see many things at once. Insects do not have noses, instead they have two **antennae** they use to feel the world around them. Some insects also have **wings** they use to fly around and collect pollen and food.

Directions: Create a colorful insect. Follow the directions and color the correct parts of the insect.

Color the head **green**.
Color the thorax **orange**.
Color the abdomen **blue**.
Color the six legs **brown**.
Point to the eyes.
Color the antennae **purple**.
Draw wings for this insect.

154

Create Your Own Insect

Use your imagination and knowledge about insects to create your own!

Directions: Draw your insect below. Use the words in the word box to correctly label your insect.

| eyes | thorax | wings |
| head | abdomen | legs |

Drawings will vary.

Check out pages 42 and 43 in the Craft Zone to make your own nature picture! You can make your new insect!

155

Insect Chart

Directions: Each time you find one of the insects below, fill out the chart.

Insect	My observations: (colors, wings, body parts)	What kind of insect is it?	How do I know? (wing patterns, size, jumping legs, colors)
(ant)		Answers will vary.	
(butterfly)			
(beetle)			

157

Insect Chart

Directions: Each time you find one of the insects below, fill out the chart.

Insect	My observations: (colors, wings, body parts)	What kind of insect is it?	How do I know? (wing patterns, size, jumping legs, colors)
(ladybug)		Answers will vary.	
(dragonfly)			
(bee)			

158

ANSWER ZONE

244

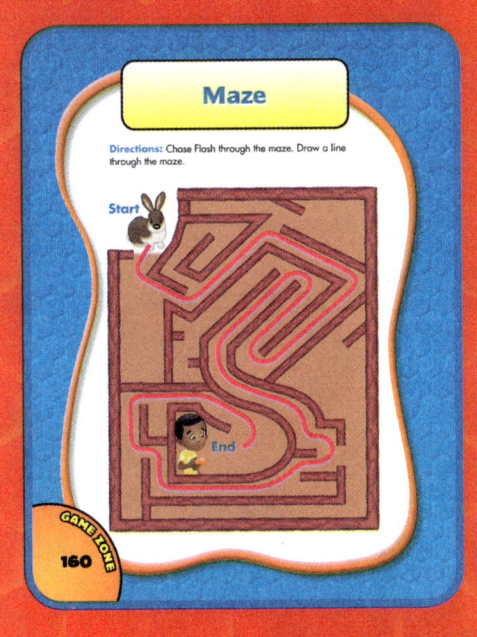

Maze

Directions: Chase Flash through the maze. Draw a line through the maze.

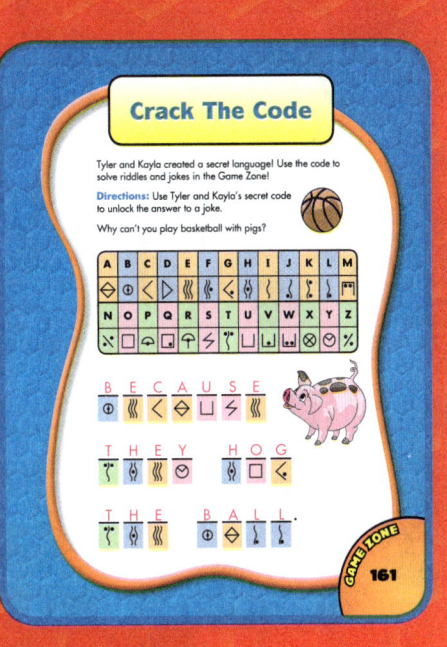

160

Crack The Code

Tyler and Kayla created a secret language! Use the code to solve riddles and jokes in the Game Zone!

Directions: Use Tyler and Kayla's secret code to unlock the answer to a joke.

Why can't you play basketball with pigs?

BECAUSE THEY HOG THE BALL.

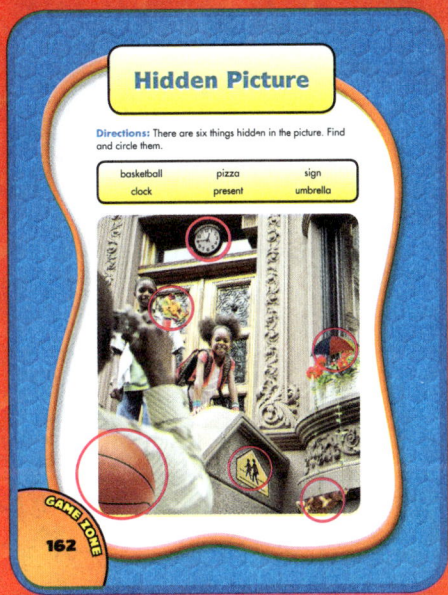

161

Hidden Picture

Directions: There are six things hidden in the picture. Find and circle them.

- basketball
- pizza
- sign
- clock
- present
- umbrella

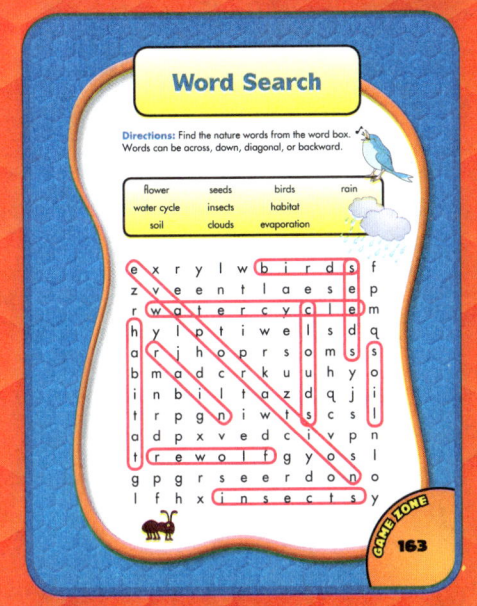

162

Word Search

Directions: Find the nature words from the word box. Words can be across, down, diagonal, or backward.

- flower
- seeds
- birds
- rain
- water cycle
- insects
- habitat
- soil
- clouds
- evaporation

163

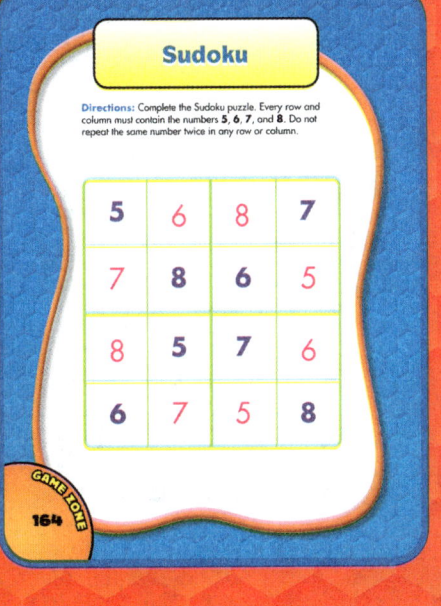

Sudoku

Directions: Complete the Sudoku puzzle. Every row and column must contain the numbers **5**, **6**, **7**, and **8**. Do not repeat the same number twice in any row or column.

5	6	8	7
7	8	6	5
8	5	7	6
6	7	5	8

164

ANSWER ZONE

245

Picture Puzzle

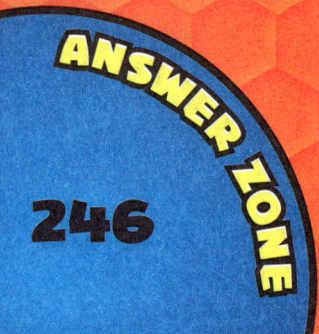

Directions: Cut out the pieces and mix them up. Then, see how fast you can put them back together.

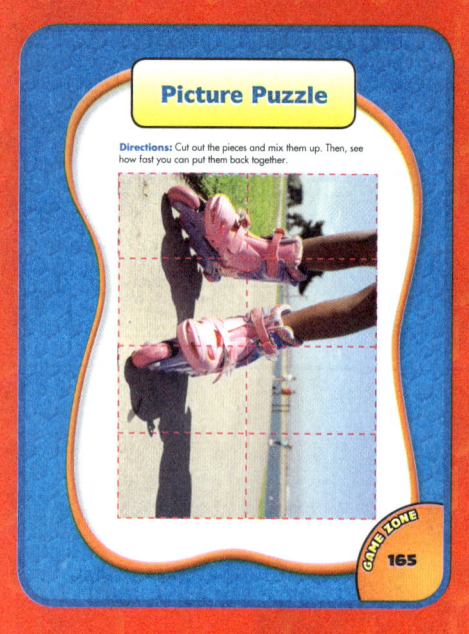

165

Grid Art

Learn how to draw Kayla! Follow the directions below.

Directions: Finish drawing the picture by using the grid as a guide. Then, color it.

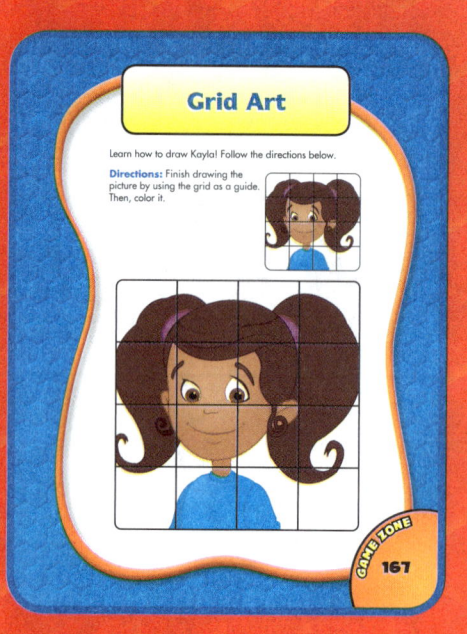

167

Crossword Puzzle

Directions: Write the correct opposite into the crossword.

Across
1. If something is small, it is not _____.
4. opposite of over
6. _____ is the opposite of in.

Down
2. If you are _____ then you are not near.
3. _____ is the opposite of loud.
5. opposite of up
6. opposite of new

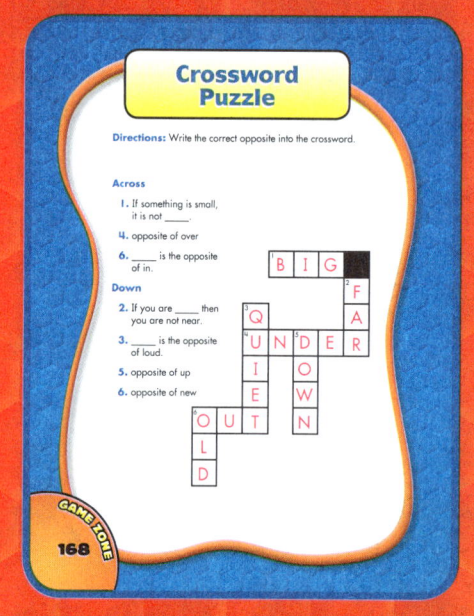

Across: 1. BIG, 4. UNDER, 6. OUT
Down: 2. FAR, 3. QUIET, 5. DOWN, 6. OLD

168

Maze: Flash's Riddle

Directions: Help Flash answer a riddle. Draw a line through the maze to find the answer.

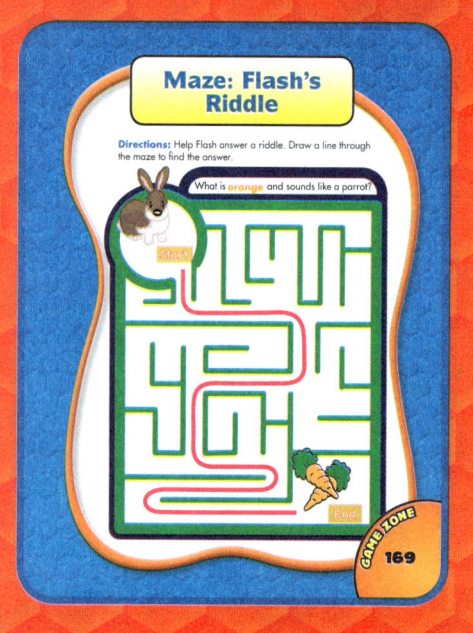

What is *orange* and sounds like a parrot?

A carrot!

169

Snow Day!

Directions: Fill in the nouns, adjectives, and verbs below. Then, write them in the story to create your own fun and silly Tyler and Kayla adventure.

Adjective (describing word) _____
Noun (person, place, or thing) _____
Verb (action word) _Answers will vary._
Verb (action word) _____
Adjective (describing word) _____
Verb (action word) _____

Tyler looked out the window, it had snowed! "No school today!" Tyler said. Tyler went outside to play in the _____ snow. Kayla met him outside. "Let's build a _____!" she said. Kayla _____ in the snow. Tyler _____ in it. They finished their _____ creation. "Let's go get some hot chocolate now!" Kayla said. They _____ inside.

170

ANSWER ZONE

246

Tic-Tac-Toe

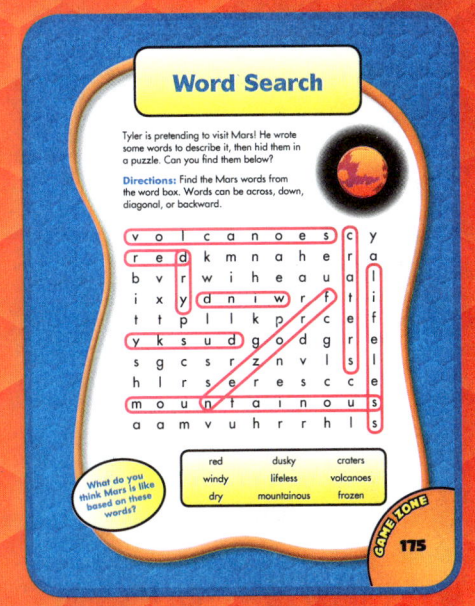

Directions: Play with a friend. Take turns writing **X**s and **O**s. Three in a row wins the game!

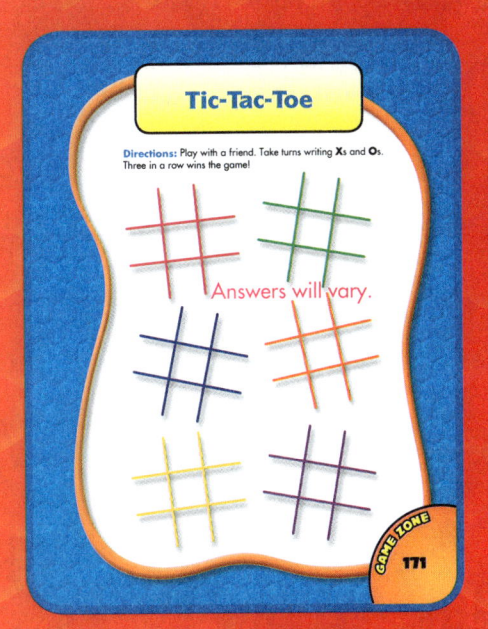

Answers will vary.

171

Which Is Different?

Directions: Look at the two pictures. There are five things different in **Picture 2**. Find and circle the five things that are different in **Picture 2**.

Picture 1

Picture 2

172

Crack The Code

Directions: Use Tyler and Kayla's secret code to discover a silly but true fact.

A SNAIL
CAN SLEEP
FOR THREE
YEARS.

174

Word Search

Tyler is pretending to visit Mars! He wrote some words to describe it, then hid them in a puzzle. Can you find them below?

Directions: Find the Mars words from the word box. Words can be across, down, diagonal, or backward.

red	dusky	craters
windy	lifeless	volcanoes
dry	mountainous	frozen

What do you think Mars is like based on these words?

175

Animal Riddles

Directions: Draw a line from the riddle to the correct answer.

I love to walk in the snow and slide on the ice.
What am I?

I slither on the ground because I have no arms or legs.
What am I?

I save lots of bones and bury them in the yard.
What am I?

I hop on lily pads in a pond with my webbed feet.
What am I?

I am very big and I live in the ocean.
What am I?

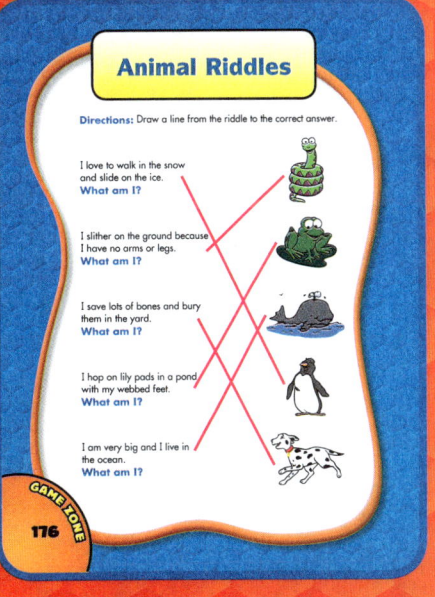

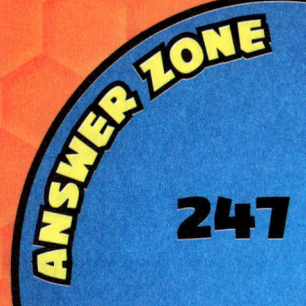

176

ANSWER ZONE

247

248

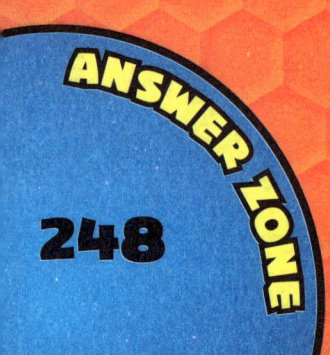

Finish The Picture
Directions: Draw and color the other half of the ladybug.

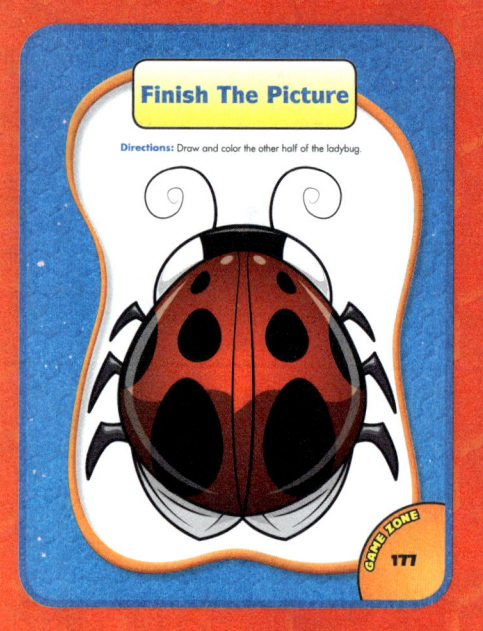

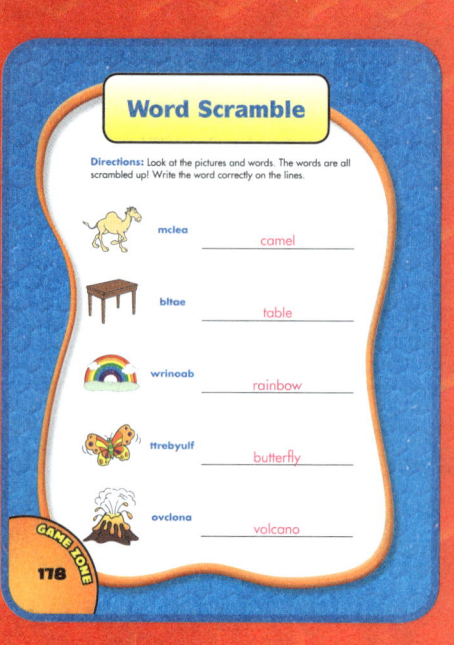

Game Zone 177

Word Scramble
Directions: Look at the pictures and words. The words are all scrambled up! Write the word correctly on the lines.

- mclea — camel
- bltae — table
- wrinoab — rainbow
- ttrebyulf — butterfly
- ovclona — volcano

Game Zone 178

Picture Puzzle
Directions: Cut out the pieces and mix them up. Then, see how fast you can put them back together.

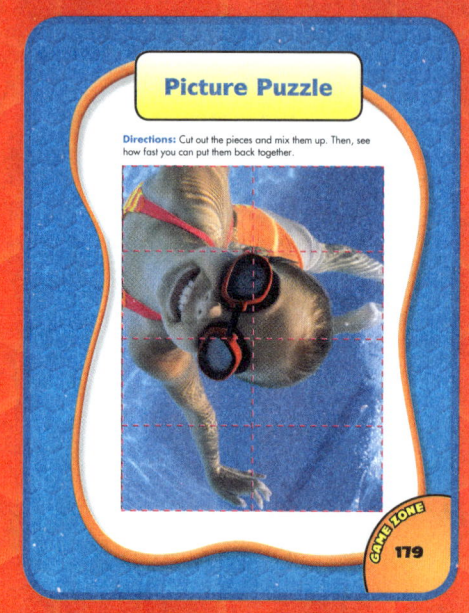

Game Zone 179

Crack The Code
Directions: Use Tyler and Kayla's secret code to unlock the answer to a joke.

Why did the banana go to the doctor?

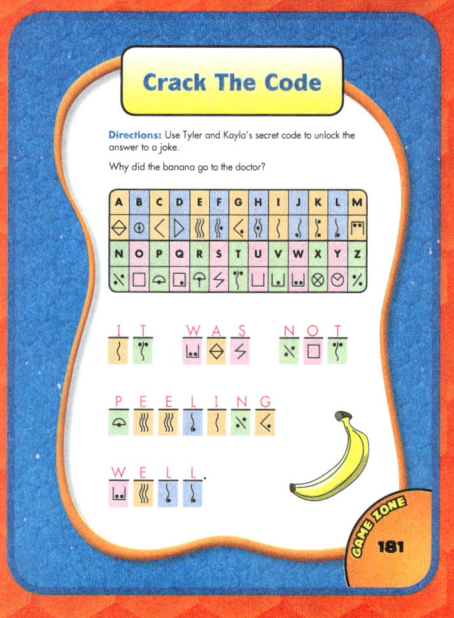

IT WAS NOT PEELING WELL.

Game Zone 181

Maze
Directions: Help the bird find the feeder. Draw a line through the maze.

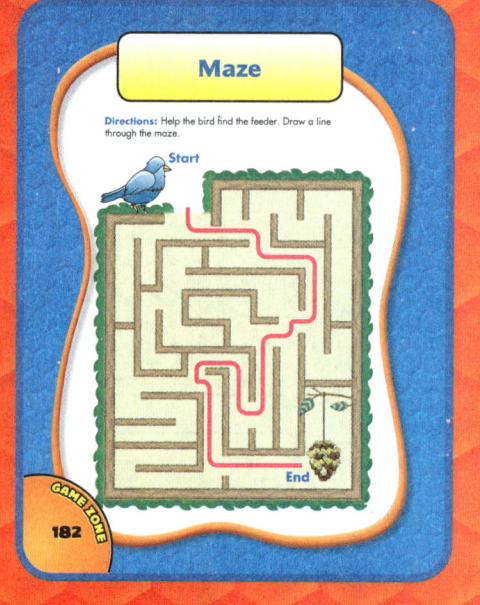

Start → End

Game Zone 182

ANSWER ZONE

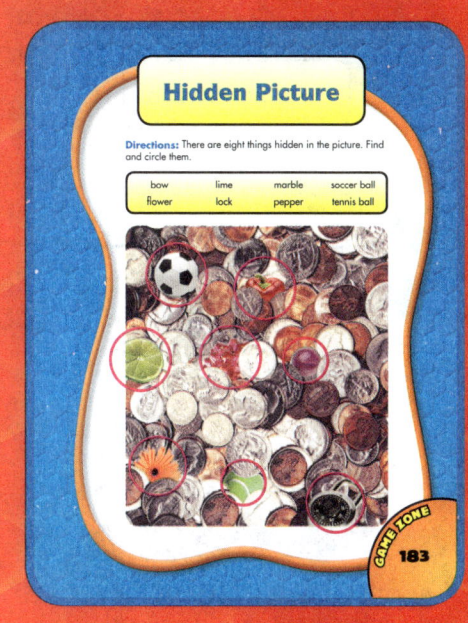

Hidden Picture

Directions: There are eight things hidden in the picture. Find and circle them.

bow	lime	marble	soccer ball
flower	lock	pepper	tennis ball

GAME ZONE 183

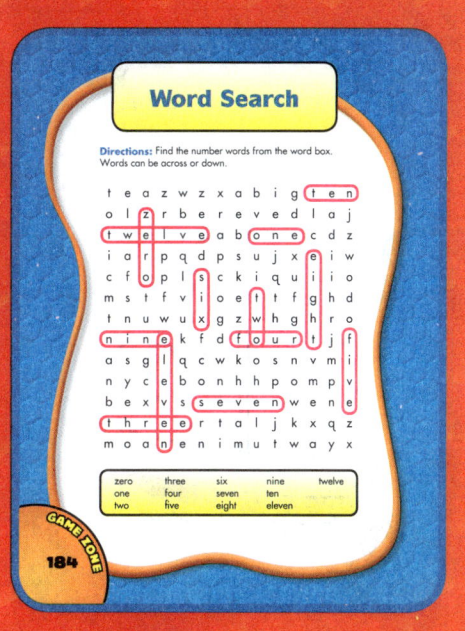

Word Search

Directions: Find the number words from the word box. Words can be across or down.

```
t e a z w z x a b i g t e n
o l z r b e r e v e d l a j
u t w e l v e a b o n e c d z
i a r p q d p s u j x e i w
c f o p l s c k i q u i i o
m s t f v i o e t t f g h d
t n u w u x g z w h g h r o
f n i n e k f d f o u r t j f
a s g l q c w k o s n v m i
n y c e b o n h h p o m p v
b e x v s s e v e n w e n e
t h r e e r t a l j k x q z
m o a n e n i m u t w a y x
```

zero	three	six	nine	twelve
one	four	seven	ten	
two	five	eight	eleven	

GAME ZONE 184

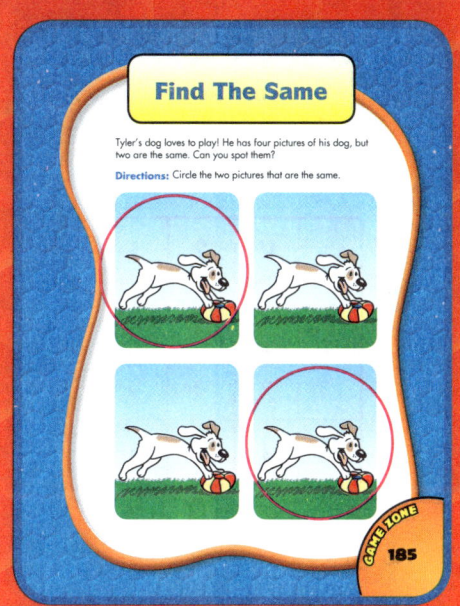

Find The Same

Tyler's dog loves to play! He has four pictures of his dog, but two are the same. Can you spot them?

Directions: Circle the two pictures that are the same.

GAME ZONE 185

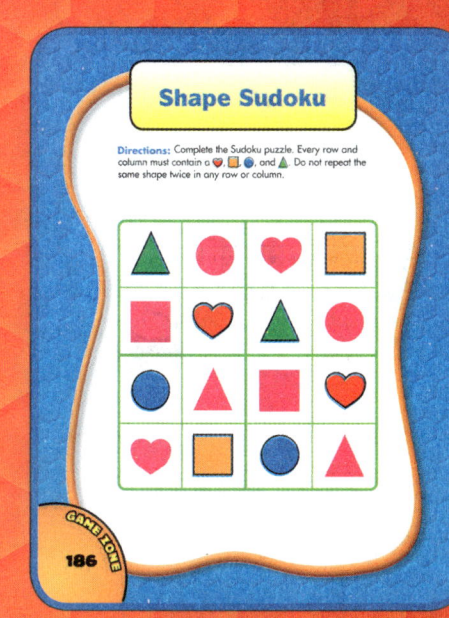

Shape Sudoku

Directions: Complete the Sudoku puzzle. Every row and column must contain a ♥, ■, ● and ▲. Do not repeat the same shape twice in any row or column.

GAME ZONE 186

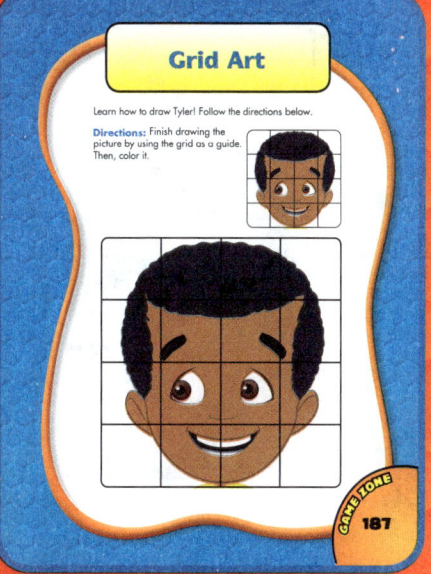

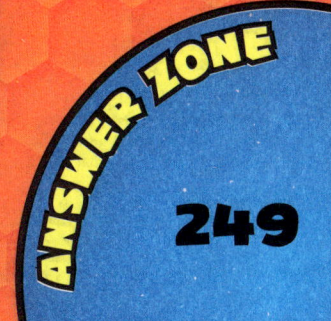

Grid Art

Learn how to draw Tyler! Follow the directions below.

Directions: Finish drawing the picture by using the grid as a guide. Then, color it.

GAME ZONE 187

ANSWER ZONE

249

Finish The Picture

Directions: Draw and color the other half of the sailboat.

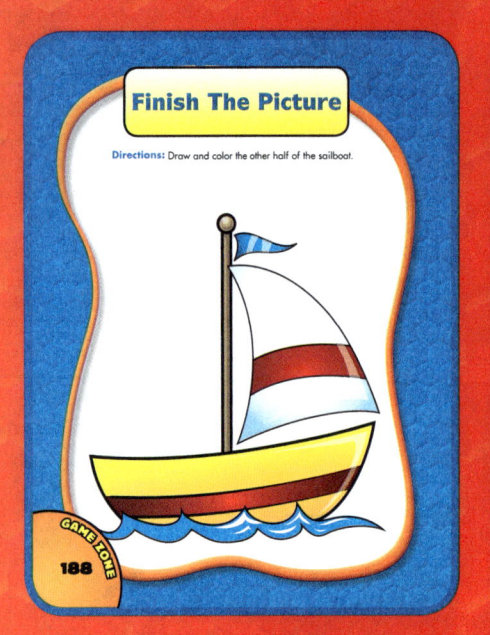

188

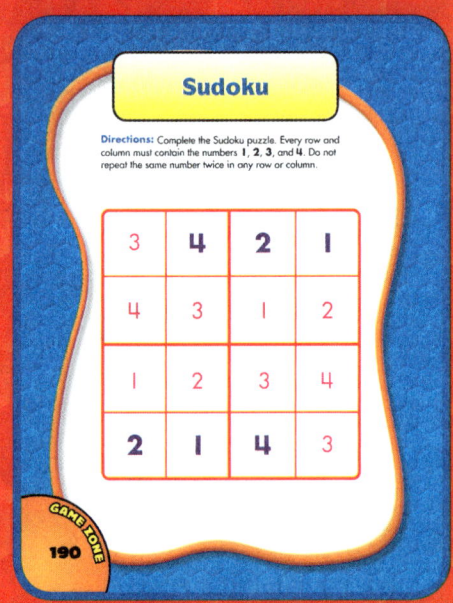

Hidden Picture

Kayla lost some items in her room. Can you help her find them?

Directions: There are six things hidden in the picture. Find and circle them.

| shoe | apple | flower |
| soccer ball | clock | hat |

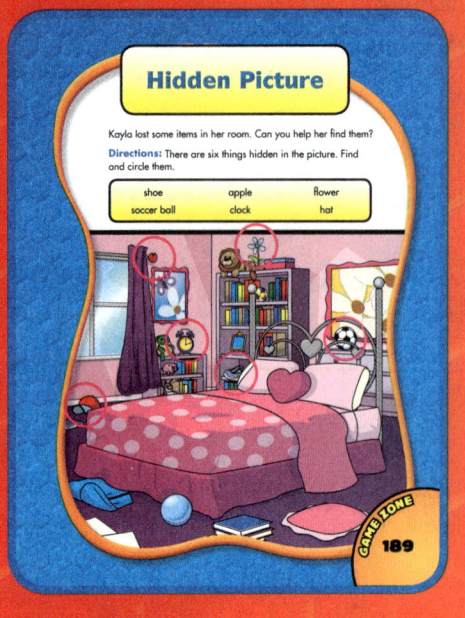

189

Sudoku

Directions: Complete the Sudoku puzzle. Every row and column must contain the numbers 1, 2, 3, and 4. Do not repeat the same number twice in any row or column.

3	4	2	1
4	3	1	2
1	2	3	4
2	1	4	3

190

Picture Puzzle

Directions: Cut out the pieces and mix them up. Then, see how fast you can put them back together.

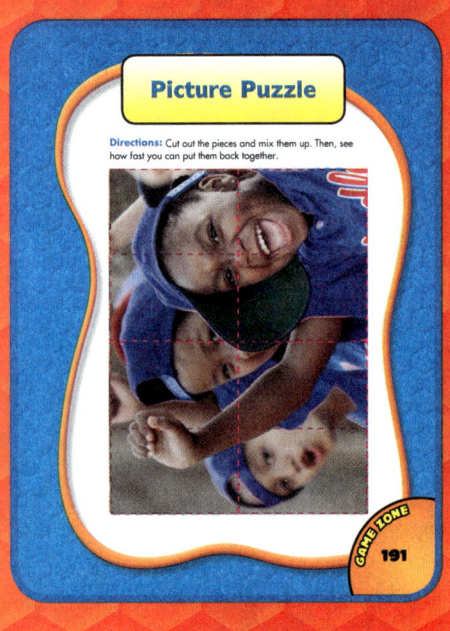

191

Crack The Code

Directions: Use Tyler and Kayla's secret code to discover a silly but true fact.

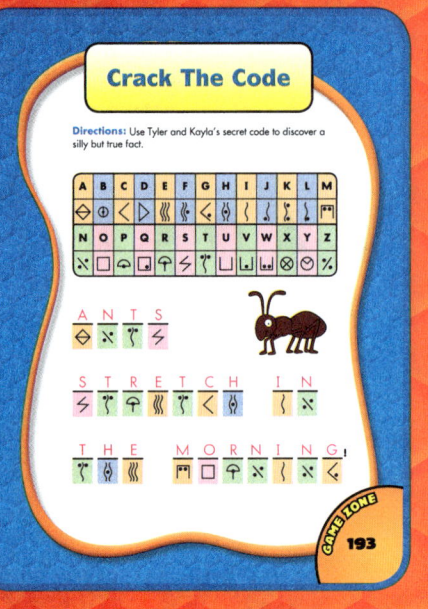

ANTS

STRETCH IN

THE MORNING!

193

ANSWER ZONE

250

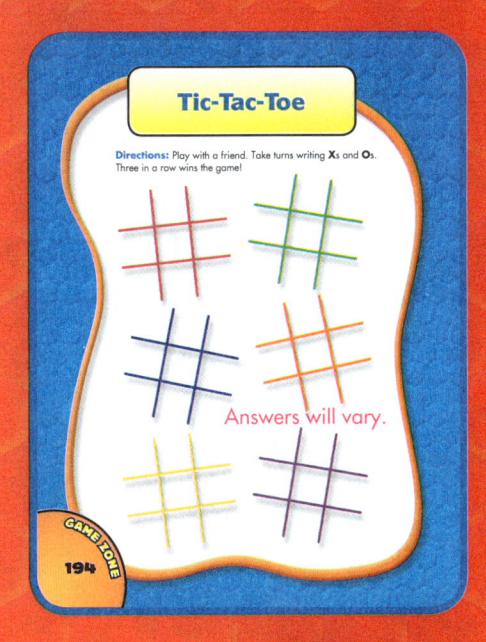

Tic-Tac-Toe

Directions: Play with a friend. Take turns writing **X**s and **O**s. Three in a row wins the game!

Answers will vary.

194

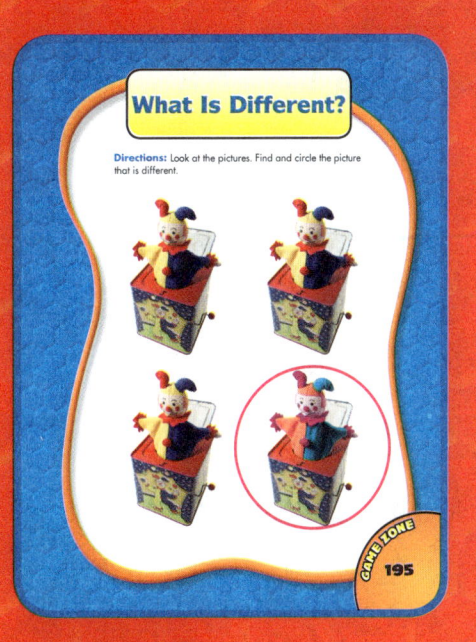

What Is Different?

Directions: Look at the pictures. Find and circle the picture that is different.

195

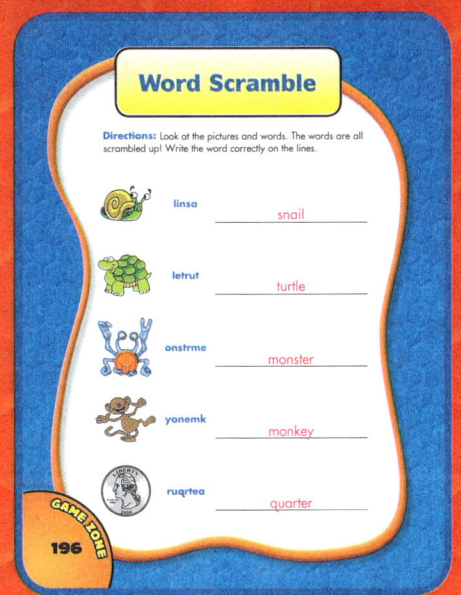

Word Scramble

Directions: Look at the pictures and words. The words are all scrambled up! Write the word correctly on the lines.

linsa	snail
letrut	turtle
onstrme	monster
yonemk	monkey
ruqrtea	quarter

196

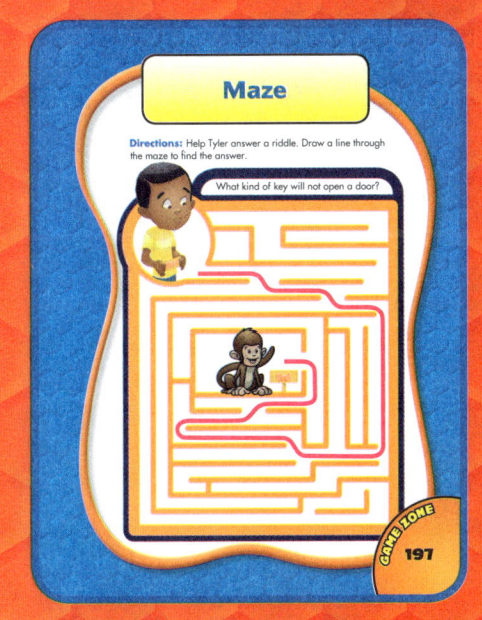

Maze

Directions: Help Tyler answer a riddle. Draw a line through the maze to find the answer.

What kind of key will not open a door?

197

Word Search

Directions: Use a **red** crayon to circle the names of three animals that would make good pets. Use a **blue** crayon to circle the names of three wild animals. Use an **orange** crayon to circle two animals that live on a farm. Words can be across or down.

bear   lion   bird   cow
cat   sheep dog   tiger

```
a m e o w w n l i o n
b m d o g g x i i s o
a i b e a r v l m h r
r m r m o o u s e e k
k c a b b i r d s e m
i o t t i g e r m p q
b w n o w w r q n e n
b d n c p h h i d u n
s f k c a t t r o a r m
```

198

ANSWER ZONE

251

Picture Puzzle

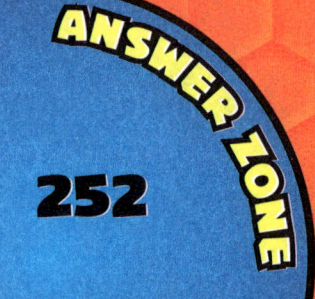

Directions: Cut out the pieces and mix them up. Then, see how fast you can put them back together.

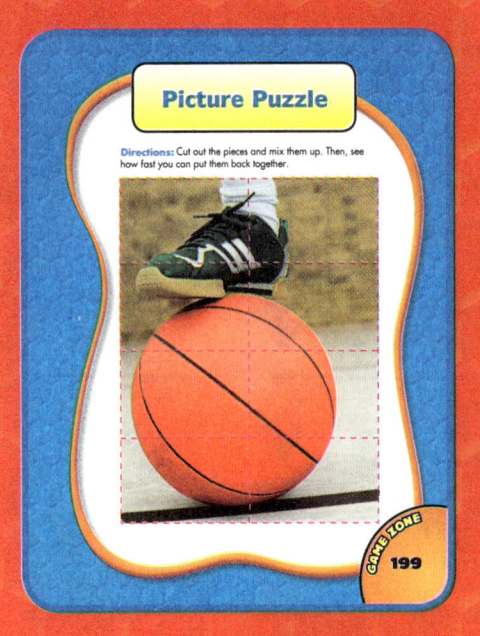

199

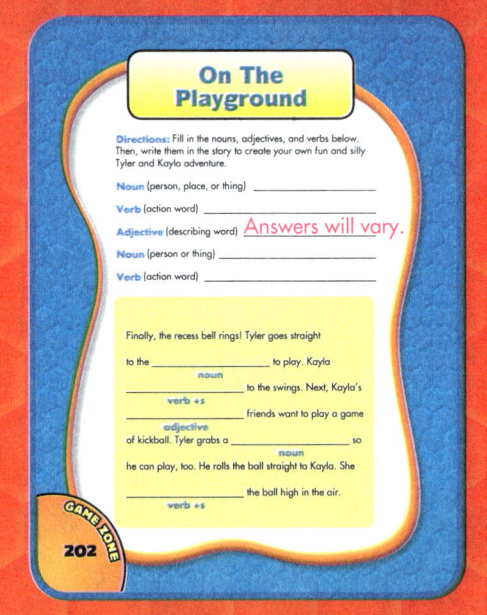

Grid Art

Learn how to draw a monster! Follow the directions below.

Directions: Finish drawing the picture by using the grid as a guide. Then, color it.

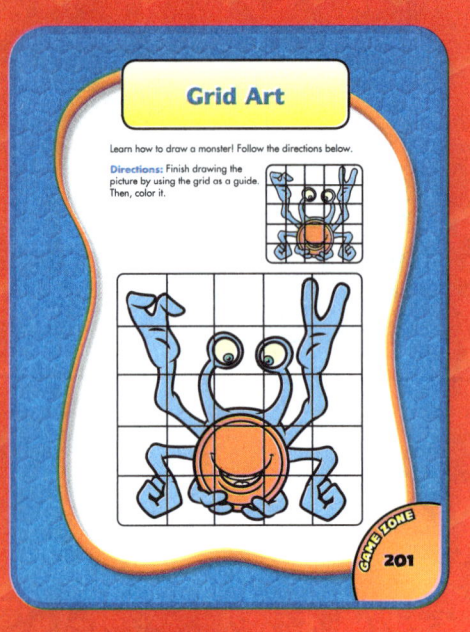

201

On The Playground

Directions: Fill in the nouns, adjectives, and verbs below. Then, write them in the story to create your own fun and silly Tyler and Kayla adventure.

Noun (person, place, or thing) _____
Verb (action word) _____
Adjective (describing word) *Answers will vary.*
Noun (person or thing) _____
Verb (action word) _____

Finally, the recess bell rings! Tyler goes straight to the _____ to play. Kayla
    noun
_____ to the swings. Next, Kayla's
verb +s
_____ friends want to play a game
adjective
of kickball. Tyler grabs a _____ so
                                noun
he can play, too. He rolls the ball straight to Kayla. She
_____ the ball high in the air.
verb +s

202

Hidden Picture

Tyler needs to find six insects. Can you help him find them?

Directions: There are six insects hidden in the picture. Find and circle them.

| ant | grasshopper | ladybug |
| butterfly | dragonfly | bumblebee |

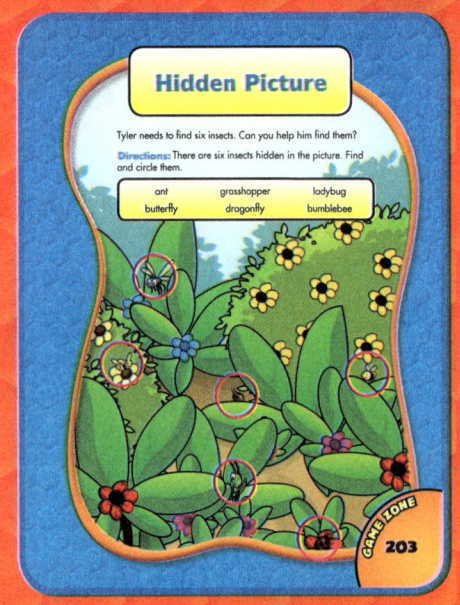

203

Crack The Code

Directions: Use Tyler and Kayla's secret code to unlock the answer to a joke.

Why was the baby ant confused?

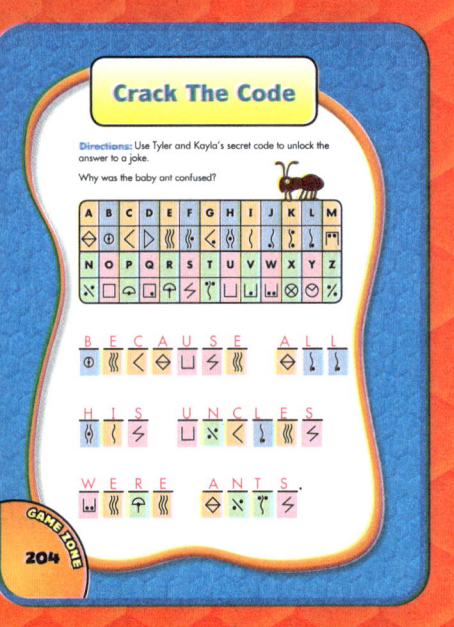

| A | B | C | D | E | F | G | H | I | J | K | L | M |
| N | O | P | Q | R | S | T | U | V | W | X | Y | Z |

B E C A U S E   A L L

H I S   U N C L E S

W E R E   A N T S.

204

ANSWER ZONE
252

Maze

Directions: Chase Flash through the maze. Draw a line to the finish.

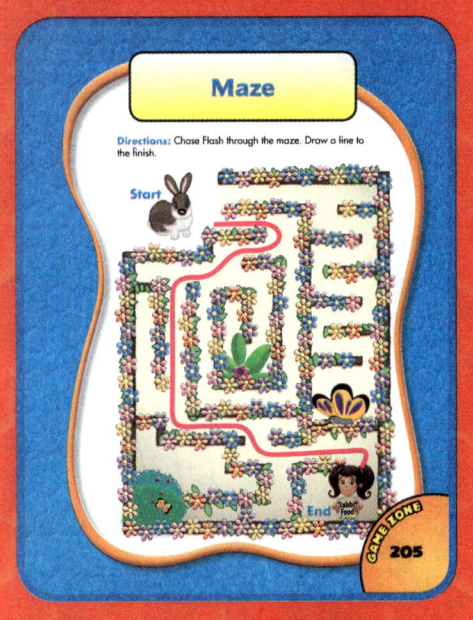

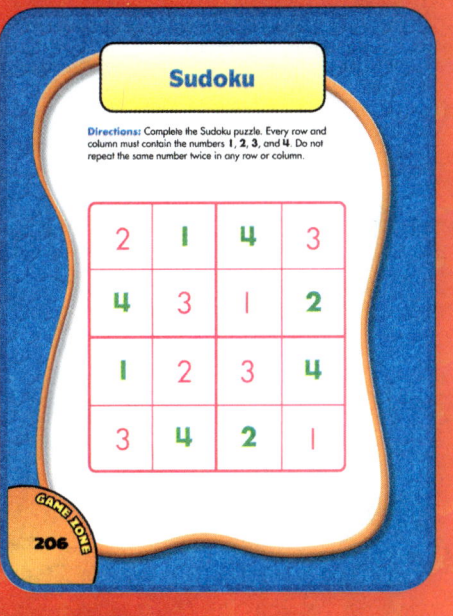

205

Sudoku

Directions: Complete the Sudoku puzzle. Every row and column must contain the numbers 1, 2, 3, and 4. Do not repeat the same number twice in any row or column.

2	1	4	3
4	3	1	2
1	2	3	4
3	4	2	1

206

Find The Same

Directions: Circle the two pictures that are the same.

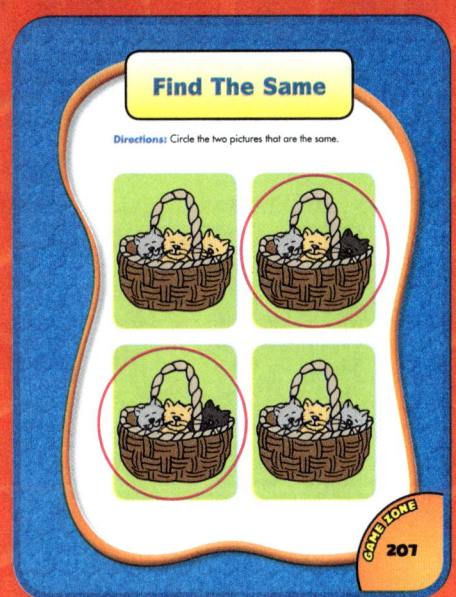

207

Color Code

Directions: Solve the subtraction problems. Then, color the spaces according to the answers.

Color Code:
1 = white   4 = green   7 = pink   10 = red
2 = purple   5 = yellow   8 = gray
3 = black   6 = blue   9 = orange

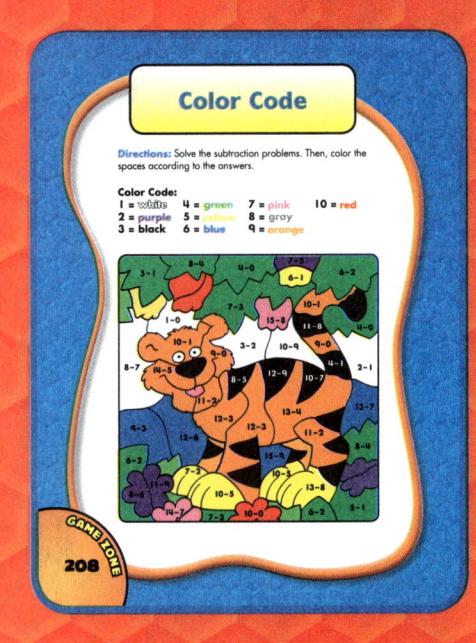

208

Crack The Code

Directions: Use Tyler and Kayla's secret code to unlock the answer to a joke.

Who is bigger, Mr. Bigger or Mr. Bigger's baby?

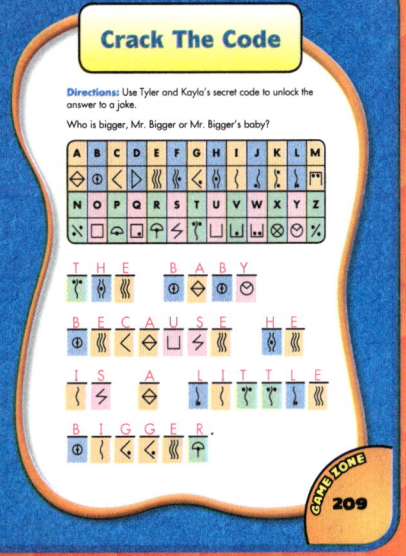

THE BABY BECAUSE HE IS A LITTLE BIGGER.

209

ANSWER ZONE

253

Word Search

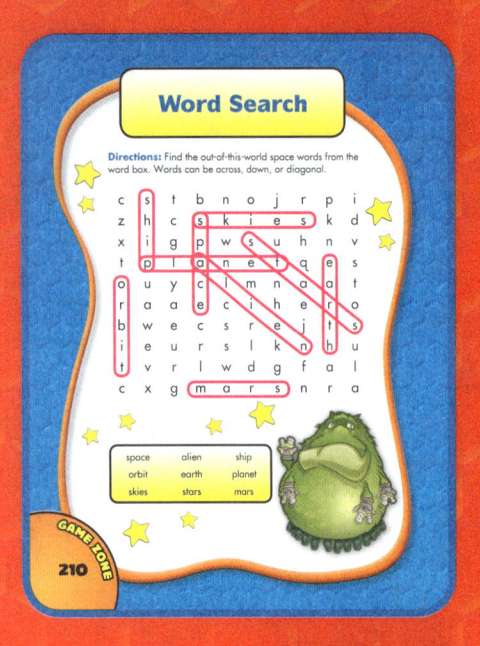

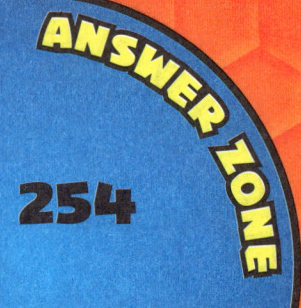

Directions: Find the out-of-this-world space words from the word box. Words can be across, down, or diagonal.

space	alien	ship
orbit	earth	planet
skies	stars	mars

GAME ZONE 210

Tic-Tac-Toe

Directions: Play with a friend. Take turns writing **X**s and **O**s. Three in a row wins the game!

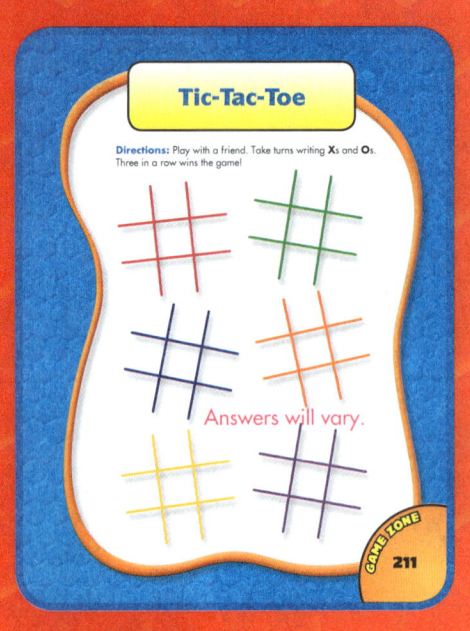

Answers will vary.

GAME ZONE 211

Hidden Picture

Directions: There are five things hidden in the picture. Find and circle them.

| caterpillar | drums | soccer ball |
| dog | pear | |

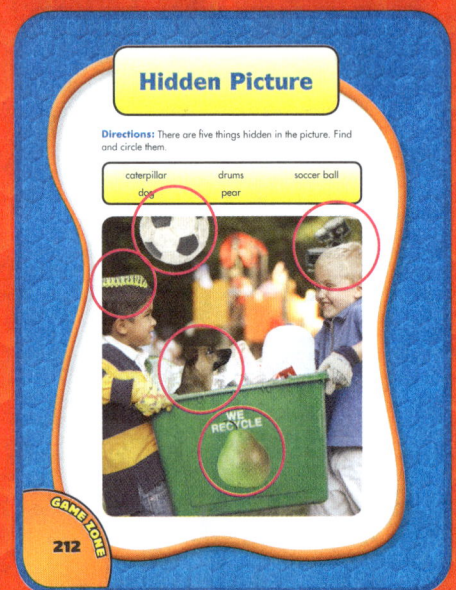

GAME ZONE 212

Grid Art

Learn how to draw Flash! Follow the directions below.

Directions: Finish drawing the picture by using the grid as a guide. Then, color it.

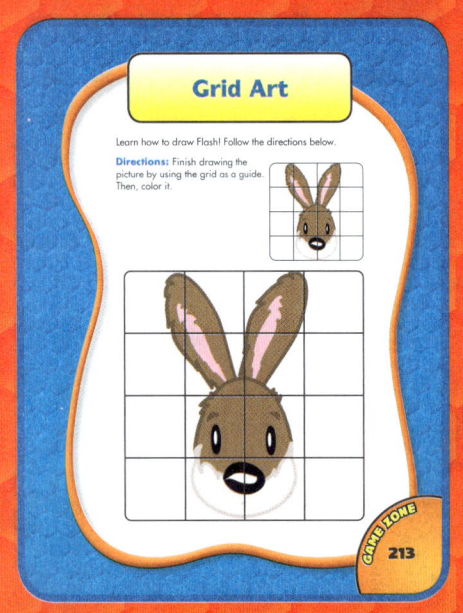

GAME ZONE 213

Space Riddles

Directions: Read each riddle. Write the answer using one of the scrambled words from the word box.

| srast | nuS | erscrat |
| rMas | rEath | nruSat |

This huge star lights the day. S U N

These shine at night. S T A R S

These are on the moon. C R A T E R S

This is our home planet. E A R T H

This planet is red. M A R S

This planet has rings. S A T U R N

GAME ZONE 214

ANSWER ZONE

254

Number Search

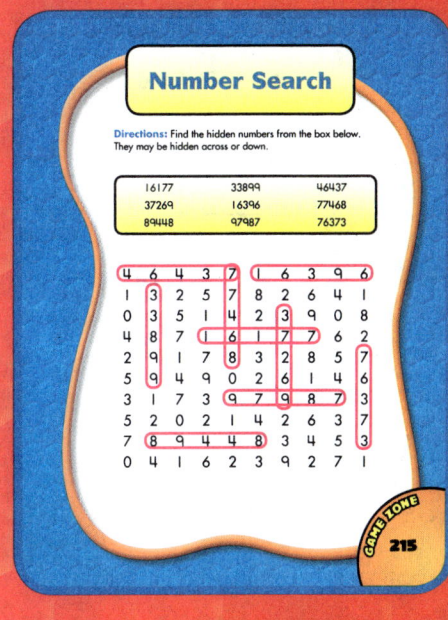

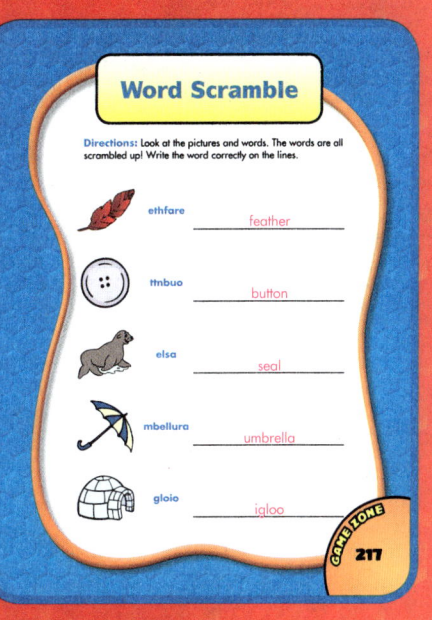

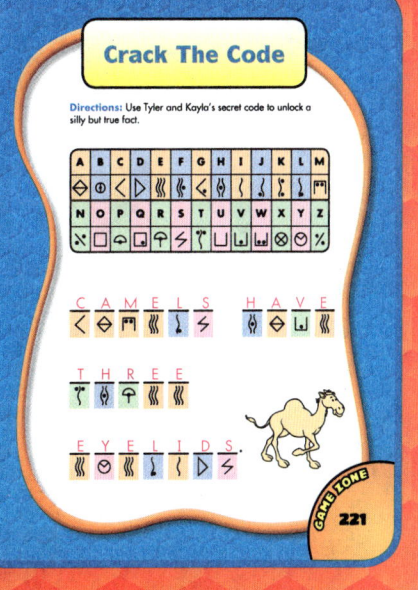

Directions: Find the hidden numbers from the box below. They may be hidden across or down.

16177	33899	46437
37269	16396	77468
89448	97987	76373

```
4 6 4 3 7 1 6 3 9 6
1 3 2 5 7 2 6 4 1 0
0 3 5 1 4 2 3 9 0 8
4 8 7 1 6 1 7 7 6 2
2 9 1 7 8 3 2 8 5 7
5 9 6 4 9 0 2 6 1 4
3 1 7 3 0 9 7 9 8 7
5 2 0 2 1 4 2 6 3 6
7 8 9 4 4 8 3 4 5 3
0 4 1 6 2 3 9 2 7 1
```

215

Word Scramble

Directions: Look at the pictures and words. The words are all scrambled up! Write the word correctly on the lines.

ethfare — feather

ttnbuo — button

elsa — seal

mbellura — umbrella

gloio — igloo

217

Maze

Kayla has a riddle for you! See if you can find the answer.

Directions: Solve Kayla's riddle. Draw a line through the maze to find the answer.

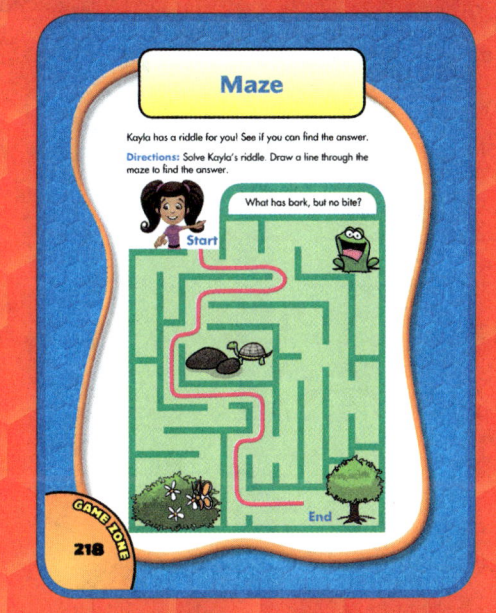

What has bark, but no bite?

Start
End

218

Picture Puzzle

Directions: Cut out the pieces and mix them up. Then, see how fast you can put them back together.

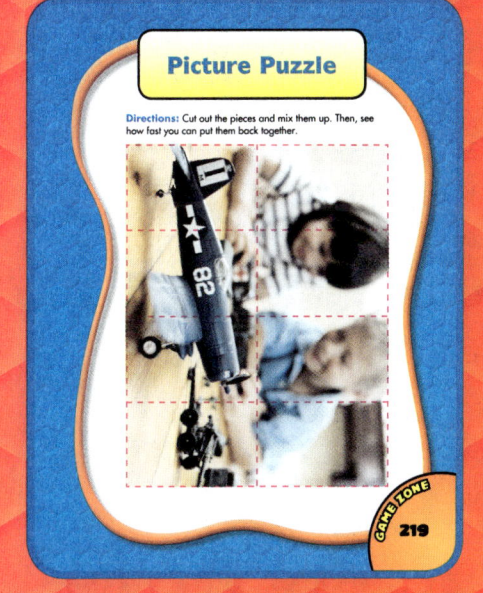

219

Crack The Code

Directions: Use Tyler and Kayla's secret code to unlock a silly but true fact.

CAMELS HAVE
THREE
EYELIDS.

221

ANSWER ZONE

255

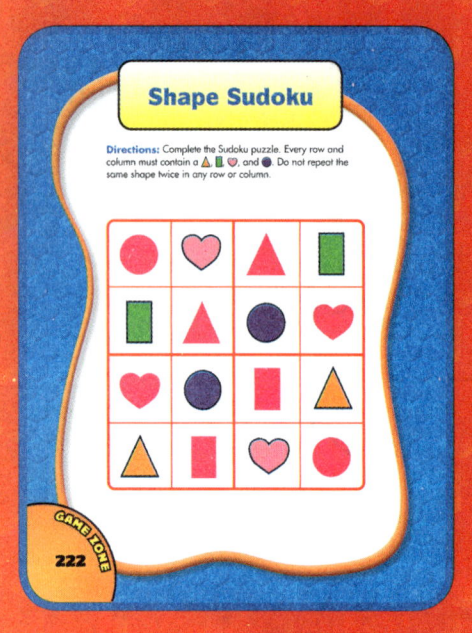

Shape Sudoku

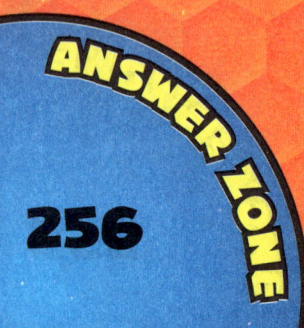

Directions: Complete the Sudoku puzzle. Every row and column must contain a △, ■, ♥, and ●. Do not repeat the same shape twice in any row or column.

222

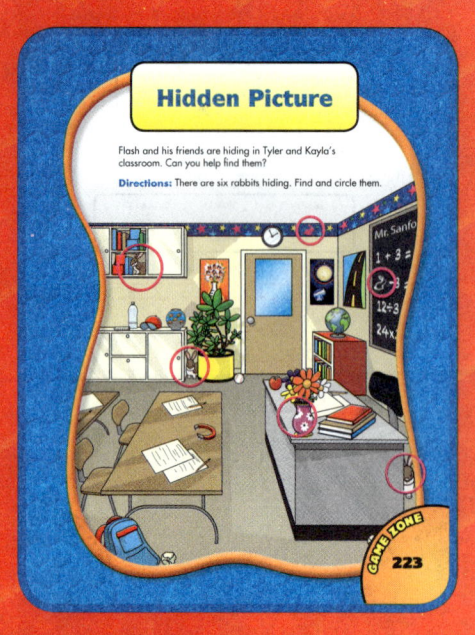

Hidden Picture

Flash and his friends are hiding in Tyler and Kayla's classroom. Can you help find them?

Directions: There are six rabbits hiding. Find and circle them.

223

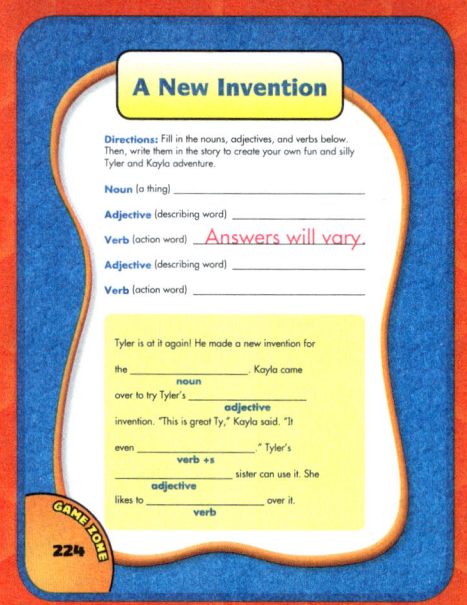

A New Invention

Directions: Fill in the nouns, adjectives, and verbs below. Then, write them in the story to create your own fun and silly Tyler and Kayla adventure.

Noun (a thing) _____
Adjective (describing word) _____
Verb (action word) _____Answers will vary._____
Adjective (describing word) _____
Verb (action word) _____

Tyler is at it again! He made a new invention for the _____. Kayla came over to try Tyler's _____ invention. "This is great Ty," Kayla said. "It even _____," Tyler's _____ sister can use it. She likes to _____ over it.

224

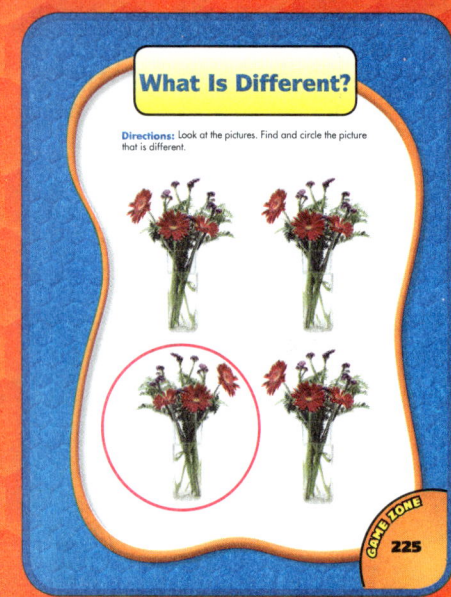

What Is Different?

Directions: Look at the pictures. Find and circle the picture that is different.

225

Create Your Own Message

Tyler and Kayla want you to write a secret message! Give your message to a friend.

Directions: Use Tyler and Kayla's code key to create your own secret message in the space below.

Answers will vary.

226

ANSWER ZONE
256

In Story Zone, Kayla and Tyler take care of Flash, the class pet. Flash needs exercise, but, if he is out of his cage, he is too hard to catch. Use your imagination to draw an invention to help Flash exercise, one that won't let him run away! Ask an adult to help you hang up your creative poster when you are finished!

Creative Kids Zone